ALONE IN THE GREAT UNKNOWN

# ALONE *IN* *THE* GREAT UNKNOWN

ONE WOMAN'S REMARKABLE ADVENTURES
IN THE NORTHWESTERN WILDERNESS

CAROLL SIMPSON

**HARBOUR
PUBLISHING**

HARBOUR PUBLISHING CO. LTD.
P.O. Box 219, Madeira Park, BC, VON 2HO
www.harbourpublishing.com

EDITED by Pam Robertson
COVER DESIGN by Heather Lohnes
TEXT DESIGN by Libris Simas / Onça Publishing
PRINTED AND BOUND in Canada
PRINTED on 100% recycled paper

HARBOUR PUBLISHING acknowledges the support of the Canada Council for the Arts, the Government of Canada, and the Province of British Columbia through the BC Arts Council.

LIBRARY AND ARCHIVES CANADA CATALOGUING IN PUBLICATION
Title: Alone in the great unknown : one woman's remarkable adventures in the Northwestern wilderness / Caroll Simpson.
Names: Simpson, Caroll, 1951- author.
Identifiers: Canadiana (print) 2022025088X | Canadiana (ebook) 2022025091X | ISBN 9781550179941 (softcover) | ISBN 9781550179958 (EPUB)
Subjects: LCSH: Simpson, Caroll, 1951- | LCSH: Outdoor life—British Columbia, Northern—Anecdotes. | LCSH: Fishing lodges—British Columbia, Northern—Anecdotes. | LCSH: Women—British Columbia, Northern—Biography. | LCSH: British Columbia, Northern—Biography. | CSH: Authors, Canadian (English)—21st century—Biography. | LCGFT: Autobiographies.
Classification: LCC GV191.52.S56 A3 2022 | DDC 796.5092—dc23

This book is dedicated to all my family members, who made great sacrifices to give me the opportunity and inner strength to live my dream in the Canadian wilderness. Without each individual, I could not have begun this journey and certainly would not have been able to see it through.

# Contents

*Our first view of Ookpik Wilderness Lodge.*

# Introduction

This book is primarily about my first ten years in residence at Ookpik Wilderness Lodge. Living by myself in the middle of the forest was a beautiful thing, but it came with responsibilities unknown to me at the start. Survival began with understanding this vast unknown wilderness and learning to live in harmony with the natural world. Then came the demands Mother Nature placed upon me to help protect it.

This is a true story. It is a book about loving life—a story about the all-encompassing experiences of following your dreams into an unknown country and into an unknown wilderness.

David and I had bought a fishing camp, called Ookpik Wilderness Lodge, in Northern British Columbia, above latitude 54. Ookpik means "snowy owl" in the Inuktitut language. The property was accessible only by floatplane, boat or a long hike. The lifestyle was unknown to us but we took on the challenge with great determination. We fuelled our dreams of the future with promises and plans.

From the moment we arrived, we witnessed the beauty, as well as the tragedy, that lives within the northern wilderness. David and I had many wild-animal encounters, each one giving us a new perspective on our place in this world. We experienced such isolation in the middle of a forest, with no roads and no people for miles. As a consequence of this isolation, we needed to learn how to live with ourselves in this solitude and come to terms with who we were and what we were capable of. David and I lived in bliss for eighteen months.

Then those ephemeral days of bliss came to a screeching halt. It was up to me to pull an inner strength from a dark place I'd never ventured to, and discover who I was and what I was capable of as a determined single woman in the wilderness. For the next decade, for every minute of every day, it was a mental and physical challenge for me to follow the dream built by two.

One of the methods I used to survive the loneliness was to record my emotional journey within a number of small notebooks with pretty covers. Late at night, I'd write in my private journal. The utmost moments of joy and pain were poured onto the pages. When I closed the cover on the written experiences of the day, it gave me a peaceful night's sleep. Year after year the volumes filled, charting my path: learning to tolerate my loneliness and heartache, gradually moving into confusion and anger, and then changing to acceptance. The journals were splattered here and there with tears of fury, mainly when I had to deal with logging and mining disputes. It was also important for me to try and record the wild beauty held in this wilderness. Without someone beside me to witness fantastic events, I had to share them with the pages of my journal.

As I reviewed my journals while writing this book, I was surprised to find, on almost every page, expressions of the love and joy I experienced every day at Ookpik. I had recorded an emotional account of living in the wilderness, the beauty of this world, the love of life and the happiness simple things could bring. The sentence I wrote over and over in the journals, I also expressed hundreds of times to the starry night, shocking the frogs into silence at any given moment: "God I love this place!"

I lived at the lodge for a total of twenty-four years. I was told as a child, "Good things come to those who wait." The last fourteen years at the lodge fulfilled that cliché.

# PART 1

# The Dream

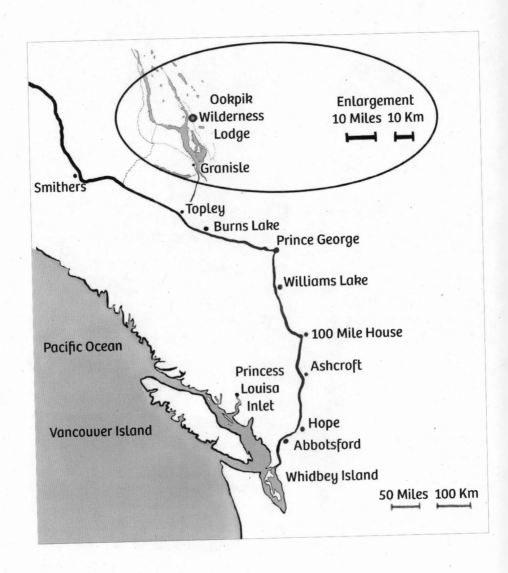

*It was 1,190 kilometres (740 miles) from Whidbey Island, Washington, to Ookpik Wilderness Lodge in the Cassiar District of British Columbia.*

# CHAPTER 1

# A Kingdom in the North

The *Resolute*, a 41-foot sloop, was moored on Whidbey Island, Washington. We'd bought the fire-damaged boat in 1991, and David worked on it in his spare time. Two years later, with it polished and complete, we moved on board. *Resolute* was the culmination of a dream David and I had shared from the very beginning of our relationship. I had even drawn a sailboat on our wedding invitations. David, a carpenter, invested in older homes and remade them into unique dwellings for resale. At this time, we had three houses but no real home. But with our children grown and living their own lives, we no longer needed an empty nest. We were in our forties by then, and our plan was to sell all of the houses, finish outfitting the *Resolute* and buy a little cabin in the woods to come home to in the winter. Hopefully we would end up with enough money left over for a nice cruising kitty. Maybe we could sail from port to port for several years, if David picked up a construction job here and there, and I could teach special classes on Northwest Coast art and culture, which I did on occasion for the school district. It would be a wonderful thing to share up and down the coastline. Or maybe I could take my voluminous notes on the subject and alchemize them into children's picture books.

Over the winter, David and I charted our first trip up the Inside Passage to Chatterbox Falls in Princess Louisa Inlet, on the BC coast. We were getting closer to departure and trying to get our ducks in a row. We were excited about casting off, but first we needed to sell the houses and find a place in the woods.

In the spring of 1994, David and I were considering several possibilities. One early Sunday morning, I ran across an ad in the *Seattle Times* classifieds:

WILDERNESS LODGE FOR SALE OR TRADE

WATER ACCESS ONLY

WRITE: PO BOX 127, GRANISLE, BC V0J 1W0, CANADA

I was excited; David wasn't. "But it isn't even in the United States of America!" he said. I sent away to find out more and promptly forgot about it. Six weeks later, I received a small package in the mail. When I opened the manila envelope from Granisle, BC, the most amazing photos fell out. As I glanced through, I felt my heart skip a beat, then thump in double time.

The first picture was of a big log cabin with expansive windows overlooking a glassy body of water. Immediately captivated, I devoured each photo. The images of the rooms inside the big cabin showed that they were spacious yet cozy, and I felt the heat from the fireplace; smelled the smoke from the wood cookstove. The pictures showed four guest cabins, each at the edge of a rocky beach framed with tall evergreens. Smiling fishermen held up huge rainbow trout for the camera, which made me grin unconsciously. Glossy photos of three gangly moose in a protected cove, with boats moored nearby, completed the montage. To me, everything was absolutely faultless.

After a timeless journey viewing the pictures—living within the photos, really—I picked up the enclosed note. I felt doped, and my eyes would not focus. I was lost—happily, dreamily lost— inside the way of life I saw in the pictures. Slowly, I collected my emotions and began to scan the words on the note. Even so, it took a few moments before I realized the water described was a lake: an inland sea. Babine Lake was 180 kilometres (110 miles) long!

Three hours later, I found myself walking around in a daze, placing dinner on the table in front of David. I just couldn't release the dreamscape the photographs created, and I couldn't wait another minute to share my experience with him. I held back the enclosed note, waiting for him to become infected, as I had, with this reverie. After he had explored each three-four coloured glossy, and I could see he was thoroughly enthralled, I reluctantly gave him the enclosed note. As soon as David also realized Granisle was a village on a lake, not an island in the ocean, his enthusiasm vanished. He ate his supper in silence, and I reluctantly put the pictures back into the envelope.

Whenever I was alone, I would find myself spreading the glossy photos out on the table again, losing track of time. Fingerprints smudged the images and the corners had become rounded with handling. The enclosed note asked me to please return the envelope with the photographs. But I just couldn't do it.

My daughter, Amanda, came by with her young baby, Silver, after work. I brought out the photographs. My enthusiasm was contagious, and soon she, too, was caught up in the wilderness magic. Jason, my son, was working out of state on his own adventure. When I spoke to Jason he was in love with the idea. They both shared their excitement with David, which strengthened my case for a new adventure in the wilderness. This grand change would give a totally new perspective on life. It would be an experience our grown children could benefit from.

I kept showing David the pictures and expressing such passion, and he was finally drawn in—somewhat. After a couple of weeks, he was resigned to a quick trip to see the place.

—

We each wrangled a week off work in late August. We left Washington State in the heat of a beautiful summer day. After twenty-four hours and 1,200 kilometres (750 miles) of driving, we made it to the Northern Interior of BC, east of Smithers. Much to our surprise, it was already a gorgeous fall afternoon in this part of Northern BC. We took a room at the Granisle Resort overlooking Babine Lake and marvelled at the fantastic colours within our vista.

We woke early the following morning and drove down to the beach. Everything was draped in a light, misty fog. The lodge's owner, Paul Adams, waited in his boat at the Granisle marina. He greeted us with a crooked smile, and we loaded into his small craft.

The mist evaporated as we powered up Babine Lake. Paul set a northeast course and pointed to the continental divide to our right and the Babine Mountains to our left, and told us the snow-dusted range ahead in the distance was the Driftwood Mountains. After a few quiet moments Paul casually mentioned, "My wife threatened me not to talk too much." And then he was silent.

After an hour, the speedboat pulled into Ookpik Cove. Paul quickly lashed the vessel, walked up the long dock and vanished. We hardly noticed in the height of our excitement.

Coming from the Pacific Coast, we were used to the smells of seaweed and salt water. The contrasting scent of fresh water and pine trees was distinct and heady. My eyes were drinking in the mist rising off the water lilies when David reached for my hand to help me out of the boat.

Walking directly in front of me down the dock, David stopped, turned and said, "My boat's in big trouble, isn't she?"

I had not said a thing until that moment.

"You can always find another boat," I said.

"I can always find another woman too," he retorted.

The smile on his face told me he was thinking about the possibility. But the furrow in his brow and the confusion in his eyes showed turmoil. This was not just a passing adventure, but a colossal reversal in our future's direction. My body was trembling as I followed him.

Paul and his beautiful wife, Ardys, were in their mid- to late sixties and walked slowly down the path, showing us around the area. The property was 7½ acres but only one acre had been developed. The remainder was a diverse, old-growth forest. The couple shared particulars about themselves as we wandered along the trails—the same trails I would learn to know and love dearly.

The Adamses, also Americans, had flown themselves all over Alaska trying to find a perfect place for a wilderness fishing lodge fifteen years before. With the long search fruitless, they headed home to Seattle. The blue beauty of Babine Lake lay in their charted course.

Circling over an old fishing camp where the lodge now sits, Paul and Ardys became intrigued. Taxiing their floatplane into Ookpik Cove, they were hooked. They both fell in love with the location. At the time it was just a beautiful cove, with a few old cabins built in the 1930s. Within a few months they tracked down the owners and bought it.

Our hosts escorted us along the edge of the forest to the second cabin on the south side of the lodge. Ardys and Paul went back to the lodge for a small break. This gave us time to breathe in the forest air and try to process our experiences. David and I scanned the old log cabins, placed deep in the wilderness. David's demeanour shifted profoundly. It was like he became intoxicated with the essence of the forest. He pointed out a beautiful pair of kingfishers diving in the cove and chuckled at a squirrel who called out our intrusion. They say a picture is worth a thousand words, but the pictures inside that manila envelope created a dream that could only be surpassed by the world in which we now stood. To my delight, I saw David embrace the idea of living in this place.

As we walked towards the main log house, which we would come to know as the lodge, it seemed impossible to believe all this could be ours. With each step up the stairs our excitement doubled, and then we knocked on the lodge door.

Paul greeted us with a quiet foreboding that we didn't understand at the time. (Later we came to know he suffered migraines from a previous head injury.) Ardys opened up and started talking more freely. Over coffee and cookies we all became more relaxed. Paul mechanically explained how all the systems worked. With no public road, electricity, water, sewer or fire department, everything sounded complicated. While David processed the physical details, I took in the romantic side of my surroundings. All of my senses were lit and everything seemed magnified. I could see myself placing the fragrant cedar kindling into the firebox of the shiny, enamelled wood cookstove. A wave of emotion swept over me: I wanted to live this life. I took notes about what they said but didn't hear their words.

And then they stopped. Paul and Ardys became quiet. We sensed they had finished their spiel, and it had taken a toll on them.

I went back to our little cabin in the woods in a state of euphoria. David went back mentally filing away detailed information on the systems needed for this location so far off the grid. Neither of us fully understood what that implied.

We were exhausted that night and slept like rocks in the feather bed. In the early dawn hours I awoke to the aroma of fresh coffee. I don't know how long David had been awake. We talked and dreamed and drank coffee for hours. We packed our bags slowly as we lingered in the small, cozy cabin. Our two days and one night were spent, and it was time to go.

The morning sun took every opportunity to dress our surroundings in pageantry. The flat lake held only the ripples of fish collecting breakfast and geese heading south after an evening's rest. How could we not be swept away?

Our long boat ride back to Granisle gave us an opportunity to try and grasp our location: 10 kilometres (6 miles) of pristine shoreline passed before we saw a manmade structure. On the northernmost divide of Babine Lake there were a few old log cabins and a small white church with a tall steeple. Paul explained it was an old Hudson's Bay Company settlement, and it was called Old Fort. The church and village had been given back to the Tachet Band (of the Dakelh people) years ago. We didn't see any smoke or signs of life. Paul told us people didn't live there full-time, but came to hunt moose and harvest salmon. Paul also pointed out an old, closed gold mine. That was it. There was no other sign of habitation.

Paul explained that if our boat broke down on the west side of the lake, we would have to walk for days to find civilization. If we landed on the east side of the lake, we would have to walk for weeks to find another human.

"If... you weren't eaten by grizzlies before you got to safety," he added casually.

—

After saying our goodbyes, David and I spent the next several hours during the long journey south spilling all our feelings about Ookpik Wilderness Lodge. Our conversation spun a mountain of possibilities during the drive back to Whidbey Island. By the time we got home, David was lost trying to organize his thoughts, and I was spellbound.

From that point, it took thirty days and nights to process and calculate the many documents, and then finally everything fell into place. Consumed with the thrill of adventure, we signed the contracts. David and I sold everything we owned, including the sailboat, and paid off half of the mortgage for this remote log house carved out of the forest. In late September 1994, we took possession of Ookpik Wilderness Lodge.

# CHAPTER 2

# The Adams Family

**D**avid and I arrived a few minutes early at the Granisle Lakeside Marina, where Paul was going to pick us up. The body of water before us was much bigger than we had remembered, and the wind blew a steady ten knots to the north. In the distance we saw Paul coming towards us. All we could see was white spray around his boat as it pounded over the water. Gradually it became larger, yet remained dwarfed by the immense vista. He was passing a small island we would come to know as Bear Island. The trees along the shore had started to change colour, the aspen and birch showing gold against the darkness of the spruce and pine.

We loaded a week's worth of gear and jumped into the small boat, almost speechless with excitement. Paul, much more verbal this time, adopted his new persona as tour guide. He took us back to Ookpik Wilderness Lodge with a following sea and explained how to use the skyline at night to navigate, how to use the small bits of exposed shoreline to traverse in the fog. The wind drove the surf north, carrying the boat along. I felt my life being ushered forth as well, by the power of Mother Nature.

Our arrival that day felt fresh and new. It was different: we were the owners of Ookpik Wilderness Lodge. We began to consider for the first time the reality of living here. Life was magnificent. Nothing could have prepared me for this bliss.

Nowadays, I become frightened and panicky when I get this close to perfection. It feels like being in the eye of a storm, seemingly peaceful but there are secret edges of dread all around, as though something devastating is going to happen. But at that time, it felt like we were in paradise. Nothing could be better. It was heaven on earth.

The Adamses seemed more comfortable with us than previously—although both were very sombre, they were sincere. It was as if they had finally come to terms with the sale of the property. We learned volumes from them during our visit, including how the lodge came into existence.

As a team, Paul and Ardys had hauled logs using a small, powerful boat they called *The Duck*. They pulled a log boom 130 kilometres (80 miles) by water, north from Pendleton Bay, on the southern part of Babine Lake. They beached their load in Ookpik Cove. They rented a small apartment and took on jobs in Granisle and waited for spring. When spring came, they hired a barge to help bring in the majority of their belongings and equipment. Soon they began the adventure of building Ookpik Wilderness Lodge. Ardys hadn't used many power tools before, let alone a chainsaw or a backhoe. Even the radio phone was a new experience.

Paul and Ardys placed the foundation for the lodge in 1978. Paul used the backhoe to raise and lift the monster logs into place. On the last log of the first round, the chain holding the 80-foot timber slipped. It swung around, smashing into the cab of the backhoe and crushing Paul's head against the ground.

Ardys, in shock, was still able, after just one lesson, to use the chainsaw and cut the end off the giant log. Then she moved the backhoe into an upright position to free her husband from his near-death trap. Somehow, she dragged the unconscious Paul into the boat. She called ahead by radio phone, and an ambulance awaited their arrival at the village.

Paul was in the hospital and under medical care for over a year before he saw their place on the lake again. He was never the same. Major migraine headaches caused this formerly happy-go-lucky man to be irritable. He said to me one time, "You think I am handsome now, you shoulda seen me then."

Paul may have been a handsome and capable guy, but Ardys—she was exceptional.

Amazingly, with just a little help from their friends, Paul and Ardys finished the lodge in 1984. But Paul never fully recovered from his migraines and they never opened the lodge for business.

Paul told us again that Ardys threatened him if he "talked too much." Evidently he had already scared off a few prospective buyers. But now he opened up. And David and I were like two giant sponges, soaking up all the information we could. This was imperative for understanding the unusual systems and idiosyncrasies of the lodge. Between the two of them, they helped us gain as much knowledge as possible.

This isolated world off the grid also demanded a crash course in wilderness survival. David and I took notes as fast as we could write them down, and we also used a tape recorder. One of the lessons we recorded was Paul and Ardys saying, "You both have to agree on the way each of you will deal with a grizzly attack. You need to make a pact on whether or not to shoot the bear, with the chance the partner might be shot by accident."

We went to our little cabin after that meeting and replayed that segment of the recording over and over. The thought of a grizzly attack had never occurred to us. We shook hands and agreed if one of us were being mauled by a grizzly, the other would try to shoot and kill the bear and not shoot the other.

A few days later we modified the agreement when we realized we had only a shotgun. It would be kind of hard not to hit the human while trying to kill a bear with double-aught buckshot. We put a regular rifle on our list of needs. All this conversation seemed strange because neither of us had ever seen a bear, nor shot a gun. But David and I were infatuated with the place. By then nothing could have interfered with the transaction or the transformation of our way of life.

Paul and Ardys stayed on for a week, ensuring their baby would be passed into capable hands. The lessons in how to shut down the lodge for winter were paramount. I took copious notes. Sprinkled between all the serious concerns, we gleaned many things about the couple and what they'd achieved. For instance, Ardys had scribed every single log. She had marked and cut them to fit every knot and slight bend.

Ardys said when Paul rolled each giant log into place, the sound made at contact would tell if it fit just right, or if it had to be rolled over and scribed again. When all the logs were placed, Paul wanted to use a sander to finish. They had weathered into a grey colour while sitting in the cove during the years of Paul's convalescence. Ardys refused to use the sanding machine to remove the grey. She wanted to maintain the wonderful texture and beauty of the log surface obtained after slicing off the bark with a draw knife. So she scraped and cut through the greyed wood to retrieve the golden colour they originally had. Day after day, she scraped and scraped until at last she was satisfied. Paul finished the logs with a clear protective sealant. The process took several weeks. Finally, they were ready for the roof. It took a mountain of shakes. They split every single one by hand.

While telling these stories, Paul and Ardys were so animated and enthusiastic. Their two memories interacted, combining into an amazing recollection. They seemed bigger than life, with their adventures and accomplishments.

After intense study under the tutelage of Paul and Ardys, the day came to take them to the village. The morning was misty and rainy with no wind. The drops pounded the flat, grey surface of the lake. We got into the boat, feeling enveloped with a heavy saturation of both rain and emotional duress, wondering if we were doing the right thing. David and I were elated with the thrill of our new adventures to come, while wondering if we could even make it back through the 30 kilometres (20 miles) of unfamiliar weather and water.

Paul and Ardys seemed smaller and deflated, with all their words spent. Paul sat for the last time in the captain's seat, with Ardys straight, tall and striking alongside him. She wept all the way and Paul was sombre as always, but with a single tear trailing down his scarred face. With rain rolling down the canvas and windshield of the boat, it felt like their world wept along with them. It was a lengthy, heartbreaking trip.

I felt so sad for them that cool, grey September morning. Leaving this world—where they had shed real blood, real sweat and real tears—had to be devastating. The memories of dreams realized, and dreams abandoned, must have been terrible. Although they were moving to another log cabin in Northern BC, nothing would ever compare to the adventures of Ookpik.

On the other side of the boat, David and I were consumed with the immense journey before us.

# CHAPTER 3

# Quiet Waters Run Deep

D avid and I spent another week at the lodge, lost in the grandeur of it all, and then went back to Whidbey Island for the winter. Conveniently, the new owner of the sailboat would not take possession until spring.

The first thing I did after returning to the States was to haunt the Humane Society shelters for the perfect dog to take up north with us. On our journey south we had decided it would be a good idea to get an alarm dog—one that was not too big, but not a small, wimpy yapper. After several weeks and several different dog pounds, I found the perfect animal. She was a two-year-old American Eskimo and weighed about 20 pounds. With a coat of long white hair, the winters would be no problem. And with a curled tail, she looked the part, so I rescued her and took her home. The only problem with this beautiful canine was her name: Princess. David would never call out a name like Princess! So, before I introduced our new companion, I christened her Foxy. She was a terrific addition to our upcoming northern life.

That winter we worked with enthusiasm. Our mission was to organize our personal possessions and collect the tools and supplies needed before spring, which came within a blink of an eye.

We arrived up north early the next spring with a lighter key ring, dreams overflowing and a list of chores ten pages long. Our hope was to open our place the following spring as a fishing lodge for floatplane enthusiasts and fly fishermen.

We found the difference in the seasons in the north was profound, and unlike anything we had ever experienced. While the tulips bloomed in the fields in Washington State, the land and water in the Babine Valley was still frozen. We watched this sleeping world come to life. The flourishing energy of spring painted the blank canvas. An unfamiliar melody of songs filled the crisp air, followed by the frenzy of nesting birds. Time sent winter back with warmer and longer days, letting spring leap forward until the cold was just a memory. Asleep for many long months, the incredible scent of pine trees exploded with the hot spring sun and filled this world anew.

Giant dragonflies carried on through the long days of summer, with dazzling sunsets that lasted for hours. Summer consumed us with its grandeur and was a precious reward for our endurance through the long winter months. A heavy frost in early August was no surprise to the local inhabitants.

The months went by in a torrent of education, work and play. Every morning was a joy to behold. With the exuberance of young children on Christmas morning, we bounced through our days. Everything was a fresh and new encounter with a world unknown.

Our hearts were entwined with love for each other and the dreams we shared before us. At the crest of this emotional bliss, we greeted our second fall with open hearts, with no indication of what was to come. The sprinkle of colour became more vibrant each day and reverberated across the lake. Bears came to harvest salmon along the shore and wolves howled in the dead of night. With great anticipation we awaited our first full winter at Ookpik. We were not disappointed. With startling force, Old Man Winter confiscated the land with a heavy eiderdown of clean white snow. Moonbeams moved through the laden forest, illuminating the night with tiny jewels on the frozen surfaces.

—

Our first winter spent at Ookpik was magical. Twelve feet of snow accumulated. The weight of the compressed snow created a glacial turquoise colour along the sides of our shovelled paths. David made the trails extra wide to accommodate the two 5-gallon pails of water we needed to carry up every day from our water hole cut in the ice of the lake. Water splashed and formed smooth boils of ice on either side of the path. The splatter would freeze to David's pant legs during the short trip to the house. There was a particular ice hazard area on the path. This is the spot where a pair of ptarmigans, dressed in their snow-coloured invisible plumes, were spooked by the water carrier one day and burst into flight directly in front of David. He managed to save most of the water, but a treacherous gallon escaped to glaze 3 feet of the path.

Just drilling the hole to make the well required a remarkable amount of work. First, David and I took turns using a 6-inch auger to drill a hole through the 3 feet of ice. Then David chainsawed a 3-foot square with an X in the middle. After that, he used a crowbar to pop out chunks of solid ice. I kept the chunks for the ice box. When we saw it would be impossible to reach the last 11 inches of remaining ice with the 2-foot chainsaw bar, we took turns using a swede saw. The hole filled with icy water that froze as we worked.

Finally, we fished out the remaining ice chunks and used the crowbar to chip and finish the hole. Every single day the opening shrank and we had to remove the accumulated ice around the edge. After collecting the water, we covered the hole with a 4-foot circular wooden lid and then packed snow over the cover, to insulate the water from severe freezing conditions. That helped some.

On the way to the well one morning, David noticed we had forgotten to replace the water cover. He thought we would have to re-cut the well. But when he looked down at the water he saw liquid—it hadn't frozen! David was surprised to see a small black head pop up. He was no less stunned than the river otter was to see a man looking back! Consequently, a new hole had to be made. (Otters don't mind pooping in and around their water access.) This meant a longer walk to retrieve our daily water needs. We didn't mind. The shenanigans of our new otter neighbours were priceless on quiet, snowbound days.

We had three cold snaps that winter. It is easy to say a cold snap is −34° to −51°C. It is difficult describing exactly what it means. One winter in the northern latitudes gave us a brand-new perspective. And when you are snowbound for months, you have loads of time to analyze everything.

When you live in the north, the word "cold" has several definitions:

At 15°C, the room is cold.

At 1°C, the snow is sticky, so it's not cold enough to cross-country ski.

At −10°C, it's not cold enough to take dogs for a long walk, because snow freezes on their fur, making snowballs collect, and it's too heavy for them to carry.

At −25° to −29°C, it's great to snowshoe, cross-country ski and exercise the dog.

At −40°C, it's too cold to leave the cabin for more than a few minutes. Logging stops, metal breaks like uncooked pasta and propane freezes.

At −51°C, it's dangerous to be outside—any exposed skin will freeze. If you draw a breath unprotected, too deeply or too quickly, your lungs will freeze. Humans were not made to live in that kind of cold.

One of my favourite ways to play on a winter day was blowing soap bubbles at −40°C. I would start with warm, soapy water and hurry outside. I'd need to be quick with the blowing process, but it was very rewarding. Each bubble seemed to hold many more colours than a rainbow, maybe because of the lack of colour everywhere else. As the iridescent bubble formed, it would freeze and fall to the snow-covered ground. Upon hitting the surface it would break like an egg and lie there with all its peacock colours. Talk about a step back into childlike joy! Quickly, I'd repeat the process. But this kept me entertained for only a couple of moments—not for lack of enthusiasm, but because the bottle would soon freeze solid and I would not be able to pull out the wand.

That first winter an ice formation built up over the outside kitchen wall. Evidently, the gable was not insulated sufficiently. This caused snow to melt and run down. Not just a few icicles or a little sheet of ice, but a giant wall 20 feet high and 4 feet thick. This frozen wall bubbled up over the top of itself every day for months. David and I worked hard to try to stop this phenomenon in the beginning. One of us would climb a 14-foot aluminum ladder and work daily to melt the collection of ice. We tried to remove the rain gutter, with no success. During all this effort, the ice—a living creature—continued to grow in and around the steps of the ladder, making it part of the miraculous structure. In the end, we had to abandon the ladder along with the gutter. It wouldn't be until the following June, when the ice finally released its grip, that we'd be able to retrieve the twisted and destroyed gutter.

Meanwhile, I broke some of the monster icicles off the edge and pushed them upside-down into the snow, along the path, making a little fence to the outhouse. Each day, for fun, I took coloured water and poured it over the ice spikes, creating a fantasy trail in the winter wonderland. I tried to take pictures of my creation, but my camera would not function under such severe weather conditions. It was too cold and the lens fogged over.

David and I had married on Valentine's Day twelve years earlier. In February I dug out the hidden valentines and anniversary cards. I was kind of smug because I knew David had not been thinking of our anniversary the last time we were in town, several months prior.

On our warm, sunny porch, where the thermometer read −33°C, I sprung out the cards. Then I waited, ready to produce a predetermined pout. David gave me a big hug and swung me around to face the snow-covered expanse of the lake in front of the lodge.

To my delight, I saw a monster heart tramped in the deep snow. It even had an arrow going through it. He whispered over my shoulder, "I love you. Happy anniversary, darling." I shall never have a card as wonderful as the massive valentine he created for me in that vast, white vista.

We loved ice fishing and it turned out to be very necessary for winter nutrition. Without access to a grocery store, we had few options for fresh protein. The excitement of a catch produced a main entrée for a week. It's amazing how tasty a meal becomes when you work for it.

Each day I saved a little bit of the 8 gallons of water David brought to the house daily from the lake. On Sundays, I received a double delivery. With this extra water, David and I would celebrate with candlelight and a steamy bath.

I shall never, in my lifetime, turn on a water faucet without thanking the water gods. Flipping on the thermostat in a modern home in the city always makes me feel like a pampered woman. Turning on a light switch is still magic for me. Life in the north taught me to notice and appreciate these simple acts.

And then there was the apparently inevitable cabin fever. I first saw this term written in big copper letters on a medical building in Anchorage, Alaska: CABIN FEVER CENTER. I never knew the true meaning, or knew anyone who admitted to having the affliction, until we met Paul and Ardys.

They warned us about cabin fever. Listening to our recorded lessons, we heard Paul say, "You need to be prepared for cabin fever after a few months of isolation. You might have a frying pan come zinging across the room for just the simplest thing. Pulling at your earlobe one too many a time is a perfect example."

I laughed at the absurdity—until, that is, David and I were into our fifth month of isolation and he just ran out of things to say. That doesn't sound too dreadful unless you have no other form of communication. Without a phone, radio, TV, neighbours or even a mailman, a person needs conversation. And I had found myself with a husband who ran out of words.

"You ran out of... WORDS? How can you run out of words?" I asked.

Cabin fever had set in. I had no control over the situation, and poor David had nowhere to hide! I lit into him like a fish wife with no fish! Poor kind-hearted, unsuspecting David didn't know what hit him. Thank God it was a lashing of high-pitched gibberish and not a frying pan.

After a few choice words, I was off—mad as hell, for no reason at all! Jamming on my cross-country ski boots and not enough clothes, I flew down the frozen steps.

The next thing I remember, I was puffing up a steam cloud roughly 8 kilometres (5 miles) from home. It was getting dark. Even through my earmuffs, I could hear wolves howling nearby, probably making plans to pick off this helpless idiot. That was when I stopped and wondered, *Why am I out here alone?* The second my situation sank in, I turned back towards the lodge and, in the distance, saw a black speck on the frozen lake.

The silence of the snow blanketed the landscape, making all sounds unheard, all except the wolves communicating to each other—about me!

I had dressed unwisely, and unhealthy consequences developed with every second that passed. My earlier accumulation of sweat now froze and my inappropriate house pants were frozen to my legs. With my energy fading, I slowed to a crawl on unwaxed skis. Hypothermia set in and my brain refused to register events properly. The sun sank into the snow-covered mountains. I forced onward while I repeated the mantra, "You can do this, you can do this." I huffed towards home.

The next thing I remember was my sweet David on his Ski-Doo, asking me in his warm, deep voice, "Want a ride?"

My king—so wonderful, so nice, my sweet David of few words.

# CHAPTER 4

# Season of Change

The winter melted away, along with the rivers of melted snow and ice. Our long-awaited spring arrived. It was time to address the massive job list created during the previous months. We checked off the chores done throughout the day and added to the never-ending ledger every night. I was the expeditor, and with the shop a few hundred feet away from the dock, all the cookies I ate were burned off running to fetch this and that. And someone had to bake said cookies.

David was in his element. Dock repairs, roof repairs and deck repairs filled our days. He loved to be busy and see things finished. We wanted to have everything ready for our first paying guest, in the spring of 1997. We were astonished at just how hot it was at midday. David and I expected the northern summer to be chilly, and indeed, when the sun finally set—after 11 p.m.—the mosquitoes buzzed in the cool air. Summer days burned away as fast as they came, with stolen swaths of time spent fishing in the late evening sun. As exhausted as we were every night, we were filled with happiness. These arduous days were not a burden but a gift.

As the aspen leaves turned a more intense gold with each cool night, we gathered piles and piles of wood, preparing for our second winter like a couple of squirrels in overdrive. For weeks David split logs and I stacked firewood. We needed more than eighteen cords.

One morning, while preserving highbush cranberries, I heard an explosion coming from our dining room. I ran to investigate and was just in time to see feathers drifting away in the breeze. Two distinct spots of blood and a few tiny feathers smeared the window where two birds had hit the glass at full force. I looked outside and saw David on his knees, two kingfishers cradled in his lap.

Tears filled his eyes and dripped into his beard. The birds lay together, unmoving. Drops of blood ran down the male bird's beak. I moved out of sight so I would not embarrass David in his private grief. I watched as he willed life into one of the birds by gently blowing into the stilled beak. It soon flew off. Maybe the kingfisher revived on its own, or maybe David's ministrations worked. The tenderness my husband exhibited made my heart swell. The male bird did not move, though, and I watched as David cradled the king of fishers down the path and into the woods.

We never mentioned this event to each other. David did not want to bring forth the anguish of death. I didn't want to renew the pain I saw in his demeanour.

In early October, my cousins Zack and Josh, and Josh's friend Lisa, were coming to visit. I hadn't seen my cousins for thirty years.

"How will I know you?" I asked Josh over the phone.

"I am the one who loved you when I was six years old," he answered.

David and I picked them up from the airport in Smithers, three hours away from our remote lodge. Josh was right. I recognized him by the way he smiled at me. I could still see the young blond boy and instantly remembered how he squeezed my hand so many years ago as kids on a California beach. Now holding the hand of Lisa, an Italian beauty, Josh beamed as he introduced her.

Zack, his older brother, was glad to get away. He worked as an emergency medical technician for the fire department in Monterey, California, and needed a break.

It was getting dark as we drove back to Babine Lake. Zack, Josh and Lisa were delighted to learn the last leg of their twelve-hour journey included a boat ride in the moonlight. By the time we loaded the boat, the sky was a blackish blue, with a full moon rising above the mountains. The moonlight hit the tops of our wake, creating a brilliant trail that shimmered across the waters. Everything else was velvet black.

My cousins were astounded to encounter no signs of human development on the way to Ookpik Lodge. To them it seemed strange, to have come so many miles on the water and not to see lights or any human disturbance. As we approached, they were entranced by our little story-book village of log cabins lit by moonlight. We escorted Josh and Lisa to the second cabin, lit their lamp and let them melt into the feather bed. We continued along the forest trail to the last cabin, where Zack was excited to take up position for the week.

The next morning our local loon family gave the wake-up call. Our guests were greeted with a view of the lake, which was reverberating with reflections of the dramatic fall colours and framed by the pristine wilderness.

Our home was filled with family and laughter. My aunt Ginger and uncle Ray, who had arrived the day before, were settled in already and happy to see their sons. I was grateful to have this time to reminisce. Not only did we all get to tell our sides of funny family tales, it was also a perfect time for me to get to know Zack and Josh again, and to share David with them. David and I were caught up on our chores and had set aside time to visit. By the end of this day, we were quite relaxed and had enjoyed our day off immensely.

That night, after everyone had gone to their little cabins, David and I threw a blanket down in our bedroom in front of a grand, crackling fire and lay down together. It seemed like it had been a very long time since we had gazed into each other's eyes without falling asleep.

The brilliant blue skies continued the next day, without a breath of wind, and the sun made it feel much warmer than it really was. We stood on the deck, where David told our visitors about how wonderful water-skiing could be on that glassy lake. One arm around David's waist, I listened while he spoke, thinking how lucky I was to share *this* dream with *this* man by my side.

The ski boat beckoned, and David, Josh, Zack and Lisa answered its call. Despite the warm sunshine, the water was cold. Everyone pulled on light wetsuits. David was a wonderful skier, and I usually drove the boat for him. This time, Josh, David and Zack took turns driving and skiing, while Lisa took pictures of the scenery and the skiers, and I stayed at the lodge with my aunt and uncle.

When it was David's turn to ski, I went out to watch. He waved to me as he passed the front dock, casting a beautiful rainbow spray just for me. I caught his eye, and still remember his gaze over his shoulder as he made his turn. He swooped past, then straightened up and hooked his right arm into the pull bar, and I went back to the warm kitchen. Inside, I visited with Aunt Ginger, placing cookies just so on Grandma's best china. Uncle Ray, a writer, worked on a new manuscript, a keen eye on the cookie plate.

I was expecting the cold, wet and tired skiers back at any moment, and I listened for the boat heading to the back harbour where we usually moored it. I was surprised when I heard the boat roaring, full throttle, towards the front dock. I rushed out and knew immediately something was very wrong. Josh was driving the boat and I could not see David or Zack. Lisa waved madly.

I flew to the dock and heard someone screaming, "Call an ambulance." I raced back to the lodge to get the hand-held radio phone. My aunt and uncle followed me back out. I called the ambulance number as I ran back to the dock. I was transferred from one city to another. My voice became louder and higher pitched each time they transferred me to another contact. As my feet hit the dock, I saw Zack, Josh and Lisa doing CPR on David. No one knew what had happened. He had no visible injuries, and there hadn't been an obvious collision or incident. He'd just collapsed on his skis, they told me.

Finally, the operator connected me to an emergency team several hundred kilometres away. They told me to have my family keep up the CPR until the helicopter arrived and for me to stay on the radio phone. This proved to be incredibly difficult. I had to stand still and remain on the line with the emergency operator. I could not release the radio phone to try and help. Zack was in charge and instrumental in directing the family, united in trying to save David's life. Everyone became exhausted, yet no one stopped. Even though I knew Zack was trained for this, it was extremely difficult to keep from throwing down the radio phone and assisting.

"Send the helicopter *now!*" I begged the operator.

Then I heard a helicopter over the roar of emotion. Yes, I could see it. The aircraft was headed our way. It would be here any second! My radio phone told me we had been engaged in exactly twenty-five minutes of non-stop CPR and radio communications. Suddenly, the helicopter took a right turn away from us.

"What is happening? Can't he see us?" I called to the operator.

"That pilot is on another mission of mercy," she answered.

It was not our helicopter. The sweat dripped off my cousins' faces as they worked to keep David alive. Keeping my focus on what had to be done, while my own heart was breaking, was a huge effort. Another helicopter appeared, but it did not turn towards us either. We waved and hollered at the sky, as my cousins continued CPR, but to no avail.

Forty minutes had now passed since I had connected to the emergency operator. Josh and my uncle were working on David, but I could tell they were both about to collapse. Zack relieved my uncle. "One, two, three, four, breathe. One, two, three, four, breathe...." David still showed no response.

"I hear a helicopter!"

This one had to be ours. Yes, the helicopter was coming our way! The pilot signalled, wanting to know where to land. I marked the spot with water skis and stood back. My radio operator asked if it was our aircraft. "Yes," I replied, and we disconnected.

Looking at the radio phone, I saw fifty-four minutes had passed. David's skin was not the same colour it was an hour earlier.

The rescue crew piled out with their equipment and took over from Josh and Zack. They cut off David's wetsuit. As they loaded him onto a stretcher, I followed, too close. The crew pushed me gently back, saying I couldn't come with them in the helicopter. They had to tell me sternly to stand clear as the helicopter rose in slow motion.

With my bare feet spread on the cold October grass, I felt a vibration from deep in the earth. A horrible, thunderous sound roared closer and closer until it found the soles of my feet and spread like the heat of a wildfire up my legs. David rose in the helicopter 20 feet in the air above me, his arm fallen from where they had placed it upon his chest, his face turned towards me.

A horrific and deafening pain exploded in my chest. It rose into my throat, and my mouth opened with an outpouring of anguish. I fell to my knees.

Time stopped.

I found myself in the ski boat. I moved David's swim towel and placed his sailor cap on the dash. Mechanically, I started the engine, thoughts tumbling one over the other. *The medical people will not let me ride in the helicopter. The helicopter is gone. David is gone. I know he is really gone.*

"I must go. I must kiss his lips before he leaves this world forever," I said out loud.

Josh and Zack jumped into the ski boat, still wet from water-skiing, and we sped over the surface of the lake, now darkened with black clouds. A storm was coming in. The forty-five-minute journey to the village evaporated. I then drove us in the old Suburban to the hospital in Smithers, another two hours from Granisle, my brain just a silent roar. I exchanged no words with my two cousins. Drawing on their strength, I focused on the tricky dirt and gravel roads.

When we arrived at the hospital, we learned David had not survived the journey. The RCMP separated my cousins from each other and placed me in yet another room. Now, in that sterilized space, I felt truly alone. I wandered around the room with only hollow grief to keep me standing. Time passed, and I found myself still alone, sitting in a brown plastic chair in a beige room.

Because David's death had been deemed suspicious, each of us underwent interrogation. The RCMP thought David was just too young and too healthy to die of natural causes. Plus, he was an American citizen. It would take an autopsy to determine the cause of death.

When the officers finally left, I asked the nurse in charge if I could see my husband's body. I needed to say goodbye and to kiss his lips. The nurse immediately called the RCMP to ask if I could enter David's room, as it had been sealed for the investigation.

The nurse also had to prepare him for me. They had placed him in a body bag.

"You need an escort to view the body," the nurse said.

As the nurse opened David's room, a cold breeze hit my face—an unusual chill, for a hospital. The emptiness of that room engulfed me.

David lay on an elevated bed, a plastic plug in his mouth. I asked the nurse to remove the plug. She refused. I insisted. The nurse called the RCMP again and they said she could remove it. She did and left.

I stood beside David for quite some time. I spoke to him: words of love from David's wife to David's soul. And then I kissed his lips tenderly.

On the road home, I saw a herd of caribou—the only thing I remember from that drive. The animals were magnificent, running with the dark night wind. They bounded up and over the dirt road and into the black forest, their enormous antlers thrown so far behind their small, stout bodies that they almost touched their backs. I remember the whites of their eyes as they looked over long noses before turning to follow their leader. I had never seen caribou before, and I never saw one in the wild again, though I lived in that wilderness for twenty-four years.

# CHAPTER 5

# Visitor in the Moonlight

Eventually, the doctors would determine that David had died of a heart attack while spraying beautiful rainbows, just for me, with his water skis. But it would take some time for the coroner to arrive at that conclusion.

I do believe that only the good die young. It's true: David was such a good man, and at only forty-seven, he was much too young to die. I used to tease him on his birthdays, "You will always be older than me." Not true anymore.

His death was a life-shattering event. We always said, "Life goes on." How could we have guessed it would not?

I didn't have a funeral or hold a wake. We didn't believe in them. We believed in a supreme being, but we were not religious—we were spiritual. If David had a totem, it would have been the wolf.

David and I had left everyone we knew and loved more than 700 miles away, across an international border. Still, many people came up to pay their respects and to extend their sympathy. Neither my younger brother nor my son, who was on a fishing boat in Alaska, could come, but they were there in spirit. My parents, who had purchased a home in Granisle two months earlier, were there when I returned. They had been packing, as snowbirds do, getting ready for their yearly holidays in Mexico. My older brother arrived shortly thereafter. My daughter, Amanda, always so strong and steadfast, was there to hold me up. I could not have managed at all without Amanda. She also brought her two young daughters, Silver and Chavala, for which I was grateful. My sister, who had never before accepted an invitation, also came. It was good they were all there I suppose, although I remember nothing of my sister. I know she must have been doing the cooking and cleaning, along with everything Amanda was doing. It meant so much that they were there—more than I could ever say—and sadly, I said nothing.

I remember yelling at my sister's husband, also named David, who had done nothing to deserve it. He asked me if he could do anything to help, and I suggested he become the fire tender. I called him by his last name, Churchill, as I could not bear to call him by my sweet David's name.

I showed Churchill a vent knob in the back of the stove that no longer functioned properly and asked him not to touch it. A few hours—or days—later, I went into the room and saw the wood stove shuddering as if it had come alive. It was dangerously red hot and woofing air. I panicked. Fearing the lodge would burn down, and many of my family would perish, I reached behind the huffing stove to close the errant knob.

"You must have messed with the knob!" I screamed at Churchill. I am sure now he did not touch the damn thing—poor guy.

As I reached behind the stove, I laid my tender forearm against the red-hot metal. Feeling nothing, I reacted to the smell of burning skin and pulled my arm back. Silver saw my arm and started to cry. I still felt nothing.

The radio phone rang, and no one answered it. Robotically, I walked over to the station and picked up the mic and replied flatly, "Ookpik Wilderness Lodge."

"This is the coroner. I have a few questions for you. Do you know how your husband died?"

Everyone on the radio frequency within a 200-mile radius was listening to this conversation. In the wilderness, rumours related to a death spread like wildfire.

I had to force myself to become emotionless and disconnected in order to speak at all. I remembered the consultation with David's doctor at his last checkup and I replied with the most concise reasoning possible for me at the time.

"I believe the artery going from his heart to his brain blew up." My answer fell flat—a monotone.

The coroner came back fast and professional, and my family gathered around to hear as he said, "You know, I have two other doctors here and we have looked extensively, and we do not think that is what happened."

My emotions flipped into overdrive. Here was a doctor looking at my husband's body cut open, with his heart in his hands, questioning me—on cause of death.

"You asked me, and I told you what I thought. You and your two other doctors, with a collective education of over thirty years... and you've cut him open... and looked at his heart, and you are telling me you can't figure out what happened to my husband?" I wailed.

My mother removed the mic from my shaking fist and hung up the radio. It was time for me to remove myself from the crowded house.

Silver and I moved into the small cabin next door. She saved me. I had to be strong in her presence, and I succeeded in that endeavour. What I didn't expect was such a little girl being strong for me; she was only five years old. No one had told her David had died. No one knew how. She loved her Papa David.

I found it impossible to sleep. When I was stroking the sweet soft baby skin of Silver's forehead one night, she woke up and said, "Papa is not coming back, is he?"

"No," I replied.

"He must have water-skied all the way to heaven," she whispered.

"Yes, honey," I said.

With a soft, sleepy voice she said, "There must be a big lake up there for him to land on, huh, Nana."

Without another word, Silver's heavy eyelashes closed onto her sweet baby cheeks, and she fell into a gentle slumber. I slept for the first time in days. (For many years thereafter, I would be blessed to have Silver come and stay with me for several weeks in the late summer.)

The next morning my mother came to our cabin and told me I needed to answer the radio. It was the coroner again. He apologized profusely for the last call and said that they now believed David had a blockage in the heart's major artery to the brain, and that he had sustained substantial damage to the heart muscle, causing a massive coronary thrombosis. Although Zack and Josh had kept his blood flowing with CPR, he had died instantly.

I know my family was perfect and wonderful during their stay, but I just do not remember many details. A week later, they each returned to their homes. I stayed on at the lodge, alone; it was mine. I had invested my heart and paid for it with such deep trauma, the thought of leaving my home and going back to the States never entered my mind.

—

David came to me two or three weeks later. Normally, I don't tell people this because they would look at me strangely. At least I know that if someone told me this story, I would think them odd. But here is the truth: One November night, when the moon was full and I tossed restlessly in my bed, sleep eluding me, I heard my bedroom door open.

David was there in the blue moonlight.

"Don't be upset, everything is OK," he said in his velvet voice.

David looked happy, standing as he often did, with his weight shifted to one leg. He gently closed the door and sat down on my side of the bed.

"Don't cry anymore. I'll help get you through this," he said softly. He lay down beside me, so extraordinarily close. I remember no skin-to-skin contact. It was more like soul-to-soul melt. My strongest memory is a flood of sensations that started at my head, his cheek near mine, and flowed through my body, through every vein, muscle and bone to my fingertips, to the bottom of my feet. When it reached the full length, the sensation

sparked, then ignited my body and soul. It was a physical experience not unlike an orgasm or a rush of adrenaline. It was a combination of both and neither—something powerful and unknown to me before, or since. And then I slept—a deep and long-missed sleep—with no thoughts, no fears and no tears.

I never saw David again. I believe his spirit had passed peacefully into the all-encompassing energy of pure beauty, love and happiness.

# PART 2

# The Reality

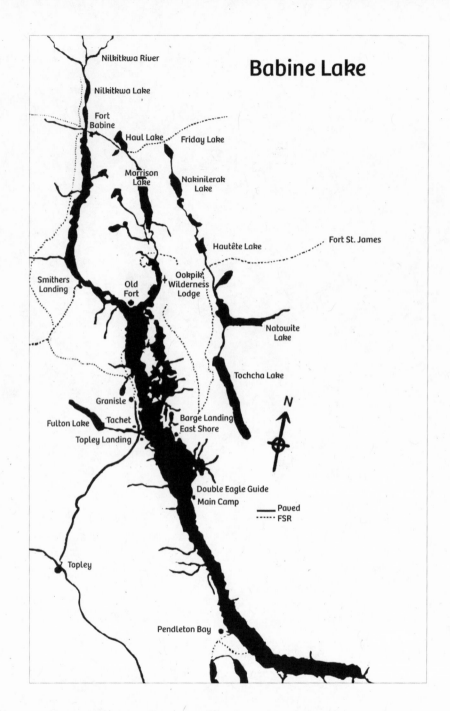

**Babine Lake**

Nilkitkwa River

Nilkitkwa Lake

Fort
Babine

Haul Lake   Friday Lake

Morrison
Lake          Nakinilerak
              Lake

                                    Fort St. James

              Hautête Lake

Smithers              Ookpik
Landing      Old     Wilderness
             Fort      Lodge

                                  Natowite
                                  Lake

                          Tochcha Lake

          Granisle                 N

Fulton Lake   Tachet   Barge Landing
Topley Landing          East Shore

                       Double Eagle Guide
                       Main Camp
                                    —— Paved
                                    ---- FSR

   Topley

              Pendleton Bay

*Morrison Arm on Babine Lake and the nearby small lakes shown on this map
were all in my angling guide's territory.*

# CHAPTER 6

# *The Duck*

ater that month, as the days became shorter and the nights longer, loneliness created an emotional mist that filled my days with a cool, damp emptiness. My family had left, and I was alone for the first time in my life. The numbness was all-encompassing. I felt no desires, no intention and no will. Days came and went. I was glad to have our dog Foxy with me. She gave me reason to carry on through the day.

One morning, in early November, the snow fell again. Big flakes floated in a zigzag motion, like down feathers from a goose, falling slowly to earth and creating a sense of extreme depth and space. I stared out my bedroom window and became lost in the immense cosmos of time.

I could see the front dock, now frozen in a crystallized water world. On sunnier days, from a platform placed on top of a dock piling, we had fed the golden eagles fish scraps. David and I had treasured the time we spent watching these majestic birds from inside the warmth of our bedroom. They would swoop down and grab the fish in powerful talons, then, without stopping, continue their flight. We would watch as they carried the fish to their massive nest on top of a tall pine on the far side of the lake.

Through the falling flakes I could see the female kingfisher standing on this same platform, which was now covered with 3 inches of snow. Motionless, she looked north. The last of the migratory birds to leave the area, this kingfisher stood with her feathers fluffed against the cold as she waited for her partner, the one who had died in David's arms weeks earlier. She and I waited in vain.

As I watched her ready herself for the migratory flight so ingrained in her species, I realized that we shared the strength of our will to survive. This female kingfisher carried on by herself in the frozen emptiness of snowflakes and space. Faced with hundreds of miles and a life alone, she had to shake the accumulated weight of the snow off her shoulders and carry on. I had to gather my courage to leave all the beautiful memories created inside this warm room and travel south as well.

The next day I loaded our 11-foot runabout to the gunnels with important and ridiculous stuff. With every added box and carton, the small vessel sank lower and lower in the water. Foxy, unenthused about the gloom of my mood and the preparations of shutting the lodge down for the winter, was keeping close to my heels. The lack of a warming fire, the commotion of packing, doors opening and closing, the journey back and forth down the dock, with the weather building—it all added to her unrest.

To top it off, I was not in a normal state of mind, and she noticed everything. It was three in the afternoon and the shortest day of the year was just a few weeks away. If I'd had my wits about me, I would not have cast off into the unpredictable lake so late in the afternoon. I would have waited for the weather to pass and left earlier the following day.

In this boat, the journey usually took no more than forty-five minutes at thirty-five knots, using one and a half tanks of fuel. With two tanks on board, I would have enough fuel even if I hit really rowdy seas—or so I thought.

My trip would take me south down Morrison Arm, through the main body of Babine Lake, past Bear Island and across to the village of Granisle. As I came around the dogleg of Morrison Arm, the full force of unexpected weather conditions hit.

Upon reaching the entrance to the main body of Babine Lake, I witnessed the fetch, the wind's constant direction, generating a mountain of water, which was trying to flow over the shallow reef at the entrance to Morrison Arm. At this point I realized I had made a life-threatening mistake.

Breaking waves rolled over the shelf, but due to the spent fuel, I was committed and there could be no turning back. I reduced speed and plowed into the wind-ripped froth. This would be the worst of it, I thought. After crossing the mouth of the arm, I came to the lake's widest span. Ignoring my prayers, the wind picked up even more, adding to the stormy conditions.

Babine Lake is British Columbia's largest natural lake. By the time the wind blew up from the south—a full 140 kilometres (90 miles)—the fetch was tremendous. The freeboard on my heavily laden boat was about one foot off the side and 6 inches off the stern. I was forced to cruise, quartering the seas, crossing over 6-foot waves with giant rogue breakers thrown in sporadically, just to spice things up. To turn back now would be suicide. The boat would swamp if I tried to follow the seas north, so I lugged on.

My straight course would have been southwest, but because the waves were so tall, I had to cross over them into the wind southeast, then turn southwest in a zigzag fashion. My headway was slow due to the zigzag course and the dramatic increase in wave size.

With a surge and then *putt-putt-putt*, my engine died. Adrenaline already pumping, I was flooded with fear.

My first fuel tank had gone dry. The boat breached and swung sideways as I stepped to the stern to switch tanks. Coming broadside up the wall of a giant wave and falling down the other side, I was surprised my little runabout had not capsized. The boat wallowed in the trough while I pumped madly at the bulb in the fuel line and then dashed back to start the engine. I refused to acknowledge the water pouring over the stern as I turned the key. Nothing.

Stillness filled me. Strangely calm, I turned the key again. The engine coughed as it tried to suck the fuel, and it seemed like an eternity before it finally came to life. Foxy tried to jump into my lap. Her feet were wet. This meant water was flooding the floorboards.

I knew it would be foolish to burn the remaining fuel by trying to make it to the eastern shore. Walking out of that area would be impossible. With no one for miles and no roads along the lake, hiking through the driving sleet would be the only option. If I ran out of fuel, I would be lucky to have this option, because the wind would push me north, away from civilization. If the boat didn't swamp, it would hit a lee shore somewhere miles downwind, and hiking for miles through snow-frosted forest, in the dark, was not something to look forward to.

Finally, on my right, I spotted the small bit of land called Bear Island. Its south-facing shore was a barren rock bluff now being pounded with monster breakers. The waves surged almost to the top of the 25-foot bluff. (I've wondered since whether it was actually called Bare Island because of this beaten and bare rock wall.) I pushed my speed as much as possible to avoid ending up against the lee shore of this cliff.

It was getting dark, with just a hint of grey light left in the clouds. I was in the middle of the lake with 3 kilometres (2 miles) of angry broadside rollers left between my little boat and our destination, the safe harbour of Granisle. I was able to turn the craft within a trough of steep black greasy water, and the boat was again on course for the marina. Surrounded by the threat of certain death, I felt strangely detached, like a character in a movie.

With the clouds blocking out any light from the moon or stars, I lost all visibility. My only course was to follow the pattern of the waves. As I crested a mountain of black water, a blast of fierce wind hit the boat, and I saw, at last, the twinkle of village lights in the distance. The bow plunged on the downside of this mountainous wall, leaving me weightless and light-headed with the thought of a nosedive.

My fuel was almost gone, and strangely, any fear I may have had went with it. I had recently experienced death. I was not afraid of it. I was but a part of... the little boat... moving... ever... so... slowly... towards... the small... twinkling lights... of... a village... on the southwestern shore.

—

Somehow, I managed to make it to the marina with nothing measurable in the fuel tank. As I climbed the hill to my parents' new summer home in Granisle, I thought how my mother and father would scold me for being out late in a storm. My fathers' comment, upon my arrival, surprised me. "Well, now you can say... ya seen worse."

Curiously enough, that experience and my father's words have helped me more than once while bringing clients over the lake during bad seas. I am able to stand as a strong, steadfast captain and say to them, "I have seen worse... much worse."

# CHAPTER 7

# The Canadian Consul General

A t my parents' house, I found myself walking about in a mechanical state, following a list of chores as if tethered to it by a leash. I helped my mother and father winterize their cottage and sent them off to their winter home in Mexico. It took me a few more days to get *The Duck*, my last boat still on the lake, tucked into my parents' empty carport.

Heading south, like the female kingfisher, I travelled back to the US alone. Her image remains close to my heart: She gave me the strength to start a new chapter in my life.

Thanks to friends, I moved into a convenient house-sitting position in Oak Harbor, Washington. My daughter lived close by, and I was able to see her and my grandchildren. Now a widow, I had several daunting tasks before me, including paying off a remote fishing lodge in a foreign country. For the sake of my mortgage, I immediately went to work for a supermarket chain. My job description was broad: re-modelling, re-setting and designing grand-opening decorations, along with whatever else management needed. My responsibilities were difficult, challenging and consuming. I also contacted my schoolteacher friends and booked special project classes at the local elementary schools. This paid little in monetary funds but was crucial in focusing my mental health. I made sure there were very few moments to spare for grieving. My tears were saved for the commute to and from job sites and the rest soaked my pillow at night.

Immigration would prove to be difficult, but necessary if I wanted to run the lodge solo someday. We had started the process several months ago, but a lot had changed. To purchase property in Canada was extremely easy—the government loved to generate new taxes. We had a homeowner contract with the Adamses for the remaining balance due on the lodge, which I was determined to pay off.

The Canadian regulations stipulated that a foreigner could own property, but had to have a Canadian partner to operate a business. This partner would run the company. I wanted to operate the lodge myself. I could not afford to pay someone else to do so, nor did I want anyone other than myself to run it. So by law, I needed to become a landed immigrant.

Becoming a landed immigrant with permanent resident status was easier said than done. There were several steps to accomplishing this feat, including a health screening by a designated Canadian doctor, a criminal investigation through the state and federal authorities, and filing for status under a specific category.

Our category was business. I quickly discovered that leaving my homeland and moving to a foreign country was not simple—physically, emotionally or logistically. These few words cannot describe the details and red tape involved in such a life-changing event.

The first thing David and I had had to do was produce a business proposal—something neither of us had ever done for a project like a fishing lodge. I had gone to my previous college and asked an old professor for an outline. From that outline I had written our proposal for the fishing lodge. This took me a good two weeks to accomplish. I had listed David's attributes and all the wonderful things he could do. Without exaggeration, David's work experience made him an ideal fit for a maintenance man. I described myself as the perfect innkeeper. After we mailed the application package, David and I purchased a fine bottle of champagne. We were going to celebrate right then, but we decided to save the bottle to toast our acceptance as landed immigrants, once our paperwork was approved. We even kept the champagne with us when we travelled back and forth so we would be ready to celebrate a favourable review, whenever it came.

Eighteen months later, I finally received notice of an appointment with the immigration officers. As it turned out, that date was scheduled for two months after David died. But there was no moving it: I had to rewrite the proposal within just a few days, while dealing with the death of my spouse. I had one huge mountain to climb. Living in two different countries complicated the numerous issues, creating a jumble of paperwork and new hurdles. It all felt impossible.

Removing all of David's attributes from the business plan left the lodge, on paper, without a maintenance crew. I filled in the blanks the best I could. Living on a sailboat for a few years taught me how to operate the same kinds of systems that would be required at the lodge, though I seldom had to do anything mechanical. Panicked, I overextended my qualifications.

I enlisted everyone I knew to write a letter describing my competency. I was so grateful for the many friends and co-workers who came together to write letters saying I could do the job—that alone gave me an enormous sense of strength. I wracked my brain for anything else I could use to show my worth, and I developed a portfolio of my artwork.

Finally, the day of my appointment arrived: January 8, 1997. The traffic to the consulate in Seattle was a bumper-to-bumper crawl. My directions were useless, and the map was sprawled across the front seat. If I were to describe my commute that day it would sound like this: bad seas in a thick, pea-soup fog.

Carrying three briefcases, I waited in line to take my number from the dispenser in the Canadian Consul General's office.

My head swam as I sat in the office, with its grey carpets, walls and chairs. My heart pounded and my face flushed, and I was on the edge of throwing up. I distracted myself by looking about the drab room. I immediately focused on the silky flowing gowns of some South Asian women, also waiting. The brilliantly coloured saris gave me a calming peace and the opportunity to collect my thoughts. I also noticed there were no men in the room.

Then my number was called.

Gathering the three briefcases, filled with all the reasons why I would make a good Canadian citizen, I approached the wicket and faced a woman behind the glass.

"I need to speak to the head of the household. May I speak to David, please?" She said with a crisp English accent.

I don't know why I wasn't ready for that question.

"He's not here."

"Then we will have to re-book for when David is available," said the woman, in her lovely accent. That's when it dawned on me why there were no men in the room: they were all being interviewed, and the women were not invited to join.

No words would come. Dropping to my knees on the worn-out carpet, I rummaged through briefcase number one. I scrambled to find what I had come to think of as "the sad grey envelope." On the front, it simply said, in large print, "Made with Recycled Paper." The return address was from the funeral parlour. Without a word I handed the envelope to her. She pulled out the document I had only seen once: David's death certificate. In the silence, I heard her inhale quickly, and then she left. She may have said something, but I didn't hear. I only recall my gasps for air as I stared at the empty opening in the wicket's bulletproof glass.

On the clerk's return, she ushered me into a nearby office. Everything became brisk and businesslike. All the papers were reviewed. New forms with blue carbon paper sandwiched between the layers were inserted into a typewriter. They were typed up and then pulled from the machine. After a long silence, the officer said, "I am sorry. I just can't see how you, alone, can operate a fishing lodge. I wish we could figure out how to get more points added to your application."

Feeling desperate, I played my last ace and opened briefcase number three. I brought out a sculptured leather doll I had made. The clerk looked surprised to see four more dolls carefully placed in this last case. She admired each one, and exclaimed, "These are works of art!"

I gave the officer a class outline and reviews of my elementary drama and art classes. She flipped slowly through the pages and pictures and then left the room. I was hoping she would see the value of teaching art to young people. A moment later, she returned and introduced me to the Canadian Consul General. After looking at the portfolio and the

sculptures, they pronounced me an artist! The Consul General excused himself and left.

"What does that mean?" I asked the officer.

"You will now receive an additional ten points." With a great welcoming smile, this wonderful woman explained, "This gives you the total number of points required to complete the application for residency."

I became an official Canadian resident in May 1997. And I gave the treasured bottle of champagne David and I had saved for this momentous occasion to my parents.

# CHAPTER 8

# Ookpik Wilderness Lodge

I came back to Babine Lake in early May, just seven months after David's death. Still besieged by grief, I was glad my mother and father agreed to come with me. De-winterizing the lodge alone had seemed almost impossible. Even the long drive north from Whidbey Island proved difficult. I drove my loaded red Suburban and pulled a 16-foot trailer filled to the top. My parents, recently back from their Mexican holidays, followed in their truck, which was filled with their belongings. We stopped every 100 miles so I could sleep for fifteen or twenty minutes. My parents, supportive in every way, accommodated my needs. They understood that depression had taken its toll on me.

We arrived at Babine Lake, but the dense ice on the surface was not yet ready to give up its claim to the cold, blue water. With our first attempt we powered *The Duck* 10 kilometres (6 miles) north before encountering a thick and solid cover of ice. We returned to Granisle. Four days later, encouraged by white clouds that streaked north in a sapphire sky, we tried again. We were optimistic after 22 kilometres (14 miles) of clear water but found Morrison Arm to be an ice-locked channel. Our hopes were dashed again. Five days later, on our third attempt, we crossed open water, then carefully dodged ice floes and followed narrow passageways up the arm to the lodge.

It seemed like years since I had last entered Ookpik Cove. A chapter of my life had ended here mere months before, and a lifetime of events had transpired since.

My father, a strong and powerful force in my life, full of knowledge and experience, gave me the confidence and the initiative to carry on. I'd helped David do the many chores required to open the lodge, but never imagined doing them myself. I soon realized that I really hadn't paid enough attention. Without hesitation, my father—my proficient teacher—patiently taught me how to do things: fitting and mending copper pipes, priming the water pump, setting up the inverter/converter so we could have electricity, running the backhoe to launch the boats, maintaining the generator and outboard motors, and other chores I now needed to understand fully. It was great to get the water back up and running. Outhouses are fine, but there is nothing more comfortable than the use of an indoor toilet in the middle of the night.

My mother was taking on the tasks I was supposed to do—the duties I would be doing if David were here, and the ones she had taught me to perform: the art of being the homemaker. Mom had an instinctive understanding of what needed to be done and she always followed through. She overcame every obstacle without complaint. The amazing person my mother was became an example to me now: all the things she had silently shown me, all the things I had never noticed. My mother was the current that moved the river and it's what she instilled in me. And yet she did all this with minimal recognition or appreciation. I wondered how I would accomplish all my household tasks, along with my new mechanical maintenance responsibilities.

Mine would have been a very different story without the example my parents set for me. Still, I was concerned about being able to fill the demanding duties of two people. By the end of their ten-day stay, they left me with enough strength of will and a determination to carry on.

It took another ten days for me to realize I had never been alone like this before. I wondered if anything could prepare me for this life of solitude, let alone the workload.

My loneliness must have reverberated into the wilderness. One of the locals decided to keep me company in the basement, under where my bed sat. I would not have minded, but he was not a peaceful or quiet neighbour and he felt it necessary to remodel. Under prudent consideration of the wild, and yet unknown, guest, I removed the trigger lock from my Winchester Defender shotgun, refreshed my understanding of the safety latch and tiptoed around the house. I found a new entry to the basement with a funny face peeking out. I was pleasantly surprised in a couple of ways. First and foremost, the creature did not seem aggressive. He actually looked quite shy. I had never seen anything like this giant, furry, square-headed vermin. I guessed, at the time, he must have weighed close to 10 pounds!

Eventually, I figured out that the critter was a woodchuck. With the trigger lock replaced and the gun put away, I had to decide what to do with this noisy creature. Going into the basement armed with a fish club, I discovered just how much wood a woodchuck could chuck in two busy nights: There was a heaping pile of woodchips that had been removed from the log structure supporting the house. The animal was nowhere to be seen.

When his graveyard shift began again that night, I kind of lost it. I am glad to say there were no witnesses to the wild banshee—me—pounding the carpet with a black cast-iron frying pan. The next night was silent. I suppose the woodchuck didn't like the neighbourhood and thankfully moved out.

Every day as dawn broke, I'd sit in the morning sun on the back steps and write a list of chores. I could hear the red-winged blackbirds calling out and the squirrels scolding the dog. My coffee steamed in the coolness of the morning air. The list consumed me. Filling every crevice in my brain with something other than the fear of being alone was my immediate goal.

I'd procrastinate with a decadent second cup, and number the list in red, its order dictated by daylight, work area, difficulty and desire to execute. Little did I know, in the next several years, I would make hundreds of such lists and consume hundreds of cups of coffee. After checking off each chore with red ink, I would use those pieces of paper—those lists of blood, sweat, tears and coffee stains—for fire-starter. Nothing in the north goes to waste.

# CHAPTER 9

# Angling Guide Spring

The first boat that arrived in the spring of 1997 held a couple of men from the Department of Fisheries and Oceans. They had a machine that stunned fish samples, which allowed them to record the type, quantity and size of fish in small lakes. They came into the lodge to warm up and spoke of their travels exploring and checking on the Morrison watershed. I took notes as they held the hot mugs with both hands and gulped their steaming tea.

"No fish in Haul Lake, it's too shallow and the lake freezes solid."

"You have to use the Grease Trail to get to Tahlo..."

"Tahlo Lake has cutthroat trout."

"Fission Lake is full of small hungry rainbow."

"No Name Lake 1 has tons of cutthroats."

"So does No Name Lake 2."

The next week, another boat arrived—two boats in one month is quite unusual. I walked down to the dock and greeted the two local conservation officers, who later became good friends of mine. I asked them about getting an angling guide licence. Over cookies and tea, they explained the ins and outs of being an angling guide. I was caught... hook, line and sinker. I asked as many questions as came to mind. I learned that an angling guide must make a request to the Ministry of the Environment to be granted "rod days." Rod days are a way of limiting the impact on popular bodies of water.

With enthusiasm, they told me some rod days for Rainbow Alley, the outlet from Babine Lake, had recently become available. Rainbow Alley is famous for its extremely large rainbow trout. I learned that a local doctor who had held forty rod days for twenty years had recently retired and turned the days back in. I could apply for those rod days, and my chances were good, because of the proximity of the lodge. The officers also suggested I explore a few of the back lakes. I pulled out my map and they marked a couple of the areas, then told me, "Most of these lakes have never even been fished. You'll have to check them out."

I made plans to investigate the accessibility of five small lakes, and to see how many fish were in each lake. This would be a fact-finding mission for my angling guide's licence. I needed to have some idea of how many rod days to request for each of the lakes—some of which didn't even have names.

Tahlo, nestled against the continental divide, was high on my list and not far away. An old fisheries report agreed with what the Fisheries officers had said—there were cutthroat trout in this lake.

My packing for the exploratory trip was a little excessive. I packed and re-packed my backpack and gear several times. After making arrangements by radio to borrow an ATV from a Granisle truckdriver, I went back to work. I packed a big lunch including a blanket for my picnic, my fly rod, assorted flies, a small chainsaw and hatchet, my shotgun and bug spray. I could not possibly need more. Or so I thought.

At 5 a.m. I found myself pushing a wheelbarrow down the dock where I loaded the dory boat. Nesting ducks flew from the reeds at the sudden burst of noise from the outboard engine. I cast off and headed up Babine Lake to Morrison Landing, where I'd parked my Suburban for easy access. Morrison Landing is a dot on a map with no population whatsoever. It was just a boat ramp and dock nestled in a protected cove on the northwest end of Morrison Arm. Now abandoned, it was used, years ago, for booming logs down the lake. When I arrived, the borrowed ATV was waiting on shore, strapped to a small trailer.

Hitching up the trailer was easy. The fact that I had never driven an ATV didn't stop me for a second. It was shiny and new. How hard could it be? I was so excited about my plans, I didn't even think about how to start a four-wheeler. Down the logging road I went in my Suburban, a cloud of dry dust billowing behind the small trailer.

Another 10 kilometres (6 miles) and I reached my destination, the old Grease Trail leading to Tahlo Lake. I drove the trailer into a pullout and backed up against a mound of dirt. This gave me a ramp for unloading the ATV. I started up the machine with no trouble. I was so excited to check out this area that nothing seemed difficult.

I used bungee cords to secure all my gear. I'd been forewarned that the Grease Trail had not been used for years, so I'd packed my small chainsaw. It was thrilling to drive the ATV down off the main road and onto the unused trail. Previously I'd thought how noisy and smelly they were and wondered how anyone could enjoy such racket. By the end of the day, I was a convert.

A short distance down the trail, I ran into the first windfall and was forced to stop. It was so quiet after turning off the key. I thought my ears weren't working until a squirrel gave me a piece of his mind. I then filled the forest with the dreadful noise and oily fumes of the chainsaw. After cutting a path through the wind-fallen tree, I put the wood-eating beast away.

Bouncing farther along the trail, I saw the remains of a trapline where rotting wooden traps lay abandoned. It was like stepping back in time. Set along the trail beside the creek, they must have been used for trapping mink, ermine, marten or fisher. I knew this was a Grease Trail used by the Dakelh (Carrier) Nation many years back, and I wondered how long it had been since anyone had been here. I continued down this ancient trail, feeling extremely guilty for leaving two mud-churned tracks on the old footpath.

Just around the corner, I was stopped by another fallen tree, then another. After the fifth windfall I ran out of chainsaw fuel. However, I had brought my hatchet. I searched for the trusty tool and found it under the peanut butter and jelly sandwich and chocolate chip cookies.

I hacked away for several minutes and paused for a sip of water. Then, I jumped to the other side of the fallen tree where I was going to finish the cut. As I was crossing over the mangled timber, I looked down to see 10-inch grizzly bear tracks, gradually filling with water. I could have put both of my hands inside the paw print. As the claw marks came into focus, the reality of my situation hit home. This could only mean a grizzly had been right here—very recently.

Not wanting to be his picnic lunch, I reached for my gun. As a law-abiding, safety-first, gun-packing woman, I had the trigger lock on. Did I have the key? Heck no, it was with the can of gas I'd left in my car, so I would have enough room for my honey-sweet-smelling picnic. In my hurry to escape I flooded the machine and had to wait, looking over my shoulder, until the fuel line cleared. It took forever to get the ATV turned around, but then only a couple of minutes to retrace the journey that had taken an hour coming in.

Back at the Suburban, I was shocked to see mud all over the hood. Getting closer, I recognized muddy prints, big enough to lay from one side of the hood to the other, likely from a full-grown grizzly. I knew a giant bear could weigh up to 900 pounds, about the same size as five big men. With mud smeared all over the vehicle, this was obviously not a happy bear.

I got into the car right away, thinking I would give the grizzly some time to move on. With no one around, I felt it would be safe to load the ATV later. I decided that first I'd check out a small lake a few kilometres up the road.

That lake looked promising. Several fish were rising, just begging me to cast a fly their way. I had a great time catching and releasing several 10- to 14-inch rainbows. I named this lake Mountain View, and was elated to have found my first lake for which I'd request angling rod days.

When I returned to load the borrowed ATV, I was quickly shaken back to reality. The shiny new rig was on its side. The grizzly had attacked the ATV with its razor claws, shredding the seat. Fuelled by adrenaline, I righted the machine and loaded the ATV as quickly as I could, looking over my shoulder the entire time.

That trip cost me $80 for a new ATV seat and more than a few new grey hairs.

—

In the end I had six little lakes on my angling guide licence, all in grizzly territory. My father was an artist with the fly rod, the line in the air flowing like music. He had taught both of my brothers to fly fish. They were experts, but both lived in the city. Meanwhile their sister, with little fly-fishing experience, was now a registered angling guide.

The following year, with my angling guide licence framed and on the wall, I pulled all my self-assurance together and designed my new persona. I was a strong, confident, knowledgeable angling guide. I could do anything I wanted, and nothing was going to get in my way. I even practised my casting... when no one was looking.

Then came the Butterfly Ball.

I had learned that driving down a logging road was no easy feat. I studied maps and logger language in order to navigate the unmarked roads and understand the radio. I learned to listen to the scratchy, screeching thing and determine exactly where a monster truck, going hell-bent for the mill, was going to be in a specific amount of time. By keeping track of all oncoming traffic, calculating the average speeds expected and dividing the distance between my small vehicle and the massive oncoming trucks, I'd be able to guess when I needed to find a pullout. These wide spots were placed every few kilometres. This is where I'd pull over and wait for the fully loaded, fifty- to eighty-ton trucks to pass, to avoid getting smoked in a head-on collision. I practised this exercise many times successfully—without, I might add, the chatter of excited fishermen in the Suburban—and I finally felt comfortable navigating these unmarked roads and understanding the radio lingo.

One afternoon, while driving to Morrison River and the back lakes with three fly-fishing clients, I came around a corner and had to slam on my brakes. Already unnerved by a woman driver, the two rather large guys I had in the front with me went into a white-knuckle position on the dash. The third guy in the back wished he had his seat belt on.

It wasn't an oncoming truck we'd encountered. Right there in the middle of the road was a giant ball of butterflies. The phenomenon was about 3 feet in diameter. I turned off the engine and all was silent except for occasional radio noise. I jumped out of the rig along with my clients and walked over to investigate.

After gently inserting my hand into the fluttering mass, I reached deeper and deeper into the middle of the moving sphere, determined to find out what the butterflies were doing. The sensation of having hundreds of insects crawling and fluttering over my hand and arm was disconcerting. At the bottom of the ball, I felt an unknown smooth, sticky substance. Removing my arm at a slightly faster rate disturbed them, and with hundreds of colourful butterflies flying about, the radio suddenly blared, "Where the hell are you, Suburban? Loaded and rollin'—find a hole and hide in it!" I screamed orders to my clients, still messing with their cameras. They piled into the Suburban, and as the doors were still slamming, I floored the gas pedal, then hit the brakes and came to a complete stop at the closest pullout, lest we be smashed like bugs in the grill of an eighteen-wheeler.

"Roll up your windows!" I yelled.

Cranking as fast as they could, they sealed their windows just as a roaring truck weighing at least 80,000 pounds sped by, creating a mountain of dust. Nothing could be seen in the blur.

When the cloud cleared, the butterflies were gone. All we had left to prove their existence was the black residue that remained on my fingertips. That is when I realized it was bear scat! I rubbed my hand onto the dry, dusty road, pouring my bottled water over the unwanted stink, shrieking like a baby.

The next year I took two of those clients back to fish the same little lakes. One was Paul Messner, celebrating his birthday. I let him and his friend stay late and took the opportunity to check out another lake while I waited. It was about ten at night and still daylight when I went back to pick them up.

They were supposed to have come out of the bush by then. But by 10:30 p.m. they still hadn't returned. I tooted the car horn to let them know I was now waiting. We had to travel several miles by road and several more miles by water to get back to the lodge. Impatient, I tooted my horn again.

Looking up and down the road to see if they had come out a little off the mark, I saw a big grizzly heading towards the exit where my fishermen would emerge anytime now. I reached for my Winchester Defender and thought, *You're the guide.*

I leaped from my rig, yelling, and scared the grizzly into a gallop. The bear turned and dashed straight towards the fishermen, who were portaging a red canoe over their heads and didn't have a clue of the situation. Running and leaping over bushes, I screamed at the top of my lungs.

"Bear, bear! Get out your bear spray!"

I had a shorter path to the fishermen than the bear. Even so, the grizzly and I reached the men at the same time. The men dropped the canoe with a bang, and the grizzly put on the brakes. With the unexpected sight of the bouncing red canoe, the grizzly bear turned and ran away. Paul floundered about looking for his bear spray. "What's goin' on?" his buddy said.

Although Paul never did find his bear spray, he enjoyed twelve more birthday fishing trips to the lodge.

# CHAPTER 10

# Logging the Forest

I found I had to bury my grief. There was just not enough time to allow pain to interfere with all the labour or expense involved in running a fishing lodge. That was my strategy, and most of the time I was successful. Oddly, I felt it necessary to carry David's ashes to Whidbey Island in the winter, where I had to work, and back to the lodge in the spring. There were no handbooks available on what to do with the ashes or how to let go.

In 1998, my first boat ride through the ice patches back to the lodge for the year was filled with waves of excitement, fear, sadness and wonderment with the beauty of it all. It was my second season as the proprietor of a real fishing lodge. The prior year's experiences, bolstered with a calendar bearing the names of newly recruited fishermen and returning clients, gave me strength. I was glad I'd got to the lodge in early May to prepare for my clients' arrival in June. I needed all the time I could get.

I went down the dock to unload supplies, and I watched with astonishment as giant billowing clouds of muddy water swirled and mixed with the clean, clear water in Ookpik Cove. I could see a new mud delta had already started to develop. Even the local beaver swam around and wondered what to do. If this continued, how would the boats maintain enough water to navigate within this natural harbour?

The next day, still in shock, I went to the Ministry of Forests (MOF) office in Houston, BC, to see if anyone knew what was happening. The polite employees asked me where I lived. I showed them on a map.

"You are surrounded by an industrial forest," the officer said. I always thought it was the people's forest, Crown land—not an "industrial" forest. The MOF officer gave me no further information and no reassurance. I left the office feeling more alone than ever.

I was confused. I had to take this bad news and place it into a black box, seal it up tight and set it next to David's ashes in my closet. I couldn't afford any added stress to interfere with the duties that revolved around my clients' arrival in three weeks. My second season as a fishing lodge proprietor was around the corner, and I had to use all my mental and physical abilities to fulfill that title.

My clients turned out to be fantastic. They caught great big rainbow trout and ate well. Then the weather got hot, and the favourable bugs were gone, and so were the last of my fly fishermen. I folded up my apron and put away the fishing gear. The beaver dug fresh channels through the new mud brought down the mountain that spring.

The black box of forestry issues I had placed in the closet broke out and took over. Never having been a tree hugger, I realized that it was now time to get with it and learn everything I could. A crash course in forestry practices and understanding the system became critical. I needed to protect my interest in the watershed where I lived. The survival of my business was at stake. I spent the next week investigating the current and proposed logging operations around me and thinking about the implications. I drew up a list of concerns, placed them into a briefcase, grabbed my maps and jumped into the boat one morning before dawn.

Three and a half hours later, I arrived at the closest big town, Smithers. At the local community college, I asked to speak to "someone smart." The front office sent me to the director of the college. I told him of my concerns and said that I needed help from someone who knew about clear-cutting. That kind soul sent me to see Dave Stevens. The college director said, "You won't have any trouble finding Dave in a coffee shop across from the government office. Just look for the biggest single dreadlock you have seen, or will ever see, in your lifetime."

I stepped into the village hub, surrounded by the welcome aroma of good coffee. In the coffee shop, I picked up my mug of java and I turned to see a grey-haired man in a red felt hat, deep in conversation with a large group of people. I walked closer and discovered this man did indeed have the biggest dreadlock I would ever see in my lifetime—4 to 5 inches wide and probably 30 inches long. When I faced him, he immediately fixed his sparkling blue eyes on me. I asked him if we could talk.

"One moment, please," he said.

Dave finished his conversation, then excused himself and graciously escorted me to a quiet table in the back.

With my briefcase on my lap, overwhelmed by what I needed to know, I had trouble finding words to describe my situation. Dave waited silently and patiently. Finally, I was able to gather my thoughts, and my maps, and I rambled through my story. Dave sat there with his wise eyes and absorbed my words. He looked at my maps and started to speak—and it seemed like a thousand words a minute. He was the fastest talker I'd ever met. There was so little I could process; so much of what he had to say was foreign to me. I could tell he was sympathetic and understanding. His advice, in the end, was to go see the scientist across the street in the government office.

I gulped my coffee and said goodbye to this strange man who would become a fellow crusader in the eco-friendly sector in the years to come. (Dave auctioned off his giant dreadlock for a charity event a few years later for $575. The local barber nailed it to the wall over a brass marker that read, "Beware, this could happen to you.")

That same day, I went across the street to see the regional scientist, the man who had deep, extensive knowledge of the area. I begged his secretary for a meeting. She looked at me impatiently and said, "Do you have an appointment with Dr. Pojar?"

My brain was scrambled. I had gotten up at 4:30 in the morning, jumped into my boat to travel in darkness to my old Suburban, then had driven another 145 kilometres (90 miles) to speak to the college director and my new friend Dave, only to find out this was the man I had to see. And I had no appointment.

"Could you come back tomorrow?" she said.

"Please... can I wait? I need to see him today, badly," I replied in a small, panicked voice. The secretary called his desk for the third time and finally said, "One moment, please."

The door whipped open. A tall, thin man with longish messy hair— "the Doctor"—looked at me with a frown and pointed with his entire arm down a staircase. I jumped up and went with him down into a dark basement overflowing with files stacked to the ceiling. There were maps all over the walls and no windows anywhere. (I would find out years later that Dr. Pojar and his associates called this workspace "The Crypt.") The doctor never said a word. I handed him my list of questions. After looking at the cover page, he tossed the six pages of my week's effort onto the file-covered desk. I sat trembling as he uttered his first words.

"Have you got a map? Is there a watershed study?"

Not knowing anything about a water study, I whipped out my map. He looked at it for about three minutes. I had looked at it for hours and hours. He snapped up my document and with red ink began, as if from habit, to correct my spelling and to add many other notations. Lost in trepidation, I found myself looking at a coat rack standing close by. Hanging there were a stethoscope, a white doctor's lab coat and a fluffy Einstein wig. This bit of good humour gave me hope, and I felt sure he would help me.

This man was brilliant. I saw him for only fifteen minutes, but it turned out to be the most educational and important fifteen minutes of my life. Dr. Pojar's notes gave me references to study specific logging issues and the serious deforestation risks to the watershed where I lived. I was never able to thank him properly, because of his post with the government. (It was not his position to give advice to lay people like me.)

When I left that day, I thought all I had to do was correct my mistakes, study the notes in red and then rewrite my comments; I would then turn them in to the logging company and the Ministry of Forests. What the Good Doctor failed to mention was that this would be a fight for years to come.

And indeed, coming back to the lodge the following spring, I found several new blocks of forest cut, and the creeks were again pushing muddy water into my cove. It was sad. Hundreds of hectares of forest had been removed in a few days, with just a few men operating a few gigantic machines. The destroyed natural habitat and my heartache were all that was left.

I went home and cried. What could I do? So much of the old forest was being clear-cut. I felt distraught, helpless and alone. I could not even begin to think of what I should do, or what I could do. I slept and cried for three days. On the fourth day, I felt sick. On the fifth day my will resurfaced. Walking down the dock for some fresh air, I realized, with all the mud filling the cove, I would have to extend the dock to deeper water.

Some people have asked me since, "Why didn't you just sell the place, go back to where you came from and skip the heartache?"

To leave without a fight would have been unthinkable. I was raised to take responsibility. My deeply rooted desire to share Canada's wonders with my family, and future generations of nature lovers who would want to experience an untouched wilderness, was worth a fight. Taking on the biggest forestry company in the world and the Government of British Columbia seemed insurmountable. So I began the battle one step at a time. I remembered the scientist in Smithers asking if I had a watershed study. Three days later I requested a watershed study.

—

It took three years for the forest district manager to grant my request to do a watershed study. (Incidentally, this was the exact amount of time needed for these young trees to reach Free to Grow Status, which released the logging company of any responsibility.) The regional hydrologist came and investigated. In his report he explained how the cove filled with 25 feet of silt.

I followed him up the mountain as he searched for the headwaters to the watershed. He found a diverted creek, originating from the top of the mountain behind the lodge. It had carved a new ravine and moved tons of silt down its path. In the middle of a clear-cut block, someone had felled three cottonwood trees with stumps 38 inches in diameter, obstructing the creek head. This action had triggered a chain of events. It directed the water flow into two overland channels reaching the creek that emptied into Ookpik Cove and brought tons of debris and mud down into the harbour holding my boats. Ookpik Cove used to moor sailboats with no problem. But during the last few years I had needed to extend my wharf. I now had a 300-foot dock just to accommodate my flat-bottom riverboats.

Even with these facts documented, somehow the government and the licensees denied responsibility. My cove had billowed with muddy water for four years and was still filling with silt. The licensees were asked to correct the damaged creek beds within their cut-block. They agreed to remove the trees causing the diversion and nothing else. The beaver in Ookpik Cove learned to live with the mountain of additional mud and I had to build and maintain a 300-foot dock for the next twenty years.

More and more of the old-growth forests were being placed on the chopping block. New plantations replaced old forests, but this left no room for the indigenous wild roses, shrubs, berries, deciduous trees, wild-flowers and wild orchids—or even the weeds—that make up the biosphere, let alone a habitat for the misplaced animals. In many places you walked through rows and rows of trees planted for profit, and they all looked alike. The planting of a single species is called monoculture, a practice now understood to be risky. Why shouldn't you plant a forest with only one kind of tree? The pine beetle catastrophe is one answer to that question. To be healthy, forest diversity is necessary.

My friend Alex Michelle, of the Tachet First Nation, said to me once, "I have walked these forests all my life. Now I get lost. The ancient trails are scraped and planted. There are signs... metal signs, warnings of the poison sprayed to kill the shrubs—the small bushes that shade the seed-lings. There are no giant spruce, no old standing snag with an eagle's nest, no fallen tree or bear den to mark my way. It's all the same." He expressed this with a solemn resignation.

I was told repeatedly that the major problem was that the area had no Land and Resource Management Plan (LRMP). This left all the decision-making to the discretion of the district manager and the licensees. An added obstacle for me was that in a small town, the company men and the forest office personnel were all friends. They played hockey together. I was the outsider making trouble—and extra paperwork. The district manager of forests told me they were in the business of selling timber, and their job was to decide when and where to harvest Crown land.

Just when I didn't think it could get any worse, I received a letter of intent from a mining company who was re-applying for a licence to build an open-pit mine 4 kilometres (2.5 miles) from the lodge. They had been denied several years before and I was appalled the application was being reviewed again. At least I could repurpose my documents of concern, originally written for the MOF, and send them off again to the EPD of the EAO: the Executive Project Director of the British Columbia Environmental Assessment Office.

Thank goodness the government finally opened the table for negotiating the LRMP for the Morice Forest District. (Later, to save money, they consolidated the Lakes and the Morice Forest Districts and called the area the Lakes Forest District.) There was an opening for a tourism sector chairman. Getting the specifics, I campaigned to become the chairperson and was elected to the position. I wrote up new concerns and set up a meeting to be held at the lodge. I invited the company forest planners, government environmental officers, forestry officers, fisheries officers, environmental assessment officers and some of my tourism constituency. I thought if all these people in power could see how devastating the proposed harvests and mining operations would be, they would fix it.

I took everyone by boat up the prolific Morrison River, where I took my clients fly-fishing. Most were surprised to see how close the proposed clear-cut harvest block was to the river and lakeshore. They were all shocked to see how close the open-pit mine and the new proposed mine access road would be.

Perfectly timed by Mother Nature, the salmon parted and swam along both sides of our boats. As serious as the situation was, I enjoyed pointing out the red backs of the spawning sockeye salmon. As we rounded the bend in the river, we spooked a mother moose crossing against the current with her calf. The osprey fishing in the river and eagles soaring overhead supported my case. The wildlife had a profound impact on most of the people in the four boats. Unfortunately, the ones with the power saw only the giant old-growth spruce, which they called pumpkins, in dollar signs.

Upon our return, we began our meeting. Here is what we learned from the government and business officials present:

The area in question had already been released for harvest and the mine assessment was underway. In order to make guidelines for the use of land around bodies of water, I would need to have a land plan completed. Until that time, everyone's hands were tied.

The conservation officers said, "We can't do anything till they do something wrong."

Even the fisheries officer was upset. "There are coho and sockeye salmon runs in this area, enhanced for over 30 years!" he said. "We are concerned the proposed harvesting along Morrison River and lakeshore would expose the water bodies to sunlight and rising temperatures, and the consequences could be catastrophic if the tailing ponds leaked into Morrison Lake and River."

In fact, the logging company had the legal right to remove every stick of wood along the shores of Babine Lake. Because the LRMP had not been finished, there was no large-lake strategy to use as a guide, so no one could legally contest their actions.

"Just write your comments and I will consider them," the forest district manager kept repeating. I truly thought, naive as I was, that the logging company and the MOF and the EAO would do the right thing. (I could never have imagined it would take another nine years of fighting the mining company before the EAO denied their application again!)

I followed all the rules. I wrote to every ministry I was advised to contact. I could not believe they would allow such permanent damage just for profit. Unlike the southern forests that grew to harvesting maturity in forty years, this northern forest would suffer the consequences of their greed for a hundred years. The destruction resulting from an open-pit mine would be there forever, with just a few people, for a few years, being supported.

But I had to fight one battle at a time, and the most imminent one was the logging issues. And so it began.

—

Several weeks later, when it looked like no one was going to address my concerns, I felt forced to file a Forest Practices Board (FPB) complaint. Just filing with the FPB gave my concerns more heft.

The conservation officer wrote his comments, Fisheries and Oceans wrote theirs, and in a small way, we made a difference. At the next meeting, after the FPB complaint had been filed, the logging company said, "We will leave 20 metres along Morrison River and 10 metres along the edge of the lake, just to be nice—we do not have to." Pushing away from the table, they finished by saying, "We are here to make money, lady."

These meetings educated me in the relationship between the forest and the government, the logging licensees, the miners, the government biologists, the First Nations bands, the ecologists and the recreational/tourism entities, such as my lodge. Much of what I learned was not pretty.

Along the way, I was fortunate enough to meet some excellent people who worked for government departments and elsewhere. I had to write pages and pages of formal comments registering and explaining my concerns, as well as my constituents' concerns, in my role representing the tourism industry. They helped me keep up with the ever-changing government ministries and policies, but nothing seemed to quell the hungry jaws of the corporate offices.

More old-growth forests were placed on the harvest map overlaid with bright magenta, a colour I would learn to hate: Magenta was the colour the logging companies and mining companies used to declare areas of green forest that have been proposed for clear-cutting and heavy-metal possibilities.

Before the LRMP was completed, around 1999–2000, the magenta painted over a 1,007-hectare block! It was a healthy spruce forest but held pine timber that was deemed "susceptible'" to possible beetle attack.

This block included one kilometre along Morrison Arm and a pristine protected harbour that was used by my clients, local First Nations and tourists alike. I'd named it Sanctuary Bay. It was admired for the safety it offered as a harbour through its keyhole entrance and the view of the white-capped Babine Mountains. (We were later successful in having this harbour designated with a conservancy/park status.) Again, I was forced into a fight to save this treasure and was shocked I seemed to be the only person who cared to do so. Again, I was forced to file another FPB complaint. My hope was that the government would reconsider the consequences of clear-cutting an area of this size,especially when the size of this block was against the Forest Practices Code. The code specified a 60-hectare block to be the largest, and this was a 1,007-hectare block!

In the FPB complaints I filed, the licensees were found not guilty. Not because they hadn't broken the laws within the Forest Practices Code, but because the district forest manager had given them a handwritten variance on a torn-off strip of notebook paper cancelling their obligation to the Forest Practices Code. There were no consequences to my complaints. No one was held accountable. The headline in the local paper read, "Logging Company Found Not Guilty."

Because my complaints were formally written and filed, the rules at that time stated the forest district manager had to address my issues and concerns themselves. They have since changed the rules, making things easier for their office. I was now required to give my concerns directly to the logging company and they would consider them. This method made it extremely difficult to have my concerns addressed at all.

The Ministry of Forests changed the rules in many other ways too. The licensees now hire their own biologist and archaeologist, which was a money-saving move for the government. I talked to an archaeologist, curious as to how he could remain non-biased, given who signed his paycheque.

"It is difficult, because if I were to give an unfavourable report the licensee may not choose to hire me a second time," he replied candidly. "I wish we still worked for the people of Canada, at least the government could require companies draw from a hat to choose their biologists and archaeologists. In doing so, the small companies, like mine, would be able to say what they want without being blacklisted. It makes me sad to say this, but we have to be concerned about our mortgage and our child's college tuition."

I was honoured to represent tourism for the Land and Resource Management Plan, but with no extra time or money, it was a burden. Unlike most of the panel, I was not an employee of the government or a company, so I was unpaid. There would be no lost wage compensation. Unlike most of the panel, in bad weather, I couldn't go home after every meeting, and had to rent a motel. And if I wasn't at the meetings, and my second-in-command couldn't come, my immediate world and the tourism sector of the Morice Forest District would not have representation. The LRMP was set up as a table for consensus, giving me at least a voice in both mining and logging decisions as well. Although there were many ways for these companies to get around consensus, this method gave me the determination to pursue this colossal endeavour.

While leaving my isolation for these necessary gatherings, I was fortunate to meet a few local residents who shared my concerns. Each one had a striking and unique quality. In the beginning I couldn't describe exactly how they were different. After many years, I began to understand these northern residents had an exclusive and exceptional strength providing the endurance, perseverance and determination it takes to live in a country that demands so much just to survive. It was gratifying, early on, to meet like-minded people willing to fight the powers that be to save some of the natural habitat we mutually respected.

# CHAPTER 11

# Housework and the Hummingbird

Paul and Ardys had instructed us to paint the logs on the outside of the lodge once every five years. The five years came just three years after David died, and I really wanted to do the right thing for the lodge. I took living there very seriously and tried my best to keep up with maintenance.

In August, after the guests and Silver had gone home, I decided to get the job done. To encourage myself, I purchased all the supplies in town, after dropping off my last fishing clients of the season. It took most of the money I had made the previous week to buy the supplies, which included: 10 gallons of expensive oil finish with UV protector, cleaning chemicals I was told I would need, and all the scrub brushes, wire brushes and paint brushes suggested.

Because the lodge was about 20 feet off the ground on the north side, I started on the lower, south side. The hot weather was perfect for working; most of the mosquitoes had burned off. The secret puddles and warm pools spawning the larvae of the little nasties had evaporated.

There was nothing easy about this job. I'd been told to use chemicals to clean the logs before repainting, so I followed the directions on the label. The fumes were terrible and I held my breath as I mopped the awful stuff on. Horrified, I watched the surface of the wood actually being dissolved. Without a garden hose, the rinsing had to be done with buckets of water brought up from the lake. I forced myself to continue, hour after hour, but was disappointed to find I had accomplished so little by the end of the day.

Once I started the job, I couldn't quit, because the chemicals bleached and stripped the logs so cleanly, exposing the wood to future damage if not quickly protected. After two weeks I was finally ready to paint, which sounded easier than what I had just gone through.

By late August the weather was a fantastic 30°C in the shade— perfect painting weather. I put on my shorts, and then quickly realized my mistake. All exposed skin needed to be covered. The blackflies came out with a vengeance.

Blackflies are the scourge of the north. Worse than that of a mosquito, which merely leaves you with an itch, an adult female blackfly's saliva contains an anticoagulant. Most people have an allergic response, resulting in intense pain and swelling. Still in my shorts, I worked on, unaware I was being bitten. Then I noticed a steady stream of bright red blood running down behind my ears into my cleavage and several streams of blood running down behind my knees. Within one hour after the bites, I experienced the itching, pain and swelling, which lasted for three days. I was fortunate, as some people experience bumps under their skin for months.

To protect myself from the wretched blackflies, I went inside and put on heavy overalls. I sprayed any skin not covered in material with a strong repellent, the hardcore hunter's type with DEET written on its label, under the skull and crossbones. But this burned my face so badly I was forced to wash it off and then went back to work. However, I had made a serious error in judging the ingenuity of the flies: I had to climb back down the ladder, find some duct tape, and seal my sleeves and pant legs shut—blackflies love to climb. To keep the nasty bugs from going down my shirt collar and from attacking my face, I draped a scarf sprayed heavily with DEET around my neck and sprayed my hat. Soon my brush, sticky with paint, was covered with bugs. I begged for a breeze to carry them away, to no avail.

At the end of each long day, I shed the overalls and dove off the front dock naked. The sensation of cool, cleansing water was my reward for a hard day of labour. The lake rinsed off sweat and bug repellent as a bonus. I didn't have to worry about being discovered because I could spot any boats at the entrance to this part of the arm a few miles away. That was enough time to dry off and dress. No one ever came this far up the lake unannounced anyway.

This job took another two weeks, and every day I had to force myself to continue. Every night I would sleep like, well, a log, and every morning I would get up as stiff as a board.

During all this time the weather stayed warm, and I lost 10 pounds. With only the north side left to paint—the high side—I was thinking I had it made. I placed the 14-foot ladder against the last corner and started up carrying a half gallon of paint. The job suddenly seemed pretty scary. If I fell, who would know? How long would I dangle? Or how long would I lie on the ground with broken bones, waiting for a hungry bear to come snack on me? I climbed back down and went to find a suitable rope so I could tie myself to the ladder, and the ladder to the eye hooks placed into the logs. This way I could reach as far as possible, left and right, without falling. I was unable to reach the top log on the northeast corner but was relieved it was protected by the overhanging—no need to paint it. After the remaining logs on the last side were painted, I was totally beat. Exhausted. Looking up at the massive shiny wall, I was downhearted not to have anyone to share the achievement of this monumental task. I dragged myself up the front steps, plopped into a chair and kicked off my sweaty boots.

Loneliness filled my heart. The sun's reflection on the lake was lovely as it sank behind the mountain called "the Sleeping Giant," on the far side. Swallows darted about, thankfully eating blackflies and mosquitoes. I slumped into the chair, still duct-taped up like a mummy in the sweltering heat.

In the quiet, a hummingbird appeared—it hovered at my eye level and hung there, suspended, thrumming its tiny wings. The iridescent feathers on the creature were dazzling in the late afternoon sunshine. He was there so long I started to think he was going to poke me in the eye. (I'm ashamed to admit this mean-spirited thought cross my tired brain: *If he comes any closer, I'll smack the dang thing.*) Then, the tiny bird buzzed down to my feet. It seemed captivated by my old purple socks. Spellbound, I stared at him. This wonderful little bird slowly inserted his tiny, long beak into the weave of my sock and with his minute tongue, licked my ankle.

The sensation was almost imperceptible. It took a second or two for my brain to register the fact that a tiny tongue was licking my ankle. I was thrilled. My sadness disappeared, replaced with an emotional ecstasy that lasted for hours.

After my dip in the lake that day, I poured a tall glass of iced tea and walked around the lodge admiring a big job well done.

Even after all these years, I still revel in the gift of pure joy that little hummingbird gave me.

# CHAPTER 12

# Touching Home
# Plate Winter

**W**orking on Whidbey Island became a means to an end. From mid-November to mid-April, I'd work any position needed in the large grocery division, asking for all the hours they could give me. All the overtime helped the bankroll. Having my expertise spread out between sixteen stores gave me a lot of options. It seemed there was always a store undergoing a remodel or a grand opening, which was my specialty. It was great fun to be paid to turn the high, vaulted ceiling airspace into a sea world of airbrushed creatures, with giant whales, mermaids and starfish, or to decorate a new store with some other local theme. When construction, remodelling or decorating was at a lull, I'd fill in for an employee on holidays, sick leave or maternity leave.

With any spare time, I taught special project classes at the local elementary schools. I did this to satisfy my love for anthropology, art and culture. I taught weeks-long courses in Northwest Coast culture, art and drama. They took two hours twice a week and were the joy of my working life. I also went to fire halls and community centres and made as many fishing presentations as possible, and I'd always get a few bookings. It was no wonder my winters flew by.

To work every winter was necessary for the mortgage, but I found it difficult to be absent from the lodge—my home—for so long. In 2002 Foxy and I would bring a new dog with us. Foxy was getting old, and I wanted her to have time to show the new, younger dog the ropes. I named him Nanook of the North, or Nuk for short. He was also an American Eskimo breed and would love it at Ookpik Lodge.

When I left each year and turned the lock, I tried to close the door on my emotional attachment to the place. But I knew the lock merely kept out the honest people. I'd only allow myself to think of my wilderness home when I was within 100 miles; otherwise, I couldn't sleep at night. Leaving the lodge unprotected was worrisome. All my family's treasures, all of the irreplaceable objects like Grandma's fine china and my family photos, were now in this one place I called home.

During the winter I'd sometimes attend meetings with the northern logging companies and government agencies and add a trip to the lodge. After the stressful meetings, my soul demanded the rejuvenation I felt there.

These trips were expensive, and road conditions in the winter were not to be endured by the faint of heart. Ice, sleet, snow and blizzards above latitude 50 were commonplace. And I travelled above latitude 55.

Normally, my trip from Whidbey Island to the lodge took seventeen to twenty hours in my old Suburban. Winter travel often took a few days. The 1,200 kilometre-journey (750 miles) of blizzards, snowslides and black ice was only the first step. After these gruelling miles, I ended up on the frozen shore of Babine Lake at Michelle Bay Landing to wait for the barge, which was called the *Babine Charger*. I liked to arrive at 7 a.m. to catch the fourth scheduled run for the day. The first barge, at 4 a.m., was usually packed with empty logging trucks. Ice crystals would hang in the air. The stars would be bright, daylight still a few hours away.

On the logging barge, in the black of night, I'd be the lone woman, my Suburban squeezed between giant trucks. We crossed a 4.8-kilometre (three-mile) stretch of lake filled with titanic blocks of ice. The industrial barge travelled all the way across the lake through a channel—kept open by a system of air bubbles blown under water—that was only slightly larger than the width of the barge. As I watched the huge icebergs rolling within this channel, I estimated the ice on the lake to be at least 3 feet thick.

When we arrived on the eastern shore, I would move over and allow the truckers to get to work. The third step of the journey was perhaps the most difficult. I'd travel to the lodge on a one-lane gravel road covered with ice and snow, where loaded logging trucks had the right of way. On my two-way radio I had to call out my location every kilometre, then listen hard to understand the professional truck drivers' language. I had to obey the rules, knowing my life and the lives of others would be in peril otherwise. With the whiteout of swirling snow that followed the hulking trucks, I'd wait for the air to clear.

I would travel this snow-packed gravel road for 10 kilometres (6 miles), and then turn onto a spur servicing the northeast area between Babine Lake and the continental divide. Often, I had to pull over many times before I reached my spot at kilometre 42. This pullout near the lodge cost me a fifth of Crown Royal a year to have it plowed by the grader man.

During one trip, we had a huge dump of snow and my spot had not yet been plowed. I had to ram three times into the snowbank to get off the road just enough to allow passage for the larger trucks. I was tense from the white-knuckled ride, my mind churning from the constant calculations and fear of a misstep. I left the dogs in the car for their safety and jumped out of the Suburban. I was conscious of every breath and covered my face with a scarf to pre-warm the air I pulled into my lungs. It was –31°C and still dark, but the stars were fading.

Using my headlights to see—and, more importantly, to be seen—I got my shovel and dug into the icy bank to make sufficient room for my vehicle. By the time I had dug enough space into the wayside and repositioned the Suburban, dawn had arrived. Even in the extreme cold, I was too warm from the exertion in my many layers of clothing. The inner debate over removing some layers was short.

At this latitude, pre-dawn seems to last twice as long as it does in the southern latitudes. I could almost see without a flashlight, but not quite. Putting on my headlamp made things easier. Fighting to keep the dogs inside the car still for their safety, I pulled out my snowshoes and backpack. The snowshoe straps were frozen and I had to work them back and forth with my hands to get them to function properly. I made a mental note not to leave them in the back of the Suburban again. It never warms up back there. The pack full of canned goods, stored in the front with me and the dogs, was safe from freezing. A ton of supplies had to be carried in. My dogs were excited and ready to finally get out of the vehicle and into the snow. Strapping on my snowshoes, I began the fourth and final stage of my homecoming. I wished for a dogsled but alas, none appeared. At that point in my life, I could carry a heavily loaded pack. Even so, the pack was overweight. I knew I could leave a few things in the car, things that would not be affected by the freezing, but returning for them later would add another leg to my journey. For that reason, I decided to carry on with the extra-heavy pack.

To discourage uninvited guests, there was no road or path in to the lodge. I always followed a different moose trail, and I was careful not to leave a visible trail in. Without a beaten path, I felt protected from hunters or people "just lookin' around." Not having a maintained trail did make it a little more difficult hiking in, but it was worth it for the added security. Foxy was excited to be going home, and Nuk was just happy to be out of the vehicle and playing in the snow. This would be Nuk's first lesson. Foxy bounced up and over heaps of snow in the general direction of the lodge and I never knew if I followed her or if she, cued by my movement, followed me.

The snow was not in its best form for humans, but it was perfect for the dogs. There had been a thaw and the deep freeze of the night caused an ice layer to cover the softer snow underneath. This, along with the snow wells under the big trees, made it extremely difficult to traverse. The thin crust of ice allowed Foxy and Nuk to stay on top, but even with my snowshoes, I would take two steps on the surface and, on the next step, fall into fluffy snow. I tried to be careful, but I still fell every third step or so. And even though I was aware it was going to happen, it nevertheless caught me off-guard. This was hard on my back. I would end up with one leg on the surface and the other buried 2½ feet in the snow, with bulky snowshoes as anchors. I was becoming exhausted.

At one point I fell onto my back and could not pull myself up. My pack had sunk into the snow. With my legs and arms extended, the snowshoes crossed in an impossible configuration. I was stuck like a beetle on its back. Lying there, I begged God for the strength to rise from my predicament. Then with the clarity of a bright white light, I heard the Big Guy say, "Take off the pack and rise."

OK, so I was exhausted and wasn't thinking straight. Being borderline hypothermic didn't help either. (That's my excuse, anyway.) Slipping my arms from under the straps, I was able to pull my snowshoes up to the surface and get up. Then I hoisted the pack and placed it back on my shoulders.

We finally arrived at the frozen creek marking the west-side property boundary. I crossed the bridge made with a giant fallen spruce tree. It was a worn-out woman on snowshoes who duck-walked the narrow span, dwarfed by a giant backpack that now seemed to weigh at least 100 pounds. With the sudden thrill of reaching the far side of the bridge, I felt a small boost of energy. Almost home!

As we emerged from the thick forest, my first glimpse of the lake was magical. The sun had edged its way over the east mountains just enough to flash brilliant light across the surface of the snowbound lake. The rays of light hit the hoarfrost, large thin flat crystal flakes that stood on end, and each crystal picked up its own colour of the light—ruby red, emerald green, while others were sapphire blue and saffron yellow. These jewels cast over the vast surface, all lit up, seemed to be just for me. I forgot my aching back and how tired I was.

I hurried towards the back porch of the lodge, quickly dropping the pack and releasing the snowshoes, and I grabbed my camera from where it was attached to the pack. Fumbling, I removed my gloves, wanting to capture the colours of the hoarfrost. I strode through the deep snow, back to the point where I first saw the glittering wedges of ice crystals. I steadied my hand to take the shot.

I looked up to check out a passing cloud and steadied my footing. Suddenly, I heard a soft crack and a thud at the same time, and to my horror, the earth swallowed me!

It wasn't just an insignificant hole, but a deep and hungry abyss, black as night and with no hint of depth or bottom. Terrified, I scrambled to slow the descent. The camera went flying into the snow. My arms stretched almost beyond endurance, clambering for purchase on the rim. My feet dangled in the air, seeking a bottom that wasn't there. As I clawed myself to the surface, using muscles I didn't know existed, my mind went into overdrive:

*Hell swallowed me for some unknown crime.* Then, *I'm falling into a bottomless pit and will never be discovered.* Followed by an imaginary headline: *Skeleton Found in Spring Suspected to be that of Ol' Widow-Woman, Stripped Clean by Animals and Vermin.*

Adrenaline-charged, I clawed my way up and out of the gaping hole and lay on the snow, now splattered with blood from my bloodied knuckles. Catching my breath, I was thankful I had been able to get out, and happy the dogs hadn't followed me in! The only real damage was the fingernails I'd broken in my scramble, and I had no picture of the hoarfrost ice crystals. Looking at the surface of the hole, it was a triangular gap in the snow, 2 feet by 5 feet. When I looked down into the blackness it was a cavern of unknown size.

I had no idea what caused the hole to suddenly open up in my backyard. I would have thought it was a septic holding tank, but there was no odour. Later that day, I covered the opening with a wide plank. It would have to do until my return. This extra trip home had been only to satisfy myself that everything was OK here, and to reward myself for attending another gruelling logging meeting.

Six weeks later, after another meeting in Houston, BC, I seized the opportunity to come home to the lodge again for a short time. There was still so much snow. I crossed on the barge and drove to my pullout. Impatient and worried as to what damages winter had brought to the lodge in my absence, I walked fast. Nuk bounced along like he had lived there all his life. Foxy was glad to be going home but was more reserved.

Everything was perfect. There were a few trees down, but nothing damaged. The hole in the yard hadn't gone away, but it hadn't gotten any bigger either. The plank I had placed across it had a 10-inch stack of new snow on top.

The serenity of the place rejuvenated me. And after just a few days it started to warm up a bit. For the first time in months the thermometer read above zero. To celebrate, I took Foxy and Nuk hiking at dawn before the sun came up over the ridge. The snow started to cling and accumulate on the dogs' fur. I had to stop several times to break the clumps off. Mitten-clad hands proved unsuccessful, so I was forced to use my bare fingers. Some of the spheres must have weighed at least a pound. With numb fingers, cracked and bleeding knuckles and lungs full of fresh air, I turned back on the trail and headed home. Foxy and Nuk were relieved and dragged themselves along.

As we approached the property, we were met with the overwhelming aroma of pine scent. The snow on the heavy-laden pine boughs was melting and forming icicles before my eyes: long, fat icicles with giant drops of water that slid down and off their sharp tips. The sun, pouring through the ice and droplets, formed hundreds of moving prisms. Rainbows flooded the snow-covered trail and the fragrance filled my head with the promise of spring. I saw my home at the end of this beautiful corridor, shimmering in coloured light.

Two short weeks later, it was difficult to leave once again. What carried me up the trail away from the home I loved was the fact it was now late February. And in just a few short weeks I would be coming home to stay through spring, summer and fall.

# PART 3

# Endurance

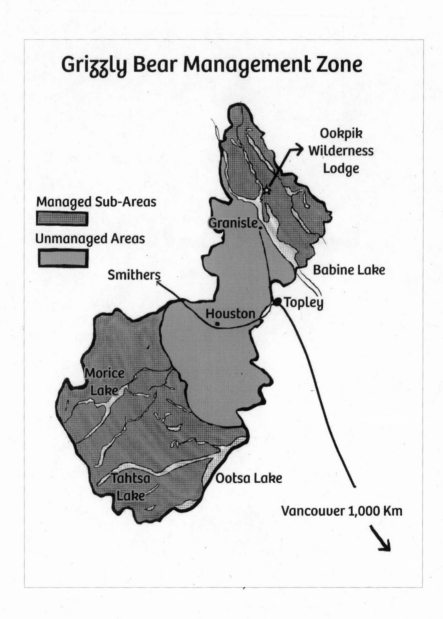

# Grizzly Bear Management Zone

**Managed Sub-Areas**

**Unmanaged Areas**

Ookpik
Wilderness
Lodge

Granisle

Babine Lake

Smithers

Topley

Houston

Morice
Lake

Tahtsa
Lake

Ootsa Lake

Vancouver 1,000 Km

*Ookpik Wilderness Lodge was surrounded by grizzly habitat.*

# CHAPTER 13

# Big Beautiful Lips

Time did fly, and coming home was a heart-pounding adventure. It always started when I came over the mountain pass and caught my first glimpse of Babine Lake, nestled several miles below in a long narrow valley. That was the moment I'd re-open my eyes to the reality of my world. I felt like I squeezed the previous winter into a whirlwind of work, with this homecoming my reward. That was the price I paid to come home, and it was worth every penny. On the long drive, I thought about the lake that drew me north, and I always smiled at the word "Babine." It is an Indigenous word meaning "big, beautiful lips."

I arrived mid-April and found the lake still frozen and the roads icy. With my SUV fully loaded, I pulled into Granisle at dusk. I was grateful my parents had purchased their summer home there. With a big shop and garage, it was a perfect staging area for my lodge business. Not only could I use it for covered boat storage in the winter, but I would also store the frozen meat supplies for the coming season. After off-loading some general supplies and placing six turkeys, six hams and a number of chuck roasts into the large chest freezer, I raced to the Granisle marina. As I gazed across at the vast, ice-covered miles that separated me from home, the expanse pulled at my heartstrings.

Every year, it was mentally easier to live and work alone. Every year it was harder to leave, and the desire to return grew more powerful. The lodge had become part of me.

As the sun fell and darkness closed in, I repacked the vehicle and backpack before collapsing into bed. I tried to grab a few hours of sleep in my parents' cold empty house; they would not be back for a few more months from their winter home in sunny Mexico. I woke before the alarm sounded, jumped out of bed and dressed for the long, cold hike over the snow between the forest service road and home sweet home.

I unplugged the block heater in the Suburban and started the engine. Because the car had been warm when I turned it off the night before, a thick layer of frost and ice had formed over the windshield. As I waited for the glass to clear, I turned on the CB road radio and the familiar logger language poured out: "Any more loads for the boat?" The barge was loading logging trucks on the east side of the lake. The dock workers were already hard at work, and it was still black as night and extremely cold. Impatiently, I scraped the remaining ice off the windshield, my breath creating plumes of fog. My nostrils froze with ice crystals.

At the barge landing on the western shore, I joined several empty logging trucks and waited a few short minutes while the barge unloaded. Seven of these loaded giants rumbled slowly off the *Babine Charger*. The barge lifted visibly as the trucks drove off.

In the dark, the flood lamps from the barge, its running lights and the trucks' headlights and tail lights, made the whole operation look like a circus. Sandwiched between miles of thick sheet ice, we moved slowly over to the far side of the lake. The smell of diesel exhaust from the barge was stomach-churning. The open span of free water, filled with rolling truck-sized ice chunks, was mesmerizing. Although I was grateful to use this transport, with its professional crew, it just didn't seem right to have a boat navigating a body of water filled with huge icebergs.

Upon landing, I pulled over and let the workers barrel down the snow-packed road. Once the truckers were long gone, the frozen forest awaited the fate of a new day. I was in no hurry. It was still dark, and I wanted some light to illuminate the snow on my hike down the trail home. During the drive to my pullout, I always worried way too much. Snow dust hung in my headlight beams. I envied my dogs, waiting patiently for their next adventure, with no qualms, on the warm floorboards. Foxy was now showing her age. Like Nuk, she was a rescue dog, and I really didn't know how old she was. The clues were most evident when she rose from a long nap.

Arriving at my spot on the logging road, I was glad to see the pull-out had been somewhat plowed. I was able to park my loaded Suburban off the one-lane road. Using the moose trails, I snowshoed in through the woods. This time, the snow was fresh, dry and dusty—easier to traverse, but still slow-going. The 6 inches of new powder fell behind me and refilled the wide path the snowshoes made. With just a light breeze, my trail would soon be unrecognizable to humans.

Foxy, my more faithful dog, followed in my wake. Nuk, on the other hand, wanted to investigate all the strange animal smells. He was snow-white, and it was hard to see him bouncing through the fluff as the early morning light filtered through the forest. My heart pounded harder the closer I got to home. I always approached the lodge with some trepidation after being away for a while. I worried about trees blowing down and crashing onto the cabins or the lodge. If it had happened early in the winter, animals and elements would have had time to wreak havoc.

As I took the makeshift footbridge over the frozen creek and into the yard, I was overjoyed to find every cabin, outbuilding and the lodge intact. I carried on. There were a few more trees blown over, but none causing any damage, and I thanked God for my good fortune—out loud.

*Ahhh, my life, once again renewed.* I would be blessed with another spring, summer and fall in this exceptional place. My dogs, truly in their element frolicking in the white fluffy snow, also loved to be home. I wished I could join them as they romped around having so much fun. Instead, being the responsible one, I cut a hole into the ice with the auger and hauled water, built a fire inside and quickly slid into my familiar routine. I would not set up my water system until the danger of the pump freezing and breaking had passed.

The rhythm of my chores felt good. I found being on a schedule not only kept me physically fit, but also kept my apprehension and melancholy at bay. I chopped firewood, the sound of the axe splitting the wood absorbed into the snowy forest. The wood box filled. The whiskyjacks, known as camp-robbers, came to watch out of curiosity. Mindless duty felt great.

"Work hard today, sleep good tonight" was what my Ol' Pa always said.

—

The snow receded slowly at first. There seemed to be more this year than in the past. Days became longer, but the temperature still plunged at night. This gave encouragement to the fire builder in the early morning chill. Meanwhile, the earth called out to the afternoon sun. Small rivers formed beneath the ice, creating caverns under the edges of the remaining snow. The ground became saturated beyond its capacity to drain. Unable to secure a solid hold during a sudden stiff breeze, trees fell.

In this icy wilderness, the first male hummingbird, defying the odds, claimed his territory. How could he fly hundreds of miles in such cold weather? How could he survive here in such harsh conditions without anything blooming for weeks? I put out a heavy dose of sugar syrup to boost his energy. Then, I was shocked to see this little hummer hanging upside down like a bat, from the little perch on the feeder. I thought he had frozen and died! Or that I had poisoned him with too much sugar. When I went out to remove the poor sad thing, he surprised me by buzzing through my fingertips and flying away! He kept coming back all day long to drain the feeder and entertain me. His loyal females arrived in the following weeks.

As the days trickled by, a steady, warm wind began to blow from the south. Spring! I could feel it in the air!

Sheets of lake ice began to break into sections the size of parking lots. At the mouth of the arm, I saw open water that glistened like diamonds in the sun. Each sparkling flash from the surface of the clear blue water sent a promise of spring. It was exhilarating. The sight made me warm, even though I was looking over a sea of ice. I walked the beach in the sunshine. I watched as the wind drove massive slabs of ice into each other with immense force. Carried by the momentum and caressed by vapour curls, they were propelled onto the shore. The frozen accumulation pushed on top of itself, over and over, until a 7-foot wall of ice stood on the beach.

Delicate prisms of candle ice, originally perpendicular to the surface, began to fall from the top of the wall. They made fantastic music that sounded like millions of glass chimes all ringing at the same time. Even when the wind stopped, the ice did not. Momentum continued to drive the slabs onto the beach.

Sunshine reflected on the enlarged channels of clear water reclaiming their ownership. Light passing through the candle ice and vapour created mini rainbows that danced about. The ice movements finally slowed to a stop. The world became still. The solitary sound of a distant raven's call pierced the silent valley, then nothing.

I was humbled beyond words. *This*, I thought, *is why people believe in God.*

Nuk broke the silence and started going crazy at the back of the lodge. I snapped out of my trance and went to make sure he was OK. The barking and yapping became fiercer as I rounded the back corner. Nuk, hackles up, in his power stance, came into view. Foxy, growling, stood firm at a thirty-degree angle.

Expecting to see a bear, I slowly stepped around the lodge. There, on the trail by the woodshed, I saw a newborn moose calf. The tiny thing had such long wobbly legs it had to hop once in a while to keep its balance. Its mother was in a rage, stomping and flinging her head! Nuk faced her, trying to protect his territory. Foxy, keeping eye contact with the moose, backed up to join me. The mother moose was trying to protect her new baby. I called Nuk off and we three retreated into the lodge.

As I looked out the window, I saw the new mother, still in a protective rage, stomp the ground, kicking up hunks of grass, dirt and rocks. And then she charged the only thing in view, the propane tanks. When she smashed into them, the tanks pounded together and made such a reverberating bang the baby fell down in fright. The mother ran to her calf and sniffed it to a standing position. Once assured the calf was fine, she took another run at the tanks and lightly smacked them again, just for good measure, then strutted away with her calf, daring anyone or anything to enter this space of motherhood. Luckily, the hoses connecting the tanks were not damaged.

As the snow receded, the hole in the backyard became more apparent. The plank I had placed over the span settled, and the opening became more ominous. It called out for my attention. At least six times a day I would walk across the plank, looking down into the black chasm. Running a wheelbarrow over the plank caused a strange echo from the depth. With a 10-foot pole, I still couldn't touch the bottom. I had investigated several possible explanations for the enormous pit, but I didn't know what to believe. I asked my geologist friend what he thought the hole might be. He was convinced it had been created during the ice age by a large chunk of ice that was covered with rock and silt, pressed down by the glacier. When it later melted, it left a hole with water that finally seeped out, creating a large crevice.

Another suggestion was that it could have been a salmon-oil pit made years ago by the Indigenous fishermen of the area. They would dig a large hole, throw salmon into it, allow it to rot and the oil would rise to the surface. I liked this idea, but when I eventually found out what the hole really was, the explanation wasn't nearly as glamorous. Upon further examination, I discovered the 12-by-12-by-14-foot hole was a grey-water tank. The tank had a ceiling of logs covered with dirt and grass. Unfortunately, two of the logs had rotted and fallen into the hole.

I was lucky, that cold winter morning, that I didn't fall all the way into it. I would not be writing this story today. Someone would have used a long pole to fish out my skeleton. Now that I knew what it was, I became obsessed with the quandary of what to do about this monstrous hole. My granddaughter suggested I put a hot tub in the space.

As soon as the snow melted, I began to build a massive and elaborate cover for the abyss—better than the plank I'd been using before. For over a week I wished for spring sunshine, but with frozen fingers, I hammered nail after nail into the final sheet of plywood.

On the first timber, under the heap, I placed a time capsule. The note said, "To my future (imaginary) husband," who I knew would have to someday re-do this mess. The capsule was an elaborate apology for the 2 pounds of nails, eight sheets of plywood and oversize 4-by-12 timbers he would have to remove to fix the problem properly. Maybe, I thought, he would just put in a hot tub.

—

I had been wishing for spring, and at long last it arrived. How wonderful it felt to be alive in this fantastic place: the birds singing, the forest scents and the spectacular sunrises. In June, the lake could rise at an alarming rate. I didn't know just how high the water was going to go. Every day I marvelled at the change.

One morning, wandering down the dock, I realized if the water got any higher, I would have to build a ramp up to the first dock. Not only would I have to situate a new ramp, but also one of the pilings used to hold the docks in place would not be tall enough. A 25-foot wooden section of the dock floated above the piling.

To add to the ever-melting snow, spring rains started coming down in buckets. Enormous black rain clouds sailed overhead to dump their load into the lake. Raindrops fell into raindrops until you had to part the water in heavy raingear to get through.

The days were flying by as fast as the dark clouds. Each day I found a dock section rising above its piling and trying to float away. In the middle of this calamity, I had to empty and drag a small storage shed by the shoreline to higher ground. The shed had been there for years, and water had never reached it before.

I'd have to replace all the short pilings to secure the docks quickly. For several days, dawn had started with a race into the wet forest. Chainsaw in hand, I cut down small trees, removed the branches and sharpened the ends. I dragged them out of the forest and down to the cove. At the dock, all six of my boats lay heavy in the water.

Before I could bail the boats, I had to secure the marina. Dragging one of my freshly cut, 20-foot logs down the dock was the easy part. Raising it into the water and dropping it straight down into the mud was much harder.

The next chore was for me to balance on a ladder, set on the wobbly dock in the wind and rain, to pummel the poles into the mud with a ten-pound sledgehammer. While teetering up there, catching my breath in between pounding, I would see yet another section of the marina trying to escape confinement. All 300 feet of dock were in major jeopardy.

Spring! I had wished for spring! My mother's words rang in my head: *"Be careful what you wish for."*

After days of pounding pilings and building another ramp to reach the docks, my old friend Alex came to see how I was making out. I asked him, with just a little hysteria in my voice, "Alex, when will the water stop rising?"

He pointed at the mountain in front of the lodge and said, with a controlled voice, "Do you see the snow on the mountain? When the snow is gone from the Sleeping Giant, the water will stop rising."

Alex had lived all his life on the lake. As a small child, his grandfather had pointed to the same mountain and told him the same thing. Somewhat surprised that a grown woman would ask such a childish question, Alex was too kind to allow his suppressed chuckle to surface.

Every day thereafter, my first priority was to see how much snow remained on the Sleeping Giant. Finally, the sun came out and the last snow patch melted away. And the water stopped rising.

Trees along the shore seemed to suck up all the extra water. Fresh verdant green filled the forest. All the shrubs and wildflowers exploded with the urgency of a northern summer. Birds had their babies. Butterflies filled the fragrant air. The lake flowed into the river and out to the Pacific. The flood was soon a distant memory. The new, tall pilings still stood, a little crooked, well out of the water, with their tops all pounded flat into a pale, soft fibre. That summer, more than one of my guests asked for an explanation as they passed these tall poles.

One afternoon at the end of the summer, a floatplane landed in the harbour. A man and wife got out, gawking at the tall poles.

The pilot, known as Hawk, said to me, "I hear there is an ol' wida' woman who wants to sell the lodge?"

I answered, "You're lookin' at her, and she don't!"

—

That spring flood was the most dramatic one recorded in decades. It was calculated, by someone smarter than me, that using the 7 feet of extra water on the surface of the 180-kilometre (110-mile) lake, stacking one cubic foot of water on top of another, you would have been able to reach the moon.

# CHAPTER 14

# My Friend Alex Michelle

Alex had first come to our front door back in 1995, during our first spring. He welcomed us to the area and explained that his family had three cabins in the small Tachet Indigenous settlement at Old Fort Village. Some of these people came to Old Fort to process salmon and moose, others came once in a while for summer breaks. But most of the time, Old Fort was deserted, and the people lived in the small village close to Granisle. This made him our part-time neighbour, 16 kilometres (10 miles) away. Alex was about sixty-five years old and very fit.

Alex asked if he could trap beaver on our property, because the land where Ookpik Wilderness Lodge sat was deeded private property. My first thought was, *Poor beaver.* I was very naive.

"Yes, but please, I want beavers left here for my grandchildren to see," was my instant reply.

He smiled and looked at me, his eyes crinkling. "That's my wish also," he said. "There have always been beaver here and there always will be beaver here." I would find out later just how many beavers were around and how the many new kits born each year would impact the area.

We invited him in. He carefully removed his boots, then entered the living room. In early spring we did not keep the living room heated, so we gravitated to the warm kitchen. Over coffee with cake, Alex told us how his father, grandfather and uncles had always trapped here.

"I have a registered trapline, just like a white man, although I do not need one. This is what I want. I am Canadian—I fought in the Korean

War," Alex told us. We visited for a while, and we talked about Alex and his family, and our own.

After David died, Alex and his wife, Hazel, still came for coffee and told stories about his family's history and about the area. I was excited to learn that Hazel was a master leather and beadwork artist. Her work was exquisite. She also made button blankets for her daughter, who danced in traditional regalia in competition. Alex told me about the olden days and about the forest and the smaller lakes that dotted the watershed. He told me this part of Babine Lake had always been a very important food source for his people. Morrison Arm had been called Salmon Arm, for obvious reasons. The First Nations people also called it the Nursery. Every spring, this area was a haven for cow moose giving birth. Alex and his family had trapped, hunted and fished here for as long as anyone remembered.

One afternoon, as Alex and I walked across the creek into the forest, looking at an area proposed for logging, we came to a small, square hole in the ground covered with thick green moss. I asked Alex what the pit was for.

"Long ago, this was a trail that led over the mountains to villages far beyond. My ancestors dug pits like these and left things they could use on the way, like a cache."

Fascinated, I encouraged him to continue. "You used this trail as a trade route?"

He hesitated and then replied, "We used this in time of war. We would steal women and take revenge. You must think we were horrible."

"Alex, have you ever heard of the Crusades?" I asked as a response.

After we'd had a few grizzly bear visits near the lodge, I asked Alex if he had ever shot a grizzly.

"He would not like that," Alex replied, with a stern face I had never seen before. "That," he said, "would be like killing family."

Alex held the grizzly as his family crest. Shooting a black bear was quite alright, but he would never consider killing a grizzly.

One winter, Alex gave me a hide from a black bear he'd shot for food. It was of such high quality he could not bring himself to throw it away. It was beautiful, with the thick, rich blue-black coat that only a winter bear can have. The hide, almost 7 feet from nose to tail, was the largest I had ever seen. I had it tanned by a furrier and I made it into a rug.

Alex would bring Hazel out to visit as much as she would come. He wanted her to see I was happy alone in the wilderness. Alex wanted to build a cabin on his trapline and have Hazel stay with him for weeks during trapping season, but she was not excited about living in the bush. In her quiet way, she would ask me questions: "Are you afraid at night? Are you afraid when you are alone in the day?"

I assured her I was happy and not afraid. I refrained, for Alex's sake, from telling her my story of the mountain lion:

Early one spring while Silver, then seven, and I were mowing the backyard, we saw a bunch of young bunnies. Silver was determined to catch one. While I mowed around each tiny, freshly sprouted wildflower, she scrambled after the bouncing little creatures. I glanced up to see her stumble over a root with a bunny just a foot or so ahead. She came up with a skinned knee and a big smile.

"I almost got him, Nana!"

Amazingly enough, Silver had a tiny tuff of rabbit hair clutched firmly in her fingers.

The rabbits grew, and then they multiplied until there were rabbits everywhere you looked. Silver had gone home. The trees began to turn colours and the lawn and decks were covered in morning frost. It seemed everywhere I went, rabbits crossed my path.

Understanding how we used the generator—which was in a shed behind the lodge—is also important to this story. In the summer, even when my guests were here, the most I ran the generator was two to three hours a day for three days a week. This generated enough power to charge my ten deep-cycle batteries. With the lengthy daylight hours, reading until eight or nine at night wasn't a problem. When I was here alone, even in the late fall, I ran the generator only once a week to keep everything charged up.

The generator shed was set as far as possible behind the lodge to keep the noise level down. It ran on diesel fuel, and I never had any problems with it. There was an extensive procedure to start and stop the machine. I needed to remember to check the oil and fuel level and never, ever run out of diesel! Just getting fuel was a big chore. First, I would drive the boat marina, get into my vehicle and get the fuel from the gas station in Smithers, which was three hours away—six hours round trip. Then I would load the diesel into my boat, motor up the lake to the Ookpik dock, off-load the heavy containers into a wheelbarrow, haul them up the docks to the trail, bounce over roots to the generator shed, lift the 5-gallon tanks over my head and siphon fuel into the holding tank. The oily diesel fuel is very hard to get off your hands and the smell lingers even after you wash vigorously.

So, for me, turning on the generator to charge the batteries to turn on a reading light took on a whole new meaning.

One evening, just before dark, on my way down the long shadowy path to start the generator, I felt the hair on the back of my neck lift. Truly, the hair on the back of my neck stood up and tickled under my collar. I felt someone, or more likely something, watching me. I had never experienced that sensation before—and hope not to again. I looked down and saw paw prints about 5 inches wide in the fresh dusting of snow. I ran back to the house to get a measuring tape, a Boy Scout guidebook and a flashlight. Upon my return I saw several circular prints without claw marks. I poured over the diagrams and read the descriptions in the chapter on animal tracks. I realized the tracks had to be cougar! Puma! Mountain lion! Whatever you wanted to call it, they are entirely the same big, wild cat. Try as I might, I could not find any other tracks that matched in the book.

I went into the tiny generator room, its door facing the bush. But I felt like a canary in a cage. Captured! After starting the generator, I rushed back to the lodge. Three hours passed slowly by as I waited for the batteries to charge. I dreaded the trip down the path—fifty-two steps, to be exact— to turn off the generator. I thought about letting the engine operate all night.

I had never run so quickly down that long path. It was worse coming back, because without the noise of the machine, I could hear my own heart beating madly. The woods were silent. Straining to hear something and dreading the thought, I rushed to the safety of the thick log walls of the lodge.

The next day, Alex came by on his way to check his traps. I knew he could hear the slight panic in my voice.

"Alex, there is a cougar in my yard. What am I going to do?"

"Nothing," he said calmly.

"What do you mean, 'nothing'? There's a cougar right here in my yard. What should I do?"

"Nothing," he repeated. "If he wants you, he gets you, and there is nothing you can do about it." He went on to explain, "It is no good to carry a gun. You'll never see a cougar. He will be in a tree, hidden. You will not see him until it is too late."

I felt my heart thumping in the quiet moments that followed. Breaking the silence, Alex slowly continued his explanation.

"He will be full of rabbits and not so hungry for you." His eyes crinkled as he smiled.

The next day, I saw no rabbits and there were no more signs of the cougar.

—

Alex had been concerned about all the old forest being removed from the land around his home and his trapline. He told me often how the animals did not like the open spaces. His family had lived and hunted in the vicinity for countless generations—he knew what the animals liked.

I asked Alex if he wanted to join me at one of the logging meetings in the village of Granisle, and he said yes. I tried to talk to all the people in the Central Babine area, informing them of the upcoming meeting. Almost a hundred showed up—a big turnout for such a small community.

The licensees had set up the meeting so we could "express our concerns." Later I came to understand the tactics they used to burn up the minutes at the two-hour meeting—they set out coffee and cookies during the greet-the-people hour, and wasted a lot of time talking about hockey and fishing. Slowly they hauled out the maps. The five men from the largest logging outfit sat at a table facing a full house. They proceeded to provide detailed but meaningless information until there were only a few minutes left for those of us attending to "express our concerns."

Alex and I sat at a table facing them. Behind us every available chair was filled, and more people stood at the back.

The executives gave a long-winded speech about how their company provided employment for so many people. In fact, only a few of those people actually lived in the immediate area. The majority of the loggers lived in a town 70 kilometres (40 miles) away. Next, they told us how the beetles had invaded the area. At the time, 100 kilometres (60 miles) away, in a forest of predominantly monoculture pine, the beetles were indeed a problem and the marketing of blue pine-beetle-stained wood had not yet been established. However, the forest around us was a diverse boreal forest—we had deciduous trees, fir trees and pine, but mostly spruce. The latter is what the logging companies were after.

I spoke about how we should cut only the beetle-infested timber. The Ministry of the Environment representative agreed: "We need to maintain a Forest Ecosystems Network. Wildlife needs to have a corridor maintained through the forest," he said. "They need an old-growth corridor to connect habitats across the forest district." He went on to explain how several species needed old-growth to survive.

The main executive from the logging company pushed his chair back from the table, put his thumbs into his wide suspenders and proceeded to tell the room how he was a trapper, and that he knew that martens loved clear-cuts.

Upon hearing this statement, Alex nudged me and asked to be introduced into the conversation. Always nicely groomed, Alex was extra done-up that night in a corduroy sportscoat with leather elbow patches.

He stood and walked around all the tables to face the gentleman with the suspenders. All eyes in the room fixed on these two men. Alex casually reached inside the pocket of his jacket and pulled out five small pieces of faded paper. His calm, deep voice clearly reached the far corners of the room.

"In 1905, before logging, my grandfather was given this receipt for the marten he trapped. He had a good year, twenty-four marten, ten beaver and five fisher..."

As Alex continued, my throat tightened and my eyes filled. The only sound in the room was Alex's voice as he read from the fragile documents. His old records listed the actual number of martens harvested before and after logging activities.

Placing the yellowed papers respectfully back into his inside pocket, Alex returned to his seat. The room full of people, from all occupations, was reminded what an honourable and stately gentleman looked like. I was not alone when I applauded Alex's presentation. And I was not surprised at his strength in facing these powerful, dismissive men. Alex hunted black bear with a .22-calibre rifle and had served in the Korean War.

After Alex sat down, the Ministry of Forests representative stood up and said, "Thank you all for coming and expressing your concerns."

In the end, much of the forest was removed in what the licensees called "a sustainable" way. Alex was the first of his family to see the damage caused by so-called sustainable harvesting of the old-growth forest. The traplines his family had used for over a hundred years had changed. They would never be the same.

# CHAPTER 15

# Lodge Business

had several clients who booked every year after David died, but to really make a go of the business, I had to fill in all of the vacancy during the fishing season. Any spare time in the winter, while working on Whidbey Island, was spent figuring out just how to get all the cabins filled for the season. I would cast my pitch at fly-fishing clubs, fire halls and even a giant sportsmen's show in San Mateo, California. And I did add a few clients at the clubs and halls. My spring and summer calendar started to fill up.

The sportsmen's show in 2000 was different. This was the big time. Thousands of people flocked around my small booth, listening to my fishing stories and looking at the amazing pictures of fish caught on Babine Lake. Mine was the only one representing Northern Interior British Columbia. I was excited and passionate. People stopped to listen to my stories about the trophy rainbow trout in Babine Lake. No one booked immediately, however; it seemed they didn't really trust a fisherwoman. I considered hiring a male model and dressing him up in appropriate fancy fishing apparel. Nevertheless, I had enough bookings by the end of the winter. In fact, I was worried about having too many clients, because I was still running the place by myself, but as my father would say, "No guts, no glory."

One early spring evening nine guests were due for dinner. Two were coming by sailboat from the Granisle marina, 32 kilometres (20 miles) south—a couple I had met a few times on the village docks were joined by two of their friends. A family of five were also joining us by powerboat from Smithers Landing, 26 kilometres (16 miles) northwest. None had been to Ookpik Lodge before.

It was so pleasing to see full sails coming into Morrison Arm. When my guests got closer, I ran to the kitchen, pulled out the bread I had baked, turned the oven on low and the burners off. The timing was important. The lodge needed to smell wonderful when they walked in from their long, windy ride.

I raced down the 300-foot dock to greet the sailboat. I had a few minutes to spare as the captain changed tack. I signalled the captain to moor in the back cove as it was protected from all winds. He understood my signals, heaved to starboard, dropped sails and came to a perfect landing. I greeted the captain and crew with enthusiasm—sailboats by nature were seldom on time, but this one was. As the sailors stretched their sea legs on the beach, the distant roar of a powerboat entered Morrison Arm. The engine's blare echoed off the hillsides. I could see an open aluminum riverboat loaded with smiling faces. The captain pulled back the throttle and slid into his moorage, and the wake washed the shoreline like applause. This was the first time I had met this happy family—Mom, Dad, two teenagers and a young boy of six, each wearing a bright orange life jacket. I helped them from their boat and made introductions all around, and I was given a big, delightful hug by the youngest in the group, Jackie, a child with Down's syndrome. Full of excitement, Jackie clung on as if I were his special aunt. It was an honest, warm and sorely missed, loving connection.

"You're all right on time and dinner is almost ready. Let's have a walkabout to get your land legs."

Holding Jackie's hand, I walked my guests up the dock to the first cabin and began my repertoire.

"This is the cabin I use for family groups. Mom, Dad and the kids fit just fine in here," I explained. "The children can play on the beach, Dad can fish off the dock, and Mom can relax on the porch to watch the entire goings-on."

Passing the lodge, I followed the trail leading to the next cabin. "This is my favourite cabin. It has a great wood heater and is so cozy and warm in the cool spring and fall," I said.

But in my head, I was thinking, *This is the one Silver and I stayed in when I was devastated and needed her company after David died.* We continued down the path to the next two cabins.

With Jackie still holding my hand, I said to the grown-ups, "I like to stay on the paths because there are so many wildflowers that would be destroyed if they were trampled on. There are three different kinds of orchids, wild lilies and numerous berries, not to mention the deep, soft moss along the edge. I never stray from the paths."

By the time we came to the third cabin, the guests were completely enthralled. I explained that the cabins had been there since 1930, when they were also used as a fishing camp. We stepped up the stairs and stood on the porch of the third cabin.

"I have been refurbishing this one for the last couple of years," I said. (I didn't tell them about how, before David died, he had put a new roof on this cabin, including two terrific skylights that made the inside bright and cheery. Or about all the hours I spent sanding the logs and caulking the spaces between each one, working late into the night using a Coleman lantern to place an old-style manila rope covering the caulking.)

"I now use this cabin for a shower-house. Someday, I will make a new shower-house and use this as a family cabin," I continued. "Last year I laid a tile floor and installed a tile countertop."

I didn't tell them about the hours spent, the mashed fingers or the lugging of the heavy boxes of tiles up from the boat. I didn't tell them David hadn't finished plumbing the cabin before he died. So, although the shower worked great, the sink had yet to be connected.

Jackie was fascinated by the large owl on the back wall of the cabin. Last spring, I had removed a 4-by-8-foot wooden panel and used a scroll saw to create a cut-out of an owl. I had placed the owl over a window at the back of the cabin, where the light shone through it.

At the last cabin my guests remarked on the fact that all the little log cabins had feather beds and down comforters. With a grin, Jackie gave one of the beds a comfort test. Each cabin had a wood cookstove and small kitchen with windows warmed by cheerful red-calico curtains. The maple rockers and braided rag rugs gave every cabin a homey feeling. I kept the cabins spotlessly clean, and with their bright windows that looked over the lake, what more could anyone ask for?

As we left the last cabin and began to meander back towards the lodge, I pointed to the numerous pink lady's slipper orchids surrounding this last cabin. I refrained from telling them about the mother bear I ran into around the corner of the cabin. One of the guests took the opportunity to use one of the tidy outhouses. Jackie wanted to wait to use the indoor plumbing at the lodge, so we moved a little more quickly.

Sometimes I would take my guests all the way to the creek at the border of the property, but today Jackie was in a hurry, and I needed to finish preparing dinner. On our way back to the lodge, we passed the workshop and the generator house, and with raised eyebrows, my guests seemed surprised to see my CASE backhoe placed in the middle of a forest with no roads.

We passed a few pots of flowers here and there, with hummingbirds buzzing about. The red-winged blackbirds were singing, and the Steller's jays scolding. The squirrels scampered about and overhead, the eagles soared.

The guests settled into the lodge's expansive, sunlit living room while I slipped into the kitchen to complete the meal. Back in the living room, I offered wine and soft drinks before returning to my chores.

I always loved to see the faces of my guests on their first visit. They invariably loved the spacious, carpeted living room and its giant stone fireplace that crackled and blazed. Jackie plunking on the keys of the piano let me know from the kitchen that there was a child in the house, which I loved. Overlooking the proceedings was the gigantic elk rack mounted on a beautiful burl.

In the formal dining room, I had set the table with fresh linen, silverware, apple-blossom Franciscan dinnerware plates, side plates, water glasses, snowy white cloth napkins, and candles. My guests admired the seasonal table decorations woven between the place settings, and the enticing smell of freshly baked bread, mixed with the hearty aroma of roasting meat and potatoes, ignited their senses.

I brought out the platters of hot food and was feeling so delighted that the entire lodge, silent only an hour before, was now overflowing with the laughter and chatter of a cheerful family and new-found friends.

Their eyes opened wider with each new dish I brought from the kitchen. Glistening baked beans smothered in a molasses sauce, candied yams topped with marshmallows and ginger, macaroni salad sprinkled with sliced black olives, pistachio fruit salad, braided rosemary bread fresh from the oven, side dishes of brown-sugar pineapple sauce, Tennessee maple mustard sauce and, last but not least, a giant ham covered with pineapple and cherries. Jackie stood up, his face glowing, and exclaimed, "A feast! A feast! A feast for a... KING!"

I have had many compliments on my food, but Jackie's was the very, very best ever.

Candles also illuminated the dessert table in the corner, which promised cherry pie, peach pie and a carafe of fresh hot coffee and sweet cream.

I was always surprised so many guests were willing to come to such a remote place solely for dinner. They made reservations by radio phone, then travelled many miles by floatplane or boat just for a supper. I always made sure the food was consistently good and plentiful, and even when guests lingered over dessert, during a northern summer there was always enough light for a sunset cruise home.

The wonderful family ambled back to their boat—Jackie was almost sleepwalking—and casting off, they promised to come back. They did, many times in the years and seasons to come. In the distance I could see Jackie as he bounced up and down, waving to me.

The sailors were going to anchor in Sanctuary Bay, just a few miles away, and were not in a hurry to leave. Walking down the long dock, we visited a while, enjoying the melody of the evening birds and bugs.

On their departure, the wife asked, "Aren't you afraid to stay here alone?"

My answer was always the same.

"I guess I could be afraid of sasquatch or UFOs... but I could be afraid of them anywhere. I suppose I could be afraid of burglars, but they usually don't have any money for boats or planes, and it's easier for them to knock off old Aunt Mabel than to find me. Besides, the rumour is out about my trusty companion, W.D."

"Who is W.D.?" she asked.

"Well, let me tell you about my Winchester Defender," I replied. "It's a stainless steel, short-barrel shotgun. It is loaded, and I'd say I'm ready for anything. I have a beaded elk-hide holster for it that fits on my back so I can keep my hands free. I have a bear-tooth charm hanging off it just for luck. So, no, I'm not afraid to stay alone."

There's one conversation that has always stuck with me: David and I had a good friend who was in the Washington State highway patrol. After David was gone, this friend told me, "If someone comes into the lodge at night, do not turn on the lights and do not give warning—just shoot to kill. When someone comes all the way out here and breaks into your house, he is up to no good and would be a deadly danger. You are not to risk your life by giving him the option to shoot first." The advice was necessary, but still disturbing.

As usual, there were no more questions—and the legend of W.D. lived on.

For a few moments that night I stood on the dock and watched as my guests sailed off into the sunset. Then I returned to the lodge, satisfied that my guests would have great memories of their trip to Ookpik for dinner, and I knew for sure my memories of the overjoyed young man would live in my heart for a very long time.

After removing the last dish from the silent dining room, I stopped with a smile, remembering Jackie's voice: "A feast! A feast! A feast for a... KING!"

All the light from the sun was gone by the time I had the dishes done, and my father's words came to mind: "Work hard today, and sleep good tonight." It had pretty much become my mantra.

Retiring to my spacious bedroom, I drew back the down comforter and reclined onto the king-sized feather bed. As I looked out the window over the dark lake, the moon rose over the midnight-velvet landscape and cast fragments of broken light on the water's surface.

It was warm, so I opened the bedroom window. I was too tired to read and too wound up to sleep, but I finally fell into a light slumber. Then a sudden whip of branches woke me. The towering evergreens sang in the stiff breeze and held my attention. It was rare to have a wind at night.

Getting up, I saw the moon at its zenith, lighting the stage. Waves were building. Lured out onto the front deck, I was surprised when the wind continued to build and seemed hot in contrast to the typically cool evenings. The wind came from the north, the exact opposite direction from earlier in the day. I stood with my dogs and watched as the waves gained in size. In a matter of minutes, the seas reached 4 feet. It was spectacular. My robe wanted to fly into the night. My skin tingled.

A salmon soared from the top of a moonlit wave into the emerald crest of the next. The wave filled with the dark shape of the salmon, and I stood astonished as the hot wind whipped my hair. It was hard to pull my eyes from the waves—I didn't want to miss another salmon's flight.

Just as quickly as the wind had begun, it stopped, and in no time at all, the moonbeams spread out over the surface of the lake like an iridescent blanket.

Wandering back to my warm bed, I savoured every minute of the unexpected wind. If I hadn't been there, I mused, who would have seen the leaping salmon? It was serendipitous. I felt fortunate I was there to remember the wonders of this night and fell into a dream-filled sleep.

## CHAPTER 16

# Nuk, Blueberry Pie and the Grizzly

It was a sad day when I took poor old Foxy for her last boat ride. Her daily life had become painful. She had come from a dog-rescue operation, and I really did not know how old she was. My guess is she was thirteen or fourteen years old and was just too tired to go on. Foxy had served me well and had a great life out in the wilderness. It was a very sad day when I brought her body back from the vet, wrapped in her favourite blanket. Nuk and I buried her down the path on a hill overlooking the lake.

It was wise to keep a dog at the lodge. Not for security, but rather as an alarm. The other good reason for me to pack in all that dog food, for miles across land and sea, was that I never had to talk to myself. Talking to Foxy and Nuk made me feel saner. They were my friends, and I would sorely miss Foxy. I was so glad I still had Nuk.

Nuk was a little bigger than Foxy—he weighed 24 pounds and was a handsome American Eskimo. He had pure-white fur suitable for northern climates, and for some reason he was able to stay perfectly white without grooming. Nuk had an uncomplicated nature: He was easy to get along with and I was grateful he could not contradict me. By this time he was also an exceptionally well-behaved dog, never wasting his time barking at the numerous squirrels, grouse or rabbits. Foxy had taught him well. He would, however, chase moose to what he perceived to be our property border, and black bears he would hold off and confuse till I had my act together. Grizzly bears were another matter entirely. Growling and looking over his shoulder, Nuk would escort me to the lodge door, following immediately. If a grizzly entered the yard and Nuk was outside alone, he would come to the door and quietly whimper.

Nuk hated to get wet. His deep undercoat, which kept him warm in winter, became saturated if submerged. Even in the dead heat of summer he would only venture into the lake a few inches.

On board the boat, he'd remain still, lying on the floorboards—just as Foxy had. When I'd begin to moor, Nuk would get out of the way and watch for my command, "Nuk come!" Only then would he jump ashore.

As I fished in the middle of the lake one morning, fighting a nice-sized trout, I noticed Nuk was too close to a loose fishing lure. Without thinking, I commanded, "Nuk come!" In shock, I watched as poor Nuk leaped for the imagined dock. His eyes rolled back as he looked at me with panic. I could not believe Nuk had interpreted my order to mean he should abandon ship.

There I was with supper on the hook and a dog floundering in the lake. I secured the rod first. That was easy. The retrieval of the poor dog proved to be a wet and scrambling affair. Visibly upset, he turned his back on me. After a long shake, releasing a gallon of water, he sulked under the bow. But by suppertime Nuk had forgotten the incident and gobbled his share of the catch.

Out for an early paddle one splendid fall morning, I heard a ruckus on shore. Nuk raced back and forth along the beach, barking like mad. Looking to see what caused this flurry of activity, I watched in horror as an 80-foot aspen crashed to the forest floor. The sound echoed across the lake and the startled birds on the other side rose from their perches. The dog was terrified. Paddling as fast as I could towards the beach, I watched as Nuk raced along the shoreline, frothing at the mouth. Another tree crashed down. Then a big, brown furry shape materialized at the edge of the grass. With all that fat rolling with muscle under the shiny fur, there was no mistake: It was a massive grizzly bear. I slowed to a cautious paddle.

After a few minutes, he thrashed around to the far side of the dock area, flipping beach logs like pancakes while searching for food. We always had a visit from the grizzly this time of year. He came to harvest ants and berries, and in a couple of weeks he'd come down for the spawning sockeye salmon.

I waited until the king of the forest had moved along. As I landed the canoe, Nuk was elated.

I pulled the canoe onto the grass by the second cabin, far from the dock area where I'd last seen the bear. I wanted to give the big brute as much space as possible. The small knoll by this cabin was so full of wild low-bush blueberries that the warm sun caused the air to smell like a fresh blueberry pie. Nuk ran up to the blueberry patch, lay his head and shoulders down and ran as fast as he could. He came up with blue racing stripes from his nose to his shoulders. He was now a proud war dog, painted for battle.

—

After all the excitement of the grizzly's visit, Nuk and I relaxed on the front deck. I loved being here, looking out over the ever-changing body of water. Even the wind whipping up frothy waves couldn't disturb the serenity of this small space. It was strange: no matter how the wind blustered, the deck never got enough breeze to ring the wind chimes. The lodge sat on a 7-foot bank. When the wind blew towards the shore it hit the bluff and swirled up and away. It seemed like this house of logs was so isolated, so alien in this world of trees, animals and water, that the wind did not want to touch it. I would have to find a new spot for the wind chimes.

Later that afternoon, the treetops above me bent away from the gusts. The golden eagle came to visit and soared motionless out front. He was so close I could see the radiant variation of the golden colours separating the wing feathers. What a magnificent creature of the sky!

The breeze came in from the Pacific, 750 kilometres (470 miles) away, and hit the west side of the Sleeping Giant, the mountain directly across the water from the lodge. Slumbering throughout the year, with just a change of attire from one season to the next, the giant managed to divide the wind at will. It could blow 15 knots to the south, suddenly stop, and then blow a steady 15 knots to the north in just a few short minutes.

Although the awe-inspiring view gave me much to ponder, being on the small bluff also gave the wild animals a secret path along the beach. This natural wildlife corridor allowed moose to wander, wolf to hunt, otter to frolic, bears to cruise for spawned-out salmon, and I could be sitting there, 15 feet away—unseen.

—

Staying at the lodge eight months of the year, I saw very few people. Other than the fishermen who booked in the spring and dinner guests coming for a Saturday night supper, I was mostly alone. My parents came out infrequently, as they travelled a lot or stayed at their home in Granisle, though whenever I had an extended forestry meeting, they would babysit the lodge for me. My son, Jason, busy with his own life, came to see me once every few years. My daughter, Amanda, who was now raising three children on her own, found it difficult to find free time. Somehow she made time every year to retrieve her older children, Silver and Chavala, from a couple weeks' holiday at Grandma's house. Cyrus, my grandson, was still too young to stay without his mother. I greatly looked forward to this special time, but with weeks adding up to months alone, it was important to have a dog for constant companionship, and Nuk was just right.

Although I sometimes had bouts of melancholy and missed David, the longer I was isolated, the more I adapted to being alone. It was a double-edged sword. I couldn't imagine living my life without a companion, but the longer I was in seclusion, the harder it was to go back to civilization to find someone. Nuk made being alone much easier to bear.

It was so beautiful at the lodge, I made a conscious decision every day to try to open all my senses to see, hear, smell and feel the goings-on within the stillness of the wilderness. I wanted to consume the abundance of nature's beauty. I tried to explain this wonder to Nuk, but he was never interested. Foxy was more attentive, but she was gone.

I did wish, once in a while, that there was a human by my side to share the many magical moments that transpired. The moving light show of the aurora borealis; a bull moose swimming to shore, then shaking like a giant dog, throwing rainbows of colour through the morning sun; a snow-filled forest, illuminated by moonlight, shadowed through the trees by passing clouds; enchanted moments inside the blackness of a wilderness night. Every day was a gift. Every night was a treasure.

I knew all too well how short life could be and how valuable each moment was. Having seen death, I found each day stunning and precious. But sometimes a darker, lonely mood would quietly enter my perfect world. I decided that I would not make a good hermit after all. I was missing my soulmate.

How strange to think that only a few years before, David and I were going to sail up the Sunshine Coast. Now I found myself in the middle of the Canadian wilderness, more alone than I have ever been in my entire life. Here I was, in the most gorgeous place in the world, without the man I expected to share the rest of my life with. David—who loved me more than any man ever would love me— was gone. Only the memory of him was left to keep me company. And Nuk, of course.

# CHAPTER 17

# Working for the Guide Outfitter

In the fall, business always slowed. Most people would not chance being caught on this big body of water with the fickle fall weather—even for my good cooking. The fish were hunkered down for the cold winter, so the diehard fly fishermen would wait to return with the spring hatch of bugs.

Becoming a widow had been a financial catastrophe. It was crucial for me to find work to subsidize the lodge income. Even with my winter work stints on Whidbey Island, the looming mortgage payments, insurance and taxes were a burden. Putting cash into the coffers whenever possible became mandatory.

Early in the summer one year, a couple came to dinner, and he was the owner of a guide outfitters operation in the Lakes Forest District. After sampling my fare, he asked me to cook at his hunting camp in the fall. The particular workplace was an outpost on Babine Lake, 105 kilometres (65 miles) south on the eastern shore.

This seemed perfect: The job would last three weeks in October and the first week of November. I could work seven days, come home for a couple days to check up on my place and then go back to the hunting camp to make more money. It sounded good to me.

A few months later, I met the owner of the outfit at his headquarters, in a small settlement on Babine Lake called Mill Bay. Here began my "cook's job." We loaded the grub into a boat along with a mountain of other gear. It was rumoured only women needed frivolous stuff in the bush, but after an hour loading huge quantities of gear into the flat-bottom riverboat, I wondered if men were just as frivolous.

Travelling over rough water was normal at this time of year, but stepping into a 25-foot riverboat with Nuk hopping over the mountain of gear threatened my sensibilities. With four hunters, the hired guide, many boxes of food, gas, guns, my trusting pup and me, we cast off into 4-foot seas. It seemed we were gravely overloaded.

Our voyage upwind to the outfitters' main camp was a pounding affair. The seas were short and steep. The boat fell off one wave with a slamming slide, only to run right into the next one. The heavy spray soaked my face and made me glad I always wore a life jacket. I inserted ear plugs and slipped under a plastic tarp at the bow of the boat, where Nuk and I rode it out.

Halfway there, smack in the middle of the giant lake, the engine died. The boat was tossed about by wind and sea. I looked back and saw Helmut, an experienced guide who doubled as the captain, hustling to find the problem. With the wind ripping off the tops of the waves, I hated having to remove my beeswax ear plugs. But in order to hear what was happening, it was necessary.

The gas hose to the outboard engine had sprung a leak. With everything in the world onboard—except for a new hose, oars or a radio—this boat was in trouble. We were in for a long, treacherous drift, blown by the wind wherever Mother Nature determined. The boat and its inhabitants would not be missed for seven days.

As part of the working team, I stepped over the mountain of men and gear to see if I could help. Helmut was holding the damaged hose. I handed my warm wax ear plug over to the captain. Helmut plugged the leak in the hose with the beeswax, and I was a heroine! These guys had not even tasted the cook's food and she was already going to receive a tip. Not only that, I had impressed the guide.

We travelled south, beating upwind for over an hour, passing pristine beaches with no cabins and no sign of humans. The trees were glorious in their fall colours. After covering 40 kilometres (25 miles), we came to a shore with surf breaking on the pebbled beach. The captain's timing of the waves was impeccable, and he made a smooth landing.

After we unloaded the boat, I put on some coffee and made lunch. Then I had time to explore my new digs. There were two fairly new log cabins facing the beach and a couple of old buildings situated behind them. One cabin was set up for the hunters and one set up as the cookhouse, with my quarters in the loft. Nuk claimed a back corner under the loft. The small log cabins were spacious and bright and my area private and comfortable.

The guides stayed in an ancient cabin they called the "Rat Shack." The second guide and two more hunters arrived an hour or so later, and our camp became a little village. The men were soon off for the evening hunt. After putting a roast in the oven, I went to work stowing supplies.

The hunting party came back to camp with nothing but enthusiasm and giant appetites. The two guides, helpful and very nice, packed my water and brought in firewood. Ken talked non-stop about his three young boys while passing pictures around. Taking a look at the blue-eyed boys, you could see why— they were so cute. Helmut, a Canadian citizen with a German accent, had immigrated as a young man. He showed pictures of his family and the love he had for them was quite evident.

Days came and went. The hunters brought in their trophies: giant moose and a couple of bears. After a satisfying supper, including apple pie, the hunting stories would come to an end and the men would wander off to their cabins, exhausted. Four a.m. came awfully early. In the middle of the week Ken and Helmut postponed retreating to the Rat Shack to use the radio phone.

It was impossible to have a private conversation because the radio station was at the dinner table, and with a radio phone you can hear both sides of a conversation. Helmut called his wife. I tried not to listen, but it was a small cabin. I could hear his wife, Mary, explain that his fifteen-year-old daughter had the opportunity to become an exchange student and go to Japan for a year. After some discussion they decided it would be a good experience. With a final farewell, he signed off. Helmut said goodnight and left the cookhouse. Then Ken called his wife to say hello, and each one of his boys just had to talk to their daddy. It was really sweet. I went to bed that night thinking how wonderful it was to see men so in love with their families.

One morning, while I was cooking, I heard a bunch of cussing and hollering. Evidentially a grizzly had hauled off the head of a trophy moose for a midnight snack. The hunter was not happy. He demanded the guide follow the grizzly tracks, and trail of blood, into the woods. Helmut, somewhat amused, refused to wander through the tall grass and into the forest to fight a grizzly for the mangled head of a moose.

After three days, Helmut hiked down the bear trail and retrieved the missing moose head. Most of the meat had been chewed away and there were teeth marks on the antlers. The hunter was glad to get his trophy rack back, even with the chiselled marks, which would confirm the grizzly stories. I am sure the tales became more gruesome as the years went on.

The seven days ended none too soon. The days were long. All the hunters bagged their beasts and we boated back to the guide outfitters' home base at Mill Bay. I promised to return in two days to greet the crew of fresh hunters and new guides, and said goodbye.

With only two days off, I had no time to waste. Jumping into my boat, I cruised home as fast as I could in the pouring rain. At least the wind wasn't blowing. It was great to go home.

The commute by water was always an adventure in itself, and this one was no different. I had to constantly scan the surface for beaver logs or debris. I watched the pristine shoreline for wildlife, and the time sped by. Once I saw a wolf cub bouncing about on the shore of an island along the way. I saw a mother wolf in the trees nearby, hackles up and growling, and three cubs at her heels.

Another time, I had to detour around a big black bear swimming mid-channel. It was common to see moose swimming from one side of the lake to another, but I'd see bears less often. Some suggested the moose swam across to escape wolves or bears tracking their scent. Or maybe they were just getting rid of ticks. I have seen a mother moose, followed by her three tiny calves, crossing a great body of water. A hunter told me the cow moose did this to remove the frail babies from the birthing place. The scent would be a dangerous invitation to a hungry predator.

Slowing to five knots, I cruised past the lodge, I always felt blessed coming home to this log house surrounded by forest. Today it was carpeted with fallen leaves. It had been cold lately. There was ice in the bilge that morning and this would be the last time I could come home by boat till the next year.

—

The next hunt, with new guides and new hunters, passed in a blur of pots and pans, bread and sticky buns, with a couple of moose in there somewhere. That season, in between the camp jobs, I also managed to attend logging meetings and make my monthly mortgage payments.

With the hunting season over, winter was coming fast. Over the next couple of weeks, I prepared the boats, cabins and the lodge. As the days got shorter, the cool shadows and darkness crept out farther and farther, and it didn't take long for the shoreline to crystallize. One morning, I watched as the crystals flashed, connecting shore to shore. Then the temperature plunged and the ice grew thick. It seemed to lay heavy on the surface of the lake. The reason for this is odd; ice floats, so it shouldn't look heavy. But as the water started to freeze deeper and deeper, the water in the lake kept flowing downhill and out the Babine River. As the water level lowered, the surface ice sank, its edges still clinging to the rocky shoreline. This gave the illusion of a heavy load, and indeed it was.

A light breeze dusted the glassy surface and banked the snow along the shore. A few late-fall leaves splashed bits of colour along the snow. My easy waterway commute was now on hold until the lake broke free of its bondage in the spring. With all the boats put away for the winter, my trips to town meant hiking to the logging road, warming up the old diesel Suburban, then driving 50 kilometres (30 miles) to the barge. One particular morning, the trip was gorgeous. Trees were laden with snow, and the forest was deep with white powder. The bumpy logging roads, usually filled with potholes and dips pounded by the intense weight of giant trucks, were now packed with ice, snow and gravel, making for an exceptionally smooth ride. The heavy Suburban did well in the winter conditions and held her own with the logging traffic. In November, highway conditions were worse than on the forest roads. People drive faster, and black ice lurks in the shadows.

After I dropped Nuk off at my friend's house in Granisle, I took off for another logging meeting in town. On this trip, I got only a few miles from the barge landing when the Suburban's transmission went out. After hitchhiking in the cold pre-dawn to the highway, I found a good mechanic, had the car towed and hitched another ride on to the next town, where the meeting was being held. With no taxis or bus, I had no choice but to rent a car back to Babine Lake. I picked up Nuk and contemplated my options before deciding none of them included taking the little rental car into the backwoods. I went in to pick up my mail and explained my predicament to the postmistress. She suggested I hitch a ride with her husband, who drove a logging truck.

It was a great idea. I would get to see the world from his perspective. Hard-working and good-hearted, Gerald refused to drop me and Nuk at the trailhead in the early morning darkness. Consequently, I went with him to collect his first load of logs, which proved to be an eye-opening experience. To witness how fast a forest could be removed, and how few people it employed, was heartbreaking.

Gerald dropped us off on his return trip to the mill. His massive truck held a small forest—a condensed one, without branches or nests, just bare trees that would never see spring again. It was still early and the sun hadn't quite made it over the winter horizon, but the first rays lit the frozen snow, and I had Nuk to help lead the way.

Glad to be going home, I strapped on my snowshoes, but I was feeling sad about the old-growth forest. Seven days later, on our way back out of the bush to return the rental car and to pick up my repaired Suburban, Nuk and I were fortunate to hitch a ride with another giant rig of logs.

Two thousand dollars later, with only two hours behind the wheel on my new transmission, I broadsided a moose. We were on the last rise before entering Granisle, going 80 kilometres (50 miles) an hour. I slammed on the brakes and slid 100 yards with the moose draped over the hood of the Suburban.

Those few seconds were some of the longest moments in my life. The moose looked back over his shoulder and into my eyes. The Suburban slowly slid into the snow-filled ditch. Nuk slid to the floorboards, and the moose slid to the ground. I made sure Nuk was OK and I jumped out of the car. The creature tried to get up, but his legs were shattered. With tears streaming down my cheeks, I tried to soothe the moose and was surprised when my voice calmed him. He lay back into the soft snow and looked at me with sad eyes.

I called the RCMP on the radio phone. It was against the law to shoot an injured moose on the road. I was still crying when the officer arrived. The moose stirred, but soon settled with my consoling gibberish. The officer got on one knee and raised his assault rifle to the moose's cheek. Holding my breath, with eyes closed, I waited for the blast that would end the moose's suffering.

What I heard instead were a few choice words from the officer. For some crazy reason he had forgotten to remove the trigger lock on his gun. He ran to his patrol car, jumped in and zoomed away with his sirens blaring to retrieve his gun lock key from the office in Granisle. Once more the moose struggled to stand, but I was able to calm him. The minutes stretched like hours until finally the officer returned and dispatched the poor animal.

Shortly thereafter, elders from the Tachet Band arrived to process the meat. My mangled Suburban had saved my life and was now in the repair shop for the next eighteen months. But if I had been in the little compact rental car, this story would have never been told.

Now, I had to find a new vehicle. That is a whole other story.

Morrison Arm is called "The Nursery" because so many cow moose give birth and care for their newborns in its safety.

PART 4

# Perseverance

*When I finally reached the lodge in the spring, months of turmoil melted off my shoulders.*

# CHAPTER 18

# Winter Work
# and Calamity

O ne year, instead of renting an apartment or house-sitting, I thought it was a great idea when my brother offered to lend me his 37-foot sailboat for the winter. It sounded like a great deal for both of us: I would have central accommodations for my winter job on Whidbey Island and my brother wouldn't have to pay moorage—I would. Moorage on Whidbey was inexpensive, and I was also able to buy a new-to-me black Ford truck. The downside to the boat accommodations was Nuk would not be able to stay with me on board. But Nuk was happy as a pup spending the winter with my daughter and her dogs.

I was fortunate enough to keep my old job at the grocery chain and come back to it for the winter. Because it was a union job, I received a good wage, great benefits and I accumulated a nice pension. The people I worked for, and with, had professional integrity for the company and their community. They allowed me to incorporate my second job as a special project teacher for the school district. Although I was only able to hold nine weeks of classes a year, it satisfied my desire to teach Northwest Coast art and drama.

In the dead of winter it was cold and damp, especially on a boat. It was with great pleasure that I accepted an offer to house-sit for friends who were going on holidays for a couple of weeks. Their waterfront house was fresh and new with a stainless-steel kitchen and white carpets. From the front windows I could see the lights of Victoria, BC, across the water. I planned to take a Washington State Ferry from Anacortes to Sidney for an appointment in Victoria with the Ministry of Environment, where I hoped to address my concerns about the proposed mine on Morrison Lake. I had decided to meet a travel agent in the city to drum up some business while I was there.

The days sped by and soon I found myself on the three-hour ferry ride. To make the bus connections from the ferry terminal to downtown Victoria easier, I packed light, with a photographic presentation of the lodge and three sets of clothes in a small duffle bag. My appointment with the Ministry of Environment was at 2 p.m. on what happened to be Valentine's Day, my wedding anniversary. David had been gone for four years. I had set up the meeting with the travel agent at 4 p.m. I needed to stay busy and strong—I had no time for grief.

Upon landing, I was surprised to find there was no bus connection from the ferry to Victoria. And it was a typical winter day in Victoria: pouring rain. Fortunately, I managed to get a lift into town with an older couple in their rental car. They were nice enough to take me right downtown and drop me off at my hotel. I rushed through registration and hurried to my room to get ready for my meeting.

I addressed my concerns with finesse; after all, I had rehearsed in front of the MOF many times, and my passion was unquestionable. The sockeye and coho salmon runs, and the rainbow trout, would all be devastated by the inevitable leakage from the tailings pond. The old-growth forest would be forever gone, and the displaced wildlife would have to search for survival. It made my personal loss of business seem selfish and trifling. Overall, this meeting seemed to be a big waste of time. The government personnel were polite but gave me no clue of any possible change whatsoever to the proposed open pit. These kind government workers were only there to record my concerns.

I raced through the rain to be on time for my next meeting. Standing inside the doorway, dripping wet and trying to regain my composure, I scanned the fancy travel agency. Compared to the sombre administrators and demure government office, the glitzy interior of the travel agency was more like a theatre. I would be lying if the thought of selling everything and taking the advertised trip to Madrid didn't cross my mind.

My photographs had endured the ten-minute dash through the deluge, and with each one placed on the table, I gained greater vigour. Even so, my usual presentation felt superficial under the fluorescent glow.

Taking advantage of my pause, the beautiful agent said,

"I will book you big-time. You don't have any problems with having Tom Cruise as a guest, do you?"

I raised my eyebrows. I didn't have a single problem having Tom Cruise as a guest, but the probability of a favourable outcome from either meeting left me with little confidence, or assurance whatsoever, that I had spent my time wisely.

I returned to my hotel. It was a nice high-rise in downtown Victoria. As I passed the fine-dining room, I saw couples waiting in line for dinner. I went back to my room. It was 6 p.m.—Valentine's night. I decided it would not be a good idea for me to stay in alone. Through my window, I saw a movie theatre across the street, which was very unusual for me. Twenty days ago, I had been looking at a moose outside my window.

Even though I had been alone for a few years now, I had never become comfortable going places solo. But maybe I would meet a wonderful, handsome, eligible guy who just loved the wilderness and wanted to marry me. So, I painted my nails, put on my best blue jeans and went to the show.

I stood reviewing the marquee. The only movie playing was *Shakespeare in Love*. I took a step back thinking, *Oh yeah, it is Valentine's Day*—and then forced myself ahead with a *Buck up, you can handle this.*

The lights were on inside the theatre and I was the only one there. Having my choice of any seat, I sat dead-centre. With seating available on either side, it doubled the chance of having a Mr. Wonderful sit beside me.

With an extraordinary amount of commotion many people came in at once. People started to fill my row. Not one seat was left empty. Before the lights dimmed, I snuck a peek. I could not believe my eyes. At least sixty seniors filled the theatre, walkers and canes propped here and there. Entire rows of senior citizens surrounded me.

I had to chuckle. Looking around I could not find one person under seventy. Several ushers were helping the elders find a seat, carrying their popcorn while they negotiated their walkers.

On my left, I was soon to find out, sat George and Lois, who introduced themselves loudly by proclaiming this to be their fifty-second Valentine's Day together. George kept asking questions and Lois kept yelling out the answers. Finally, some of the other seniors told them to hush.

"George, turn up your hearing aid," Lois suggested.

Towards the end of the movie, I prepared myself for the inevitable death scene, wondering if I should just leave.

Suddenly, Lois gasped. Looking at her, I saw her mouth wide-open, her eyes bulging. George started screaming.

"Call an ambulance!"

All the lights came on and the ambulance crew arrived. I went out the door under the red exit sign that no one ever uses. I left in a daze. The ambulance lights flashed in the alleyway. Poor George, and poor Lois. I have no idea what happened to them, but at least they had each other.

I stood across the street from my hotel, where I saw lovers, hand in hand, laughing and going somewhere to do something—together. By the elevators, I saw lovers leaving the restaurant. I went up to my room in tears.

I dumped out my black bag and organized my pictures from the presentation. I pulled out my (never-worn) crush-worthy black dress and put it on. I decided to escape my room and have a glass of merlot in the hotel's lounge. This was Mr. Wonderful's last chance.

The flash of silver in the elevator mirror reflection reminded me what my daughter had said a few days earlier: "Mom, you have got to dye your hair. You can't look like an old widow-woman if you want to find a man."

My boss at the grocery store had also mentioned that, statistically, after five years of living alone, the average widow did not remarry. I had one more year till I would be a widow-woman the rest of my life.

I stepped into the lounge. Feeling extremely uncomfortable, I found the first table for two. When the waitress came, I ordered my glass of wine and glanced around. The couples had all gone to a more romantic venue. What I saw was a room with several single men. For some reason, they were all looking at me. For some reason I felt like they were all thinking, *How much?*

I jumped up and took long, fast strides to the bartender, where I cancelled my order and ran to the elevator. On my way back up, I thought how strange it was to be in a city filled with people and still be as alone as I was deep in the wilderness.

I bought a soft drink from the hallway vending machine, went to my room, watched *M\*A\*S\*H* and painted my fingernails a different shade of red.

The next morning it was pouring again. I splashed to the bus stop two blocks away. As I stood there waiting for the bus, shivering in the cold, I read the schedules, wishing I was home, reading by the fire, snowbound, deep in the woods. I found a bus that stopped close to the Washington State Ferries terminal. With time ticking on and the ferry loading, I ran six long blocks in the deluge. Rain channelled down the back of my neck as I boarded the boat.

I found a table to empty my bag of precious lodge photos onto, which were now sopping wet. I spent the next two and a half hours drying them with napkins from the cafeteria—they were the best photos I owned of the lodge. By the time I arrived at my destination, the photos were mostly dry and I'd thrown the soggy copies of my mining concerns in the trash.

—

Once I got back to Whidbey Island, I stopped at the grocery store to check my work schedule and I bought myself a rose from the flower department. Because it was the day after Valentine's Day, it was marked down. I went to my house-sitting home to grab a few hours of sleep. With my rose in hand

I searched the house for a vase, to no avail. I was exhausted and ended up with a quart jar from under the kitchen sink. It was now 8 p.m. I filled the oversized jar with water and took it to the dressing table in my room. I opened my bag, pulled out a T-shirt and tossed my black duffle onto the floor. While pulling off my shirt, I accidentally hit the rose, which tipped the jar, which spilled the water, which poured directly into my open duffle bag and onto my precious lodge photographs.

Panicked again about the photos, I shook the bag out onto the white carpet. Out sloshed the quart of water, the soggy photos, my black dress, the polish remover and two bottles of nail polish. One of the bottles —the bright red one—broke.

The red polish splattered all over my dress and, to my horror, the white carpet. I poured half the bottle of remover onto the carpet, grabbed my dress and ran to the bathroom for a towel. I stood there, under the bright light, looking at my polish-covered dress. I poured remover over the dress. As I held it in my hand I watched in shock as the black material liquefied into slime and dripped through my fingers.

"MY DRESS!" I shrieked. Then I thought, *What about the white carpet?!*

After scrubbing the carpet for hours, I was finally able to remove the stain, although the carpet pad underneath had dissolved, leaving a visible dip underneath the rug.

On my way to work that day I thought, *The good thing about having a day like that is it's hard to have another half as bad.* Like my dad always said, "You can always say you've seen worse."

I moved back to the sailboat for the winter after the house-sitting. It felt good to be back in the boat and away from the white carpet.

—

At the marina I ran into Danny, a long-time friend of David's and mine. He reserved the lodge for a week in June! He was the marina attendant and booked four of his fishing buddies to come to the lodge as well.

Years back, David and I had kept our sailboat at the same marina, and I was able to work on emptying a storage unit we had rented while moving most of our belongings to Canada. One of the many treasures stored in it was a folding kayak placed in three duffle bags, a gift from a friend who had given it to David to give to me.

After David died, it took a long time for me to move all my belongings up north. On this last trip, I was finally able to empty the unit. In doing so, I discovered two of the duffle bags for the kayak had been stolen... along with who knows what else.

The bag of parts and the bag holding the Kevlar skin were gone. All I had left was the skeleton: a shiny wooden foldable kayak, lacquered and fixed with brass fittings. I packed it up anyway in the hope that one day I would be able to buy another skin to cover the frame.

The next couple of months flew by. I worked long hours and was preparing to go home. The long months away from the lodge were over. I was looking forward to a comfortable ride north with my new rig. I had no idea the difficulties I'd face trying to import a US vehicle.

Upon entry into Canada, I needed to have my truck converted into a Canadian vehicle, matching their standards. When I did this same thing with my old Suburban, I used a reliable local mechanic. But the laws had changed in the last few years: the BC Government had given the contract to a national chain of tire stores.

I made an appointment to convert my truck in the community of Chilliwack, fifteen hours from Granisle. I had decided to buy a new set of tires as well. The repair office told me I could not wait in my truck; I was to wait in the connecting tiny room. When I entered, there were five kids with runny noses crying and fighting. This was just not where I wanted to spend the next three hours while they refitted my truck. Night shifts, followed by packing up my storage unit for the last time, had caught up with me, and I was exhausted. And I had a long drive ahead. So I snuck out and set up my back seat with a sleeping bag before giving my keys to the front desk.

Back at the truck, I crawled into the bag and covered my head. Thirty minutes into a deep sleep, someone jumped into the truck and sped onto what seemed like the highway. I didn't say a word—I was afraid to make myself known because I didn't know if this person might be stealing the truck or what! I didn't expect to have anyone take it for a joy ride.

We drove around for twenty minutes or so. Finally, the truck slowed down. The driver turned down the radio volume.

Peeking out over the sleeping bag, I saw the windows were down and we were inside a giant garage. I could only hope we were back at the store's garage. The driver jumped out of the truck and began a lewd conversation about the magnetic signs on my doors, the lodge's logo of an owl.

"Where should I attach the headlight control?" one of the guys asked.

"Wire it into the windshield wipers," said the boss.

"What if she wants to use the headlights and the wipers at the same time?"

"Ah, she'll be 700 miles away by then," said the boss.

"How many hours of labour should we charge her?"

"Well, if no one sees her, charge her for two and half hours," said the boss.

I was looking at my watch, knowing they would be charging me an extra half hour.

Finally, the lead mechanic asked if anyone had seen me in the office. It was almost 5:30 p.m.—quitting time. I kept waiting for them to move my truck into the parking lot. I was beginning to worry about being locked in the garage for the night. So, mustering my courage, I opened the door and stepped out. The faces of the four men still left in the garage were priceless. The boss ran to the office to change the bogus half-hour labour charge, without prompting. I followed to watch him squirm.

I didn't say much. I was too tired and too angry, so I took my keys and walked back into the garage to see the men scatter like roaches. The boss walked me out to open the giant doors and I asked him about the lights.

"Will my lights go out if I use my high beams... in the rain?"

His cheeks flushed pink, and he assured me they would not.

As I was pulling out into downtown traffic, my hubcap flew off. Evidently it was not attached properly when they put on the new tire. I had to make my way to a stop and step into heavy traffic to recover the $80 hubcap. I was only half a mile from the garage, so I turned back and caught the boss on his way out. I asked him, "Do you think it's possible for you to properly attach the hubcap?"

He crouched down right away and replaced the cap on the new tire. Still on his knees, he apologized to me for his employees' behaviour and gave me his card. He told me to call if I had any problems. I kept the card for a while, just in case.

A couple of years later, I had to take the truck in because, lo and behold, my lights were not working. It cost me twice as much to fix it because of course they hadn't used the correct method of attaching the daytime lights after all.

The final irony was that when I went into the department of registration and insurance the following week, I was told, "Your truck is originally a Canadian truck. It has a Canadian registration number. It was built and sold new in Canada."

I never got my money back for all that work, and in case you were still wondering, I never saw Tom Cruise, either.

# CHAPTER 19

# The Innkeeper

I spread the word about booking the lodge wherever and whenever I could. First, because I lived in the most wonderful place on earth, and second, I desperately needed clients to ensure that I could keep the place.

I even talked my dentist into a fishing trip in partial trade for dental work. I accomplished this under novocaine, with tools and a suction hose in my mouth. He turned out to be a terrific guest. He brought his son, who was studying to be a dentist, too.

The dentist and his son arrived the second week of June, which was excellent for fishing. It was balmy during the lengthening days of spring and the cool evenings demanded a warm fire. After their second day fishing, the father and son had just finished supper. As we finished dessert I settled back and told them this story:

"I had an accomplished writer come to the lodge last year to do an article about the Ookpik for a very well-known magazine. He told me he had written for this publication for ten years. Looking forward to a good article, I treated the author to the best cabin, and with the utmost attention. After all, I needed the exposure, and the article would be free advertising for Ookpik Wilderness Lodge.

"He was a pleasant guest and I expected him to expound on his superb experience with my cooking and comfortable cabins. But to my surprise and concern his parting declaration was, 'Everything was great. I didn't even have to worry about the mosquitoes because the cabin was always full of smoke.'

"Shocked and dismayed, I replied quickly, 'Sorry about that, I'm so glad everything else was OK... cookies to go? Great fishing, eh?'

"After returning the writer to civilization, I raced the boat back to see what could possibly have gone wrong. What caused the cabin to fill with smoke?

"I checked the smokestack and flashing jacks inside and out to make sure they were not damaged. Not finding any impairment, I opened up the firebox to the stove. The fragrant cedar kindling I had set up for my special guest, a one-match light, was still intact. The fire starter was a little smoked, but otherwise just as I had left it a week ago.

"After three seconds of investigation I roared with laughter. The wilderness fishing author had built his fire in the *oven* of the wood cookstove, not the firebox. I ran back to the lodge, retrieved my camera and documented the event. I wanted to make sure that if he wrote an adverse article for the magazine, I would have an eight by ten colour glossy ready to ship off in a letter to his editor. Well, the article came out and it was very complimentary. He even wrote another article a couple of years later." Looking around the table at my audience, I ended my story with a sip of cool lake water.

The story got a huge laugh from the son, but quite unexpectedly, not from my dentist. The son roared, but the father's face reddened, and I looked at him in alarm to see if he was choking.

The dentist then said, "From now on you need to promise me that this will be the *first* story you tell your new guests. And save *them* from the same mistake!"

From then on when guests arrived at the lodge, true to my promise, I would diligently recite the story of "The Wilderness Fishing Author."

—

The radio phone was my only means of communication at the lodge, which complicated making business arrangements. If you want to phone the lodge you have to get a lesson first. On my business card it says, "Dial this number, let it ring, then let it beep, then dial 03." Sometimes you can get through. Either way I have to pay, by the minute and by the call. I don't use it much.

Medium, short, long and then a pause is the specific tone sequence belonging to the radio phone at the lodge. After that sound, the radio started to ring like a regular phone. It would only ring four times. If I was on the front deck, it is a scramble to get to it in time. With no answering service possible, if I missed the call, I had no idea who was on the line. If I was out and the phone rang, it would automatically click into monitor mode instead of scan. This means my batteries used up a lot of juice while the radio babbled out all the conversations going on in a 300-kilometre radius.

When I was lucky enough to answer the phone, I first told the person on the other end, "I'm on a radio phone. Can you give me your number in case we get disconnected? I have only six minutes before we're automatically disconnected, so we have to talk fast."

The conversation was always strained because I also had to tell them, "Don't talk while I'm talking, because I can't hear you." On a radio phone-line there is only one voice going one way at a time.

One day later in the spring, the radio phone rang. It was Danny from the Whidbey marina; he wanted to make final arrangements for his fishing holiday to Ookpik. He had worked at the marina for many years and I was pleased he had drummed up some fishing clients for the lodge.

Danny arrived a couple weeks later and brought a few giant fishing nets and some random fishing gear. After dinner one night, Danny brought out a vaguely familiar duffle bag.

"I found this bag while cleaning out one of the marina's storage units. Some guy decided not to pay his bill for a couple of years and the office had a garage sale. I opened this bag and thought about the cradleboards you create. I thought it would make a good frame."

I looked inside the bag to see a brilliantly lacquered oval piece of wood. There were several other items in the bag as well. I shook it out onto the carpet and immediately recognized the parts missing from the folding kayak. I was elated. This was the stuff that had disappeared from the storage locker! Along with the dust floating out of the bottom of the bag was a note in an old friend's handwriting: *David, please give this kayak to Caroll.*

A voice from the past—and what felt like a message from David, who had now been gone for five years.

—

After a week of good fishing and eating, I dropped Danny and his buddies off at the marina in Granisle. I scurried off to pick up the mail and a few items from town.

I was happy to receive a deposit for a family of six in the post. It meant I could pay my taxes on time.

The next week I received a call on the radio phone. Jim, who had sent the deposit, was on the line.

"I'm sorry to say, my wife is not doing very well, and we can't come up." I could tell he was extremely upset.

"My son and I were looking forward to this time with our menfolk. Could we rebook?"

Flexibility is important when working with clients, so I shuffled my schedule to accommodate them and set a later date that was convenient.

When Jim and his family arrived, a few weeks later, I was blessed with the most congenial people. I placed them by twos in three cabins: Grandpa and the oldest son in the easy access cabin, the other son and son in-law in the next cabin and Jim with his son in the last cabin. Everyone was warm and comfortable.

And all of them were extremely polite: "Yes ma'am," "No ma'am," "Can I get the door for you, ma'am?"

They even packed and split their own wood. I was impressed and delighted that the grandfather had taught them all how to be gentlemen. In my experience men usually call home only once, to let their spouse know they have arrived safely. Jim, however, called his wife every day by radio phone.

The men had a great week catching lots of fish and eating well.

The following year Jim booked again, bringing his son, who was now twelve, and his son's friend. I was happy to have them back. With several other guests at the time, I put them in the cabin they had previously used. The routine was the same: lovely manners and calls to Jim's wife every day. A couple of good fishing days passed, and they relaxed into their holiday.

Late on the third night, after everyone had retired, the radio phone rang in the lodge. Receiving a call at night was unusual and frightening. A call in the night rarely brings good news, so I was immediately concerned. A nurse on the other end explained she was calling from a hospital in the States. Jim's wife had died.

I threw on my clothes, grabbed a flashlight and ran down the path to the last cabin. Knocking on the door softly, I went in and knelt beside Jim's bed. Not wanting his to son hear, I whispered the tragic news as gently as I could.

"We will meet you at the boat," Jim replied solemnly.

I stepped outside into the pitch-black. It would be hours until dawn.

Following my flashlight beam down the trail between the cabins, I knocked on the door of another guest, told him the bad news and said breakfast would be late. He was a return client and understood; he asked if he could do anything to help.

The sombre group quietly loaded the boat and with a roar of the powerful engine, we were off.

On the way to the airport Jim promised to come back for his truck at a later date. Having lived through the loss of David, I understood some of his pain. I felt so sad for this father and son who had hundreds of miles of travel to get home, hundreds of miles to begin the process of reconciling the loss of a friend, a wife and a mother.

## CHAPTER 20

# B&B and the
# Mad Loon

**B**etty and Bill were local friends we had met through Paul and Ardys Adams.

In 1958 Betty and Bill had came to Babine Lake to buy a fishing and hunting lodge 50 kilometres (30 miles) south of where I lived. They had been married for forty-five years, every moment filled with wilderness adventures. At one point, Bill flew for an old-time airplane company called Tel Air at Telegraph Creek, BC, and Betty worked as a dispatcher and caterer. Bill carried the mail by floatplane in and out of that remote mountainous area for years.

Betty was a historian and artist and Bill... just a wild and crazy bush pilot. Paul Adams introduced them to me like this: "There are good people and bad people, but these people are the best people."

When I met them, Betty was hauling the mail, dodging moose and bear on the road into the community of Topley from Granisle, making the 100-kilometre (60-mile) round trip twice a day. Bill was operating Skeena Air.

I would call Bill to set up fishing trips for my guests as often as I could. He would always take them to a small, unnamed lake with great fishing. He was famous for calling these lakes "No-tell-'em Lake." Bill also flew several trips into the bush during hunting season. He would land on unnamed lakes and drop off moose hunters for a few days. The successful hunter's return trip would include hundreds of pounds of moose meat. He still managed to take off from these short little lakes. It was a great sight to see Bill's plane flying low, with trophy moose antlers strapped to the pontoons.

While Bill was away, Betty kept the home fires burning and took care of the mail. In her spare time she made and sold works of art in all sorts of media. Betty was also an accomplished cross-country skier and ice skater. She would bring her camera on all her adventures and took some remarkable photographs.

The stories she told of the history of the territory, and the documentation she had collected over the years, made her one of the most accomplished historians of the Babine Lake area.

Ordinarily, Betty had few words, but she was still a vivid storyteller. She told me she went ice skating one year, after one of the first deep freezes, and the ice was crystal clear with no snow accumulation. Looking down through the thick ice, she noticed she was skating along with the fish. That image lives with me. One day I hope to experience that phenomenon of the north.

During the tragic events of 9/11, Bill had dropped off three men in a remote lake area to hunt. Then all planes were grounded for security reasons. Bill was not able to contact his clients or fly in to pick them up on time. He paced frantically as he waited for the prohibition to lift, but fortunately there were no mishaps from his arriving a couple of days late to pick up the hunters.

That is not to say Bill never had any mishaps. One winter, he and a friend were flying with skis in place of his pontoons. They had taken a camera along and were running a pack of wolves down the ice, getting some great shots, when a slight breeze tipped them over and the plane landed flat on the ice... upside down. There was considerable damage to the plane, but for Bill, the casualty was the camera—no pictures could be recovered.

I was delighted when they arrived for dinner one evening. A powerful summer squall had blown up the lake an hour before they were due to arrive. Betty and Bill brought their son-in-law and granddaughter by plane. Their son, Alan, brought his sister Brenda and nephew by small boat. If it had not been this particular family, I would have held off making the gravy. Hearing their expected engines, right on time, I looked out to see frothy whitecaps on 3-foot waves. Alan's boat was barely skimming the tops. Then, from the blustery cloud-filled sky, down came Bill's plane. They moored simultaneously. Both Bill and Alan had the same twinkle in their eyes and swagger in their step as they greeted me, our feet awash on the wave-riddled dock.

Good food and good company kept the spirits high. Laughter and chatter filled the lodge, which was so often silent. By dessert, the lake had calmed, with a brilliant reflection of the late summer sunset.

After they left, I took my binoculars and a glass of iced tea to the beach. The sun was going down slowly, and I was exhausted from all the day's activities but so happy to have had company. On my way down to the dock I spooked a local fish duck, a merganser mother and her flock of seven. Off they scurried into the middle of the water.

The classic and glorious melody of the loon echoed over the lake. He was still out working, bringing home small fish to his nest on the far shore. I had my binoculars in hand while I waited for the animals of the forest. This was the time of day a moose, deer, bear or an elusive wolf would come to sip the cool waters after a warm day in the dry woods. I took a sip of the cold iced tea, and then scanned the far side of the lake with my binoculars, in hopes of catching a glimpse of my shy woodland neighbours.

Suddenly, I heard the racket of the young flock of mergansers splashing about in the water. I could see mother merganser in a panic, trying to get her babies to move away. I could see nothing to warrant such a commotion.

Through the binoculars I was surprised to see a loon just under the water, his long neck exposed and his head aimed at the flock of mergansers. He was travelling fast and looked like a half-submerged submarine.

The mother merganser became frantic as she pushed her babies ahead, then lagged behind, splashing as if she had broken a wing. In one swift flowing movement, the loon rose to the surface and swam even more swiftly towards them.

The mother merganser scattered her babies and made fast for the shore. She seemed to know that if she could manage to get her flock to the beach, they would be saved. Loons cannot walk on land very well at all.

I witnessed the magnified image of the loon as he rose to a standing position on the surface of the water. With his wings hunched over he looked just like Darth Vader. He began to run on the surface of the water, chasing down first one, then another, of the poor chicks. He killed the first and then pounced upon a second chick. I watched in horror as a few small feathers drifted down, landing gently onto the water, the only proof this chick had ever existed.

The mother merganser was calling hysterically from the beach. I was shocked to have witnessed this act of brutality in nature. I could see four babies around their mother on the grassy bank. She scooped them up under her wings, and they became soundless. The loon lurked ominously offshore, just a few feet away.

His shoulders still hunched, he swam slowly back and forth, as a sentry.

Then I heard a small *peep, peep*. It was coming from the middle of the lake. Scanning the span from shore to the area of the first deadly encounter, I could see the seventh baby. It had miraculously escaped the loon's first assault.

My heart swelled with happiness, until I heard a commotion in the water close by. Turning towards the sound, I witnessed the loon's response to the chick's peeps.

He stood to his full height and spun in the direction of the chick's cry. He seemed to grow huge, then shot off like an arrow. Using his wing tips like fingers to grab the surface of the water, he pulled himself into a full run. For more than 200 yards he raced across the surface of the water, then threw himself up into the air and dove straight down upon the shocked baby merganser, never to be seen again.

Moments later, I heard the loon call out his melody.

# CHAPTER 21

# Silver and the Mother Bear

Staying at the lodge eight months of the year, I saw very few people. Other than the fishermen who booked in the spring and dinner guests coming for a Saturday night supper, I was generally alone. I cherished the weeks in the late summer/early fall when my grandchildren came to visit the lodge. Storytime was our favourite pastime because, of course, there was no TV.

Chores or outdoor adventures were always on the top of the list, so I made sure the activities always included storytelling. Parts of tales would emerge as we paddled through the mist coming off the warm water into the cool morning air. Walking down the dock in the late evening, we'd tell more stories, watching the mist move in and out of the cattails. The stories would continue as we stood on the deck at night, listening to the loon calling her children home.

At bedtime, I would watch the kids' sweet faces as sleep came over them, and tell them of the moonbeams passing through the misty columns moving down the lake in the dark. Many favourites were retold, while the children and I were enjoying the wonders of nature. The magic between this grandmother and the little ones blossomed.

When the family had gone, I would fill the empty spaces in my day transcribing these stories to ink and paint. I dreamed of publishing a children's book someday. I was blessed to be able to give my own offspring the joys of nature, and I wanted to share these tales with other children too. There are so many young people who haven't had the opportunity to experience the natural world.

When Silver visited on her own, she invariably wanted to help with every-thing. During one of her visits, we had six guests, one of whom asked if he could shower every morning at 7 a.m. This meant we had to get up early, leave the lodge and light the propane water heater in the shower-house at 6 a.m. and remember to turn on the pressure pump under the lodge in the basement at 6:55. Silver and I were successful for the first three days. On the fourth day the propane tank ran dry, and the water consequently did not heat. The client came to breakfast covered with sticky soap and sham-poo. "The water is cold!" he exclaimed. It was hard for me not to smile and Silver wasn't able to hold in her giggle.

I put the food into the warming ovens, and down the lakeside trail we went. I was pressed for time, so my plan for a quick fix was to snatch the propane tank from the last cabin and exchange the empty tank at the shower-house next door. Silver was excited to have the breakfast routine disrupted and laughed her way down the back stairs trying to keep up. Then, she skipped in front.

"Whatcha doin'?" I asked.

She replied in her sweet baby voice, "Don'tcha know the bears get the last girl in line?!"

"I don't know about that," I replied. "Sometimes they get the girl in the front!" With a concerned look on her face, she promptly fell back behind me, followed by trusty Nuk, who was always thrilled about going for an early morning hike.

I turned the corner to grab the propane tank. Instead, I saw a five-year-old mother bear and her three cubs. She stood up to her full height, raising her front paws, and roared 7 feet from my face. When I saw the bear expose her sharp white teeth and I heard the sound of her roar, surrounded by the steam coming from deep in her giant chest, adrenaline flooded my entire body and produced an immediate response to protect Silver.

I told Silver to run. The bear had not seen her. With an onshore breeze, Nuk had not smelled the bears. Upon hearing the roar and smelling my

fear, Nuk leaped in front, separating the bear from me. I was then able to respond to my plight.

Nuk began to bark. The bear looked at Nuk and came down to his level to protect her cubs. I snatched Silver by the waist and flew back to the lodge to make sure she was out of harm's way. I grabbed my gun and let my guest know his shower would be postponed until further notice.

I got back to the cabin in time to call the dog off the poor mother bear. She was foaming at the mouth by the time I arrived and trying hard to keep her three cubs up three separate trees. All the while the baby bears were fascinated by the strange white dog. They would lose their concentration and fall down to the ground, where the mother had to scurry them back up. She was becoming exhausted.

I managed to call Nuk off and get him back up the trail, which allowed the mother bear and her cubs to go back into the forest. And the half-showered guest washed the soap off in the pantry sink.

# CHAPTER 22

# Old Ed Dilley

At the end of fishing season, after the last of the guests had left, it was time to do some chores. One fall, my parents came to visit and to take Silver back home. While visiting, they were always ready to lend a hand in any way they could. Mom was fantastic help and enjoyed the great-grand-mothering. Having them at the lodge for a few days was a blessing.

One morning Mom and Silver were making beds in the cabins. Dad and I were fixing the docks. We had to add another 20 feet to the board-walk connecting to the dock system just to keep our feet dry during the spring floods.

We were using a giant 5-foot crowbar to align the dock parts and replace worn-out pilings. Dad had fallen into the chilly cove while pulling with all his weight to move a dock section. He went up to the lodge, got changed and came back. It was my turn on the crowbar.

In the distance I could see a boat coming. We continued to work and watched as the boat came closer. I was pulling on the crowbar as hard as I could when I realized whose boat was coming. And with that, I went into a flying back-flip off the dock into the cold fall water, calling out just before the splash, "It's Ol' Ed Dillllllllley!"

Dripping wet, I secured Ed's boat. We took a well-deserved coffee break and had a short visit before Ed went back to fishing. As I cast off his boat I declared, "Ed Dilley, you are the only man I have ever flipped for."

What I didn't know at the time was that soon he would be the one to answer the only mayday I ever called.

The following week, the dock was repaired and my parents took Silver back to Washington. Without the delightful chatter of Silver's voice, the lodge was still—no sounds and no movement, other than the cuckoo clock. The startling blare of the radio phone ringing broke the peace. I jumped, then answered the phone. Many times, with the voice delay and the strange clicks, the person on the other end hangs up, figuring they have been disconnected. I'd end up standing by the phone waiting for the return call—if it came.

The phone rang for the second time.

Finally, we conversed, and I booked the caller for a holiday with his elderly father. On short notice I made arrangements to pick them up the following morning. I added to my list the extra chores required to accommodate new guests. Top of the list was fuelling up the boat before I went to bed.

The next morning, I got up early to make a Thermos of coffee and one of tea—the guy on the radio phone had an English accent. As I scanned the water and sky, I was glad to see a calm lake. Seldom was there wind that early in the day. My commute to the village was serene.

I always made specific plans to minimize my commutes to Granisle. I scheduled the return trip of guests to the Granisle marina on Saturday mornings, gathered groceries and fuel Saturday afternoons, and stayed the night in Granisle. On Sundays, I met the new arrivals early in the morning before the winds picked up.

These guests would not be able to arrive until noon, another two hours away. I filled the jerry cans at the small station in Granisle, refilled the boat with fuel and continued with my chores. It took 7 gallons of gas for the boat one way, which required continuous physical labour hauling the 30-pound cans up and down the docks, in and out of the truck to fill the boat's thirsty tank. Afterward I picked up groceries from the freezer at my parents' house, and fresh milk and cream from the tiny store.

Fortuitously, on my way back to the marina, I drove by the little library and was enticed by a bake sale in progress. I bought some peanut butter cookies for my breakfast and washed them down with coffee, re-energized. I bought a lovely cheesecake and some shortbread to go.

With yet another hour to wait, I watched a formidable breeze build. By the time the gentlemen arrived, the lake was putting on a show. Whitewater was rolling in front of the small marina's breakwater.

As we entered the body of the lake, the rollers hit us broadside. I changed course to north by northeast and I rode the surf. My water taxi was called *Dandy Rip*. She was a 22-foot Silverline, and was a sturdy, reliable craft with a lot of power and space.

The older Englishman was in great humour. He wondered if the name *Dandy Rip* was actually *R.I.P.* I explained that it came from a tide rip. His adult son seemed a little keyed up. Not unusual. Often executives would come for a visit fresh out of a tense, busy, stressed world and it would take a while to relax.

The father was having a blast. We were riding the seas with beautiful blue skies and racing white clouds overhead, and it was exhilarating. After passing Bear Island, we surfed another 8 kilometres (5 miles) into the widest area of Babine Lake. However, a couple of miles before we would have entered Morrison Arm, the engine started to squeal terribly. Nuk was not happy with the noise and hid under the bow. I slowed down and asked the elder gentleman to hold the wheel. I went back and lifted the engine hatch.

A massive spray of water hit my face. Trying not to panic, I closed the hatch, and with the engine still howling like a banshee, I made for land. The depth sounder read 643 feet. Not the place to go down. I handed the men their life jackets again, and this time they put them on. I grabbed the radio phone and with a surprisingly calm voice, made the call.

"Mayday, mayday, does anyone copy?" I spoke directly into the mic with my face turned to the starboard side. The men didn't hear my words over the noise.

Calling out a mayday was kind of a joke because the only one monitoring the marine band radio on this lake was me. Imagine my surprise and relief when I heard the voice of my good ol' "salty dog" friend, Ed Dilley!

I told him my coordinates and the heading.

"I will be there as soon as I can get there," Ed responded.

He had a beauty of a boat, which he kept ship-shape. It had an old diesel engine that purred like a kitten; although it was slow, it was steady. "She'll do 7 knots towin' a load," Ed would boast.

I expected Ed's arrival to take two hours or more.

The shore looked far, far away, yet the distance was really only 3 kilometres (2 miles). I flipped on the bilge pump nonchalantly and was glad I always wore my life jacket and didn't have to put it on at that moment.

Was the engine's howling diminishing or was I just getting used to the horrible noise? My passengers were gripping the dash, the father's lips a straight white line. Trying to make light of the situation, I asked with a smile, "Do either of you have the time?"

The son pulled up his nicely pressed white cuff and showed me his Rolex. We pulled behind a small point of land and the wind and seas eased. Finally, slowing the engine, I raised the prop, then killed the engine and heard the wonderful sound of pea gravel under the hull. We had made it. Thank God. I would not have to order, "Abandon ship!"

My ears were still ringing from the screeching engine. Leaving the bilge pump on, I went back to raise the hatch. With at least a foot of water in the hold, we would not have made it much farther. I watched and saw it was receding. Sure enough, the pump was making headway.

The boat was still in the water, so that meant there was no breach in the hull—a good sign. Leaving the hatch up, I turned the key to read the gauges. Upon starting the engine, the screech resumed with a vengeance. The oil pressure was good, the battery charging and fuel OK. The temperature was a little high.

I went back to the engine. My younger passenger was looking over my shoulder at the unfamiliar surroundings, his immaculate hands placed in his tailored pants pockets. When I raised the engine hatch to investigate, he was sprayed in the face with fresh water. I could plainly see two holes in one of the risers in the engine.

"We are not going to sink!" I said in my most reassuring voice.

I turned off the engine and pulled out the toolbox, searching for the magic tube of instant welding material. I dried out the rusted holes on top of the engine with a rag, and I filled them generously with instant weld. Not wanting to put pressure on the repair, we waited for Ed.

I could finally relax. My guests looked a little under the weather, so I offered them hot tea and cheesecake! I got a smile from the father when I asked, "lemon or milk for your tea?" Nuk came out of hiding to search for crumbs.

Ed Dilley arrived soon after, and our second cup of tea was served enroute, under tow. Ed, in his freshly painted tug, gave a salute, signalling our departure.

The senior guest began to relate a series of sea adventures, and his son began to laugh at the familiar stories. We made it to the lodge safely.

A few years after my mayday, Ed died. The story of his passing is a legend now, told over coffee at the Granisle Seniors Centre.

Ed had smoked all his life, and he shrugged his shoulders when his doctor told him he was going to die if he didn't quit smoking.

"I'm going to die of old age first... I'm eighty-one years old," Ed replied.

The oxygen tank and a lot of pills were part of Ed's routine. Ed would drop by every day to the seniors centre for coffee.

"Just a few more weeks till spring," he said while placing his name on the bet sheet, putting $5 in the jar and pulling out a smoke.

Spring did arrive, and he came close to winning the annual ice floe bet. When the lake opened up and the ice was gone, all he talked about, in between smokes, was "fishin'."

Ed didn't like much help, so you would have to be tricky. Back in the day, David showed me how to start talking to him and then carry on with whatever Ol' Ed was doing. I tried to do the same thing.

With the sneaky help of all his friends, Ed launched his boat. He was too tired to go anywhere that day. The next morning, before any of his friends knew, he cast off one last time—consciously leaving his oxygen tank and his pills on the dock. They found his ol' tug free floating, with a locker filled with ice and fish.

# CHAPTER 23

# Sir Donald and Boston Execs

Over time, the LRMP meetings began to feel endless. When I didn't have fishing guests at the lodge, there would often be a spread of unrolled maps with corners held down by this and that. I would try to understand the needs of the companies demanding the extraction of natural resources and figure out different negotiation angles.

I was fortunate that I lived in a diverse forest with many types of trees. Because of this diversity, if a specific beetle infestation hit one species, it would not wipe out the entire forest. There was a sprinkling of pine on my property. My yard was built around one of these majestic pines and it drew my attention for years. I hung my laundry line on it with a pulley. The smell of its boughs in the early spring wafted through the kitchen window. For a space in time, it was a roadway connecting the safety of the sky for thousands of living creatures. The eagle found in its height a lofty place to rest. So many nests and fledglings had found a safe haven. The squirrels and the chipmunks scampered up and down the giant timber. I watched as a black bear sent her cubs up into the pine's branches for safety.

This pine lived for two hundred and fifty years. But the tiny pine beetle, which lives for only a few months on this earth, succeeded in killing this towering tree.

The stump, now a tombstone, is the only evidence of its existence. It broke my heart to see the clear-cutting of these diverse forests, only to be replaced with monoculture, which meant they were vulnerable to epidemics that could kill an entire forest. It was impossible for me to understand how some could not see the loss of a pristine forest as a tragedy.

When I made my business proposal to the Canadian Consul General for running a fishing lodge, I never once thought to include crusading for natural resources as one of my strengths and contributions. I also never considered running a restaurant out in the middle of nowhere. But here I was, rolling up the maps and preparing for supper guests. Reservations for anniversary parties, birthdays or just special boat-rendezvous dinners with friends kept pouring in.

Most often I'd have eight to twelve people at a time. The largest dinner party I booked was for forty-five people. With the help of my good friend Betty, we created an unforgettable Mexican Fiesta at the lodge. By double-parking the powerboats and sailboats we were able to fit them all, plus the floatplane, on the 300-foot dock.

One hot afternoon, just as I put the bread in the oven for that night's guests, a boat arrived at the front dock. I ran out to greet the people, who I thought were my supper guests arriving, but I was surprised. An elegant young woman and a well-dressed Englishman, who I'll call Sir Donald, stepped onto the dock instead. I invited them to join us for dinner. They declined, saying they were here for just a moment and hoped I had time for them.

My supper guests arrived just as I was about to usher the unexpected guests inside. I excused myself to dock the next two boats. I asked them to stretch their legs, enjoy a walk about, and then join me at the main house.

Back in the lodge, I pulled the bread from the oven and then rejoined my first visitors. The young lady asked about the logging going on in the area. I took them to the parlour, where I spread my maps. I gave them a rapid rendition of the clear-cutting projects proposed locally. I was met with quiet silence.

This elegant young woman knew what she was talking about and asked all the right questions. I thought she was sympathetic to the old-growth forest issues, and I needed every ally I could get on board. With no time left, I took the English gentleman and lady to their boat. Escorting Sir Donald, he purposefully held back. I asked him how he was enjoying his visit.

"I am here trying to help out," he said. "I am just a do-gooder trying to do some good." He stopped and allowed the young lady to walk farther ahead. "She wants to cut the forest herself, with her own crew," he said to my surprise. I thanked him for the inside information and was rendered speechless. I quietly cast off their boat and raised my hand in an awkward wave.

I was shocked. How could such a sensitive, smart young woman want to clear-cut giant trees? And who, exactly, was she? I would never find out. I tried to drop this mind-boggle and hurried back to put dinner on the table.

—

That same September, a few weeks later, I received a call on the radio phone from Boston, Massachusetts. It was from a gentleman who was a friend of Sir Donald and wanted to bring a companion to go fly-fishing.

I picked them up from the airport in Smithers, three hours away, and they told me their detailed plans. They wanted to stay with me for two days and nights. They were also booked for a steelhead-fishing trip on the Morice River on the third day. Their steelhead-angling guide would take them back to the airport, but I would be responsible for getting them to the Morice River by 6 a.m. I knew that was a three-hour trip.

I had them call the other guide and request a pickup at 9 a.m. At least that would give us time for the hour-long boat ride to happen in the early morning daylight. We would still need to transfer gear from the boat to the vehicle, and then drive another two hours from the village to the Morice River.

They were not able to stay more than two days at the lodge, so I spoiled them with good food and good fly-fishing while they were with me. Even though it was late in the season, they caught a few nice wild rainbow and cutthroat trout.

The morning of their departure, I got up to fuel the boat before breakfast. I watched in dread as the fog rolled down the river and filled up the valley. By the time breakfast was on the table, it was pea soup on the lake.

The guests were excited to go steelhead fishing on the river. I knew they had spent a lot of money to reserve the guide's rod days and there would be no refund. Looking out the lodge window, I tried desperately to see the boat through the dense fog. Not happening.

As the executives from Boston lugged their gear down the dock, they showed no concern at all about the lack of visibility. I couldn't tell if they were naive or had nerves of steel. I cast off the lines and jumped into the boat, then rinsed the collected dew off the windshield, but it made no difference in visibility. It made me feel better when I glanced at the compass course, which I had handwritten on the dash with my eyebrow pencil. My passengers showed no concern whatsoever.

When navigating by compass, it's important to maintain your direction at the appropriate speed for the exact time allotted for your compass course. If you don't, it will affect your course profoundly. When you are travelling at an average speed of 40 knots, it seems easy in good weather. I have even tested myself in the dead of night with no problem. Fog is a different beast altogether. Fog is all encompassing, surrounding and encircling. Up or down, it looks the same. Fog blankets, muffles, saturates, confuses and tries in every way to keep you from trusting your compass. You have a tendency to want to slow down, which would be a mistake because you would not know when to change course.

Knowing all this, off I went, a smiling, blind but bold captain. We conversed on simple topics—what kind of fly to use in the river for steelhead fishing, and so on.

My hopes were dashed when we came to the mouth of Morrison Arm and found the fog was even thicker there. It was imperative to change course at the exact moment in order to pull off a correct heading, and not run into shore or one of the many islands. We were now 10 kilometres (6 miles) into our journey with 23 kilometres (14 miles) to go.

My passengers were talking about the rod weights they were going to use. I tried to keep one eye on my watch and the other on the course, without them noticing. We were now on the longest leg of the journey. This section was 16 kilometres (10 miles) of open water and more than 600 feet deep in the centre.

With nothing visible outside the windows of the boat, the world became very small. Even the noise of the engine seemed muffled. Time passed slowly with no visible progress whatsoever. Filling all the empty spaces and seconds with words, I tried to appear calm.

It was time to change course or hit Bear Island. Relying on the accuracy of my timing and compass, I hoped we would not slam into the rock bluffs.

And with that, my trusty powerboat popped out of the thick wall of fog. The village of Granisle magically appeared 3 kilometres (2 miles) away. With the rock bluffs of Bear Island at our stern, and the wonderful sunrise off the portside, we were right on course.

My guests never showed signs of worry. I suppose their Boston commute was more dangerous.

—

There were no more bookings for that year. I had survived another fishing season. After all the weeks of hustle, it was nice to meander down the dock sipping a steaming mug of coffee.

On one memorable morning, the lake was still warm from the summer sun, but the air was cool. I watched as the sun rose from behind me and hit the lake surface at a distance. The light illuminated the tiny rising droplets. The mist formed into several cone shapes, some 20 feet tall. The fog fairies were swaying in unison as if dancing, the tops of their shapes twisting and turning with the motion of the gentle air. Their bodies slowly marched onward with the current as it travelled south.

It was a spectacular sight. I placed the empty mug on the dock and jumped into my canoe.

I paddled out into the mist. The sun took command and drove the fairies into the shadows. Along the shore, the heavy mist gathered a few

feet above the surface. The silence was crystal clear, interrupted only by a loon calling in the distance. Gradually, the sun edged over the tops of the evergreens and flooded the lake with light. This sent sunbeams through the mouth of the arm and through the 3-foot layer of mist, creating a prism of colour.

The sun shining on the wild blueberries in the forest created an aroma only duplicated by a kitchen with a blueberry pie in the oven. I heard a low rumbling growl. A bit of adrenaline forced me to look around for a bear. Good grief! It was my stomach reacting to the smell coming from the forest. I was hungry. I used the excess of adrenaline to paddle through the rainbow blanket of mist across the lake, leaving a water trail disturbing the placid surface.

By the time I arrived back to the lodge, the sun was hot. Nuk was bouncing along the shore, keeping a family of otters from landing.

Blueberry pancakes soon followed, hot off the griddle.

CHAPTER 24

# Brain Teaser 101

The logistics of living with limited access, whether by boat or by car, are always a challenge. I was continually reminded of a brain teaser my brother used to torment me with, about a farmer who lived on the other side of a one-lane footbridge. Going to market, he could carry only one thing at a time over the bridge. With a giant head of cabbage, a rabbit and a fox, how would he manage without something being eaten?

My commute reminded me of this conundrum often. The extra challenge of taking two powerboats to Granisle Village, 32 kilometres (20 miles) away, to store over the winter months was mind-boggling.

Late fall was the time of year I pulled all my boats from the water. I did this chore over a few weeks because it was so daunting. I had three powerboats and four fishing dories to get out of the water before freezing temperatures set in. (And that wasn't counting the canoes, kayaks or paddleboat.) The powerboats were the easiest to remove because they had trailers. Two of the trailers were in Granisle. One, the ski boat, would come out to the lodge on a trailer. The canoes, kayaks and four dories would also be hauled out at the lodge. The job I really didn't like was changing the leg oil in the outboard engines, which was important because water could get into the metal casing that holds the prop, causing it to freeze and break. This would have to be done soon as well.

The dories, 21 feet long and made of wood, had to be pulled out onto the beach using block and tackle, then a coffin jack (hand chain hoist), and my backhoe. Finally, they needed to be placed on top of wooden blocks, upside-down for the winter. But all of this would have to wait.

I prepared for my winter plans by towing a dory to Morrison Landing. I used another one of the fishing dories.

Typically, I removed *Dandy Rip* from the water first. It would be a relief to have it winterized and tucked away. If any of the engine blocks on any one of my boats froze it would be a financial tragedy, but if anything happened to the *Rip*, it would be devastating. After all, it was my water taxi for clients. I powered the *Rip* to Granisle, then used the black truck to haul it onto the trailer and into my parents' garage. After I drained the freshwater cooling lines and replenished them with RV antifreeze, I covered it up tightly and closed the garage doors. The *Rip* would then be safe from ice, winter snow and any foxes looking for a winter den.

Then I would take the Suburban over Babine Lake by barge, up the forest service road to my pullout, and would hike back to the lodge. The next day, I lowered the ski boat trailer into the water off the beach with the backhoe and motored my favourite boat into its cradle. David's skipper's cap still sat on the dash where I had placed it years before, on the day of his death. After parking the ski boat in a makeshift covered dry dock, I drained the engine block and filled it with antifreeze. The following morning, I jumped into the remaining powerboat. It was time to take *The Duck* to the village and put it to bed. I drove over the cold, stone-grey waters— the dark glassy surface was a pleasure to navigate but the skies grew more menacing by the minute.

As I reached the shore it started to snow. In the short amount of time it took to get the boat trailer from the storage yard to the Granisle marina, an accumulation of giant snowflakes had built a curious 5 inches of fluffy snow. It was only September 25—pretty early for such an accumulation. With no breeze whatsoever, the big fat flakes defied gravity. If I hadn't been standing in 2 feet of water on the boat trailer, preparing *The Duck* for storage, I would have enjoyed watching the early white blanket cover the land.

My toes were blue as I cranked the boat onto the trailer. That's when I realized it had a flat tire. With a touch of hypothermia setting in, I wondered how much snow could fall during a tire change. I found out soon enough.

The lug wrench for the truck did not fit the trailer wheel. Therefore, I had to disconnect the trailer, put the rig into four-wheel drive and claw my way up the hill from the marina through 6 inches of slippery fluffy white stuff. After about an hour of rummaging around in my parents' garage I found the proper wrench. I came back to see the lonely lame *Duck* still waiting for me, now in 8 inches of wet snow.

The lug nuts on the trailer's wheel were rusted on tight. Breaking the corroded grip became quite maddening. Finally, I removed every one of the bolts. I yanked with brute force, trying to remove the wheel from the axel. Like greased lightning, I found myself propelled in a 6-foot skid onto the snow. Thank goodness I was not under the axle of the boat trailer, which came crashing down. It had swung off the blocking that held the hitch. I had flung myself, along with the weight of the wheel, 5 feet out of harm's way. I watched the freed tire roll down the steep bank and into the lake with a splash.

I retrieved the runaway and threw it into the truck, then put the spare tire onto the trailer, only to find it was flat as well. I went to my dad's garage and set up the air compressor. I filled both flats. I figured I would use the one with the most remaining air when I got to the boat trailer.

By the time I made it back to the marina, the snow was melting. By the time I had the trailer back onto the truck's hitch and the tire back on the trailer, the snow was almost gone. It was nearly dark.

The next morning, with its brilliant sunshine, I questioned my sanity. Was there really a snowstorm at all? Not a sign of the white stuff anywhere. Many of the trees still had some green leaves.

Getting everything organized and set up for winter was always a challenge. I was glad an early winter hadn't jumped into the mix. I still had several trips back and forth from Granisle to the lodge.

After pulling out *The Duck* in Granisle, I brought my second vehicle, the truck, around and parked it at Morrison Landing, at the northeast end of Babine Lake. I would use it for my last trip out. Using the dory I had left at the landing, I was able to drive my truck there and take the small boat back over the water to the lodge.

A voyage in the open dory this time of year meant I had to bundle up. The journey back to the lodge was cold but breathtaking. How many people can say that? I pity the poor people who travel on jam-packed freeways with hundreds of cars all going someplace else. Even though it took extra time travelling in the open craft, it was great. I am always struck dumb by the grandeur of it. Occasionally, the weather didn't cooperate, but this time, with the sun setting, I skimmed across water that reflected the cool lavender, grey, purple and pink colours of the sky. Flying over the surface, along with the ducks and geese, was glorious.

The lake was smooth, surrounded by fall-painted hillsides, affected by the cooler elevations. The shoreline, kept warm by the sun-heated lake, held bits of summer green. The reflected sunset painted warm colours on the distant and brilliant snow-capped mountain ranges to the west and to the north—I almost wept with my love of this place. Without a ripple on the water, I seemed to hardly touch. There was just a slight cutting noise as the hull skimmed the surface.

Rounding the peninsula and turning into the cove, I was greeted by two huge moose. The male looked like a picture postcard, with the last of the water lilies dripping from his large antlers. They truly are bigger beasts than many can imagine.

Some say moose look clumsy, but I beg to differ. They are massive creatures, but they're surprisingly graceful, with extra-long legs. To me they looked like they pranced with each carefully placed step.

I watched them for several minutes before they ambled off into the brambles surrounding the cove. They paused at the edge of the woods, with soft bells of loose skin swaying from their necks. The two grand creatures took one more look at me before disappearing into the dark forest.

During the next few days, the air cooled right down to below freezing. Oddly, the water was still warm from its summer sun collection. It was so foggy out, I could not even see the beach. While gathering wood, I watched as the mist meandered through the edge of the forest. All sounds were muffled. Heavy dewdrops fell like rain and made the carpet of golden leaves glimmer.

The dog flushed a grouse and it flew so close I thought it might hit me. Turning its big body, with such small wings, the forest chicken barely missed. It did manage to make my heart skip a beat. The Steller's jays and whisky-jacks were still here, begging. It was foggy the entire day, and then came the rains.

The four Carolina dories my brother Bob built for Ookpik's fishermen's fleet were stable, seaworthy boats. I felt safe even in terrible seas and was glad to use one of them for my commute. The other dories would wait for me to have the time and energy to remove the outboards, pull them onto the beach and flip them over.

With the ski boat, the *Rip* and *The Duck* out of the water, and the black truck placed at Morrison Landing, the infamous brain teaser was partially complete. But with eight boats still needing attention, it was a persistent nag.

CHAPTER 25

# Holding the Keys to the Wilderness

The radio phone rang. I was offered a job guarding a bridge gate on a forest service road, and I accepted immediately. Being able to land good-paying fall employment this close to home was surprising. I was extremely pleased to receive this opportunity.

I went to bed and wondered what it would be like to be a guard a wilderness bridge. I wondered if the hunters would be angry the government closed access by using a locked gate. I wondered if it was the conservation officers who wanted to control regulated hunting territories, or the guide outfitters who would find it easier. Or if the logging companies just didn't want the extra hunter traffic as they cut down the forest. It was the logging companies who would pay my wages.

My last thought as I drifted off to sleep was that I hoped it would not be foggy in the morning. I had to leave really early for the new job. It would last till November 10.

It was dark when I loaded my gear into the boat. The last thing I did before I left was pull three of the dories into shallow water, but not so shallow the engines' legs would be exposed to freezing temperatures.

I took the fourth dory across the arm to my truck, parked at Morrison Landing. I gazed up into the dark, clear sky, glad to be able to count my lucky stars. It was so early the fog hadn't rolled in yet, and I made it safely.

I took an unfamiliar dirt road and splashed through mud puddles in the dark for 67 kilometres (42 miles). Dawn broke just as I reached the bridge.

The steel gate had an impressive padlock. I had been told where to find the hidden key. Even so I fumbled, in the semi-light, for the key hidden under an obvious rock. I opened the gate and jumped back into the truck. I drove through, closed the gate and parked on the other side of Hautête Creek.

When the sun came up, a lovely little valley appeared. In addition to the gate, the creek had the natural security of a deep gorge. This made it difficult for even an ATV to cross. The hills also protected the little valley by holding off the frost. The deciduous trees still had some green leaves. Tall fireweed, true to its name, coloured the hillsides red.

My hours were Monday to Friday, 4:30 a.m. to 7 p.m. with a nap squeezed in. The job would last until the end of hunting season. Due to the distance from the lodge, I stayed the weeknights in a truck camper a friend had given me—a small homemade hunter's type of structure attached to the truck, not to be confused with a holiday camper with all the conveniences. I could not stand in it, but it had a bed, a small galley and a heater for the cold nights. The work was not too hard, but the hours were long. I monitored traffic with a road radio and was able to open the gate in advance, allowing the big trucks to pass through quickly.

The hardest part was not letting any hunters through. If anyone insisted on crossing, I had been instructed to let them go and take their licence plate number. Almost all of the hunters acknowledged I was just doing my job, and accepted the boundary.

With my shotgun close by, I felt secure. During the first two weeks there were only two rebellious types, but I just teased them until they gave up and left. No matter which way they wanted to go, I just told them all the moose were on their side.

The wild songs of wolves kept me awake at night. I made Nuk stay inside with me, and he howled softly with the pack. I didn't allow him to go out when I knew they were close.

It had been raining the last few days, causing the creek water to colour now and then with mud, but it cleared quickly. The Hautête runs out of Nacariliak Lake into several other lakes and rivers on its journey south to the Fraser River, through Vancouver and into the Pacific, over 1,900 kilometres (1,200 miles) away.

Babine Lake flows to the Skeena and then on to Prince Rupert and the Pacific on the central coast, 725 kilometres (450 miles) away. Somehow it makes me feel even farther from the lodge when I think about being on the other side of the continental divide.

With my shovel in hand, I chose a site for my outhouse on the hillside close to my new abode. It overlooked the beautiful beaver pools 35 feet below. With Hautête Creek running through the deep little valley, the beaver found it perfect. The view was spectacular.

I built a sturdy commode with a nice white seat. I had to add a cardboard gasket later so I wouldn't freeze to that nice white seat. A birch still holding its canopy of bright, buttery yellow leaves gave me cozy comfort overhead. I was a happy camper. I whittled off a holder for my toilet paper roll using a lower branch of the birch. A tin can cover gave protection for the paper and completed the project.

It was ideal. From my supreme sitting position, I could see the creek flowing into a pool, passing gently over a beaver dam made from sticks and mud. The slowed creek swirled into another dam and spilled down a little waterfall, creating another small stream flowing into Hautête Creek. Fall-coloured leaves meandered down this waterway, stopping to swirl a time or two before continuing along the way. On either side of the edge, lush, tall green grass grew in clumps. Old fallen trees covered with moss and foliage created a luxuriant thick-carpeted landscape.

There were several well-worn beaver paths winding up the bank and into the woods. Some of them were wet with fresh mud; all ended at a pile of wood chips and a pointed stump.

The shrubbery had turned into its fall splendour. All shades of yellow, orange and red against the dark green of heavy grass and soft green of thick moss filled the countryside.

As I looked down, small plants with five red berries bunched together created a paisley pattern on the forest floor, shaded by the giant spruce. The purple water flowers were still blooming here and there. Highbush cranberries loaded with ripe red fruit looked as if they'd been hand-planted in just the right places.

I was proud of my accomplishment. I ended up looking at the view on quite a comfortable commode. It was a perfect place to ponder. I liked it there, though I wondered how I would feel after four weeks. On Friday night, I locked up the bridge gate and went home to the lodge.

I had put in a week's work and didn't want to do a thing, but my home chores won out. All the vessels in my little harbour had accumulated rainwater, so bailing the boats was a priority. I loved that chore even in the rain, because the kingfisher and the eagle always came to watch. I was so glad I had moved the boats into shallow water. If I had not, they may have sunk. After that it was time to split some kindling and bring in firewood. The lodge was quite chilly after being unheated for a week. I built a fire and waited until darkness fell. I spoiled myself by sleeping in.

Saturday, I got the dories out of the water. Pulling these heavy wooden boats out is a complicated procedure. First, I laid five, 4-inch-wide PVC pipes that were 8 feet long horizontally on the beach, parallel to the shoreline, placing them 3 feet apart. Then I brought the boats around, one at a time. Eyeballing the PVC pipes, I ran each boat onto the beach and raised the engine at the last moment, which allowed the bow to roll on top of the pipe. Each time, I jumped out and tied it to shore, and then I removed the engine and put it into a wheelbarrow. That was the heavy work. Next, I attached the block and tackle, removed the slack from the blocks and then pulled them tight, rolling the boat over top of the next PVC pipe. Then I'd attach the coffin jack to the boat and remove the block and tackle. It was easy to use the ratchet on the coffin jack to pull the boat over the last PVC pipe and up to the high-water line. After I repeated this process two more times, I had the three dories out of the water.

Next came the flipping of the boats. I drove the backhoe as close to the boats as I could. Attaching a rope from the bow cleat to the bucket, I raised the backhoe's bucket just enough to secure the flip. Then I'd jump off the backhoe to spin the boat over and block it in place. Putting blocks under the gunnels of the dory and lowering the bucket completed the process. After a short break, I detached the rope and tied it to the next boat, then repeated the process.

I slept well that night.

My 2:30 a.m. Monday morning wake-up came way too soon. I walked down the empty dock to load the single, lonely dory. Breaking the silence of the early morning, I powered the 5 kilometres (3 miles) to Morrison Landing, where I left my boat. I made it to Hautête Creek just minutes before the first logging truck, and so began another week at work.

Every morning at 4:30 a.m. I was expected to unlock the bridge. At 4:35 a.m., the first of many giant empty logging trucks powered by. It would be dark for the next three hours. I'd unlock the gate and hang a chain across during my shift. The gate still appeared to be locked and it was faster to open the gate for busy forestry workers and logging trucks.

The early morning was beautiful—very surreal. The moon would be so bright, its beams would light up the low-lying vapour in the little valley. With a full moon I could see fewer stars, but each one seemed large and luminous. When the moon set, the stars became more plentiful and brilliant.

The constellations were easy to make out in the clear northern sky. The Big Dipper, the Milky Way and Orion were always there each morning to greet me. I made it a point to acknowledge Orion, the only man in my life.

My daily schedule soon became routine. The alarm clock seemed to always go off too early. I'd flip the dull battery light on, and it would be so cold I could see sparkling crystals in my breath. I would light the heater and let the cabin warm up. When I couldn't see my breath, it was time to jump out of bed and put on the coffee. I had to be careful not to hit my head on the low ceiling. About then, Nuk would crawl out of his den under the bed and wait for the door to open. With a flood of freezing cold air, the dog was out and I was right back under the warm covers.

One particular morning, the dog was not anxious to leave. When the lazy mutt finally stretched himself awake, it was 4:20 a.m. Mid-leap coming out of the camper, he started barking like mad, so I followed him. It was now 4:30 a.m. and the trucks were due any minute. It was pitch-black as I swiftly walked towards the bridge. Thoughts of potential headlines in the local paper crossed my mind: *Stupid Woman Eaten by Bear, Bear Gun Left inside Camper.*

I went back to the camper and got my bear gun and bear spray—just in case.

Nuk kept up his continuous alarm as I swung the gate open. Something moved above me. It was the lights of the aurora borealis filling the sky and flickering on the land. The dog stopped barking. I was getting dizzy, spinning around to see all the sky's action and watching out for an animal that might be hunting prey.

Then there was a huge solitary crash behind me, and the dog started barking again. After my head stopped pounding with my heartbeat, I noticed there weren't any other sounds coming from the black woods. It was at that time I realized it had to be the mighty beaver at work.

The early morning mist seemed to creep along the hills in long wisps. The sun came up and started to melt the frost. As I watched, the vapour-like breath came off the aspens' golden leaves. It was magical. I walked down my little path to my peaceful little spot for contemplation and to my shocked disbelief, the beautiful birch with the freshly whittled toilet paper holder—the same beautiful birch that had been the wonderful golden canopy over my commode—had fallen, within an inch of destroying my sturdy little privy. My roll of paper trailed all the way down the hill, 35 feet below. It *was* the work of a beaver.

The little camper at Hautête Bridge was OK, but there was nothing like home sweet home. I was always glad to have a couple of days off.

I'd drive back to Morrison Landing and find gallons of water in my small craft. I'd bail the boat, load it with my things and head home.

After the dory slid into its berth, I would trudge up the long dock in my squeaky rainsuit, loaded with gear. On one trip I got all the way to the chopping block before realizing something was wrong.

I was always cautious after being gone—this was the wilderness after all. But this time the air felt different. Something wasn't right. And then, through the rain, I saw the trouble.

A spruce tree had come down by the generator house and had taken out the power lines. With the unusual deluge of rain, the forest floor behind the lodge had become saturated with water, leaving no foothold.

I gathered all the tools I thought I'd need, as well as the 14-foot ladder. With the axe, I chopped branches off the 100-foot spruce tree. I was thankful it hadn't crashed onto the lodge. I could now see that this two-ton monster lay over both power lines coming from the shed, to the lodge and the shop. Just pulling the cables out from under the giant gave me a workout. I no longer needed the sweater under my raincoat.

Several trees with insulators attached held up the power lines leading to the shop and to the lodge. These are big cables, an inch and a half thick with insulation around, making them very heavy. I set the ladder against the first of the remaining trees used to carry the cable to the lodge. Pulling the first power line 17 feet up the tree and tying it to the insulator was not easy. After doing the same to the next tree and the next, I was beat.

The end of the electric cable that had been attached to the lodge was too short to drag up the ladder to the roof's electric connector, so I tied a rope to the cable's end, hoping to throw the rope to the roof. It took several attempts. I used the antenna tower attached to the roof to climb up and pull the power cable into position. It was a real trapeze act. With the weight of the cable and the spanning distance, I had to wrap it around the standing pipe receptacle. After securing the weight I proceeded to repair the damage done to the connections on the lodge's roof.

It continued to rain, and I had no idea what I was doing. My main goal was not to slip on the slick, wet cedar shakes. I had already survived the ladder ordeal with the first three trees. Who would pick me up if I fell? I copied the wiring at the house connection, and it took about an hour to undo and redo the wiring on the roof. Going back to the generator shed, I started the entire process over on the second power line that ran to the workshop and cabins. The first pole to the workshop had been destroyed, so I had to make a new one myself. First, I cut a 4-inch-wide pine, stripped off the branches and cut the pole to be 12 feet long. Strapped for time, I left the bark on the pole. I attached the power cable, and then had to make braces so it would stand straight carrying the heavy wire. Attaching the cable to the next two trees, and then re-wiring it to the workshop, completed this portion of the job.

The only thing left to do was to turn on the generator and see if I had done the repairs properly. I was afraid to flip the switch without an electrician telling me everything was OK. My dad was an electrician, but he was in Mexico at the time. Both my brothers were electricians, but they lived hundreds of miles away. I knew several fly fishermen who were also electricians. None were home.

I figured I could not afford to bring a professional out to the lodge to inspect my work, so I started the generator and flipped the power switch. I went out to check both of the power lines and then came in and tried to smell for anything hot or burning. Everything seemed fine. By then the rain had stopped.

The generator was still charging the house batteries after darkness fell. I had turned all the lights on in the lodge, in every cabin and in the shop to make sure everything was working. In my zeal I forgot to turn them off. When the generator was running, it didn't matter if you left the lights on. When the generator was off, you became quite frugal with the battery life.

I stood alone on the deck, happy with my day's work. Everything smelled fresh from the scrubdown of the last several hours of rain. The lake beckoned with its glassy surface, and when the loon called her children home for the night, I felt compelled to join them.

Paddling my canoe out into the velvet darkness filled me with happiness. Coming around the spit to the front of the lodge was shocking: It seemed as though a village lay before me in the wilderness. With all the lights lit, the cabins and the lodge cast reflections onto the lake, intensifying the dramatic view of Ookpik village. The gentle wake from my canoe cast ripples into the reflection. My heart was full. I was not alone.

The next morning I continued down my list of winterizing chores. I primed the water pump and filled the cistern for the last time. I turned off all the intake and outlet water lines from the lake and to the cabins, then drained the shower-house hot water heater and the water lines to the cold water taps in the cabins, the washer and the fire pump. Finally, I winterized the house water pump. After bringing in a load of firewood, I was able to sit down for a while.

A stack of papers for the Innovative Forest Practices Agreement was waiting for me. Most of the work on them was done. Tomorrow, I would have to ask a truck passing over the bridge to mail them for me, so I could make the deadline.

When I returned to my job at 4:20 a.m. on Monday morning, I had camping guests. Two tents were pitched near my site. Peter popped his head out of one of the tents. Peter and his wife, Chris, were good friends of mine and they lived in the small village called Topley Landing. The other new arrival was Peter's buddy, Don. Both were professional prospectors and were up at dawn and gone till dark, looking for gold.

One of the truckers drove by and made a comment on the radio about the new community. With my camper and two tents close by, it did indeed seem like a campground. I told the trucker they were panning for gold. He stopped his rig, jumped out and handed me five sparkling rocks. I broke into a smile as an idea immediately came to mind.

Later that evening when the prospectors came back, wet and muddy and empty-handed, I flashed my light on the surface of the rocks. They glittered like gold.

"Look at the pretty rocks I found!" I lied.

They were tremendously excited and begged me to tell them where I found them. Of course, I had been sworn to secrecy. It turned out the prospectors were professional geologists who knew what they were looking at and told me to get it evaluated immediately! "These are mariposa, malachite, copper, pyrite, silver and... traces of... gold!" they said with excitement. Sadly, the next day the owner returned and re-claimed his sparkly rocks.

Such was my life being a bridge guard. With the job over on a Friday and the barge not running on the weekends, I rushed and barely made the last crossing to Michelle Bay on the western shore of Babine Lake. I needed to get to the bank and another logging meeting that would last until late Monday. That meant Nuk and I would be gone from home ten days. The temperature had dropped seriously in the last week. I was glad I had winterized the lodge, but I worried about the dory I had left at Morrison Landing.

Upon continuation of the logistical brain teaser planning, I was to drive the black truck to the landing, take the last dory to the lodge and haul it out there. I would then hike out to the Suburban I had parked at my pullout a couple of weeks ago, drive the Suburban to Morrison Landing and park it there for the winter. Reunited with my black truck, I would drive it out and take the barge across. That would have been the conclusion to brain teaser 101. It would have worked well if all elements of the plan had come together properly.

# CHAPTER 26

# Ice versus Sheer Will

I started to panic as I drove between frozen ponds towards Morrison Landing. Nuk could feel my dismay and searched out the dark windows, finding nothing to cause alarm. My foreboding culminated with great justification upon my arrival: I was horrified to see the protected cove totally frozen over. Nuk was glad to be out of the truck and bounced over the snow-covered ground. Outside the warm comfort of the truck, the silence of cold dread surrounded me. The futility of my situation and the risk to my poor boat slowly sunk in.

Unfortunately, during the ten days I was gone, my 21-foot dory had frozen in place, stuck in almost 3 inches of ice. Complete panic set in when I realized that if I didn't free the boat right away, it would be crushed and destroyed. The continuous movement of winter's ice would transform the wooden boat into a pile of toothpicks by spring. To add to the unfortunate situation, rainwater had frozen inside the boat. I needed to develop a plan of action immediately to save it. Standing in the sub-zero afternoon air, I felt numb. I should have thought of the possibility of an early freeze. There was no one to blame but myself. There was no one to yell at, no one to hold responsible. No one but me.

"Fix it!" I heard myself yell.

"Fix it!" I heard as a single faint echo bounced back from across the cove, and immediately the sound was sucked up in the snow-cushioned surroundings. Nuk ran to me ready for a command. I ordered him into the truck, and I ordered myself to stop and think my way out of this Siberian coffin.

This was my gargantuan dilemma. The 500-pound boat was tied to a dock, 50 feet from land and frozen in place. There was a 6-foot rocky drop to the edge of shore. I had to get it onto land, by myself, immediately.

This was my plan: I needed to break the boat free from the ice. Move the craft around to face the outside end of the dock. Get the bow edge on top of the dock and tie it up. Then drive the truck as close as possible and fasten a rope from the bumper to the eye cleat on the boat. I would then have to remove the outboard engine, pull the boat up onto the dock, pull it to shore and flip it over for the winter. It was a monumental project that demanded all of my mental and physical strength to make it happen.

—

Jumping inside the boat was like jumping onto land—it didn't move. Boats feel alive when you are aboard. They move and respond to your actions. Now, when I moved around inside it, this splendid little dory seemed to be dead.

Like a sounding board, the ice stressing reverberated through the wooden hull. I tried jumping up and down inside the boat, and the ice cracked and popped around the hull. I could hear the ice fracture across the frozen surface to the opposite side of the cove. After several minutes of rocking from side to side and stem to stern, the boat was floating within the tiny confinement of freed space immediately surrounding the hull. I concentrated next on the outboard engine. I broke it free, pulled it out of the well and set it inside the boat. With the stern facing the rocky shore 50 feet away, my options were limited.

The boat was tied to a 60-foot T-shaped dock. This meant I would have to break 10 feet of ice ahead, turn the boat around the inside corner of the top of the T, move along the 12 feet inside the edge, and then swing the stern sharply around the corner, breaking 12 feet of ice along the end of the T, and then turn the boat again. Standing in the stern, I raised the bow above the ice and slid it a foot or so on top of the ice. Then I jumped onto the bow of the boat and managed with brute force to break 7 inches of surface ice forward. I repeated this process over and over, creating the water path necessary. The afternoon sun was diminishing fast. Steam rose off my body and my breath puffed in clouds, which obscured my vision. I repeated the process of breaking the ice and moved the boat along the top of the T an additional 20 feet ahead. Next, I broke the ice along the length of the starboard side and swung the stern straight out. The dory floated free, surrounded by chunky ice slabs, and faced the truck on shore.

It had taken hours to get this far, and darkness fell. I started the truck, turned on the headlights, gave Nuk a quick pat and went back to work in the bitter cold. If I stopped for the night, this boat would be doomed.

Exhausted, I tapped a deep inner source of respect and love for the work and care my brother had given to create this boat from wood and fastenings. I bounced the bow and pulled on the mooring lines at the same time. I somehow managed to lift the bow up a foot and a half from the icy trap to rest on top of the dock and held it in place with its mooring lines. Two feet of the boat was now out of the icy water. I secured the line to the dock cleat so the dory would not slide back into the icy grave. After connecting several ropes, I had the length needed to connect a towrope from the boat to the truck's bumper. I backed the truck to take the slack from the frozen rope, then set the emergency brake and jumped out to release the line holding the bow on top of the dock.

Back in the truck, I cautiously started to pull the 21-foot boat up slowly. The rope stretched, the boat started to slide out a couple of feet, and then my hasty ties failed and the rope snapped. Fearing the eyebolt had pulled free, I ducked below the windshield. Thankfully, it was just the rope that hit the glass. And crucially, the boat stayed on the dock.

After reconnecting the line, I used the truck to put tension on the rope again. The boat began to move onto the deck a few feet, then it stopped abruptly. The frozen lines were being stretched tight and ice was snapping out of the ropes, creating a halo in the light of the headlamps. I set the emergency brake again and found the boat was stuck on its 4-inch keel. I placed a pole under the bottom of the boat as a cantilever and gave it a lift. The stretched nylon rope worked like a slingshot and the boat exploded onto the dock, snapping the pole out of my hands and throwing me to the deck. Glad to still have all my teeth, and covered with icy snow and frozen sweat, I backed up the truck and pulled the boat all the way out

*Fortunately, I was able to work this dory out of its frozen confinement with little damage.*

of the water and up the length of the dock. I let the dog out of the truck to relieve himself. After I removed the outboard engine and gas tanks from inside the boat, I pushed it off the edge of the dock's walkway and tipped it over onto the shore upside down. Fortunately, the boat landed on some snow-covered shrubs, which cushioned its fall. There it would sit all winter, waiting for my return.

My day was not done. I put Nuk back into the truck and tried to warm up. It was freezing cold, and my adrenaline had worn off. I started to shake uncontrollably. Unless I wanted to sleep in the small camper, I would have to hike into the lodge in the dark. In my exhaustion, I chose the camper. I slept like a frozen rock in my down sleeping bag. Nuk was happy in his cubby hole.

Before daylight I drove to my pullout and parked behind the Suburban. I then chained up the truck, put it into neutral and towed it with the Suburban to Morrison Landing, where the Suburban would be safe for the winter months. The sun broke through as I hiked in to the lodge. With the brain teaser finally complete, I kept the fires burning and slept off and on for two full days. For the next couple of weeks I worked on my journal and, for fun, sketched out a storyboard for a children's book I hoped to publish someday. By the end of November, I would be back to work on Whidbey Island. It would be sad to leave. But with some cash in the bank and a job waiting for me, the fear of losing the lodge had been put away for another year.

While I was gone, I would be able to start booking guests for the next season and sort out my return to Houston in January for a forest planning meeting. I also hoped to squeeze in another meeting with the Environmental Assessment Office in Victoria, concerning Pacific Booker Minerals. And most importantly, I would get to see my children and grandchildren on Whidbey Island.

# PART 5

# Determination

Sometimes when I came back in the winter, it was much easier to stay in the cabins.

# CHAPTER 27

# Beast Number One

My schedule was very tight. I had some days off from my winter employment, and I had to attend several logging meetings. Time at the lodge would be limited, so I had left Nuk in a boarding kennel. I already missed him. I tried to visit the lodge several times every winter. Normally, the drive from Whidbey Island to Babine Lake was a happy one. Nuk would be patiently looking out the truck window, both of us eager to again experience the beauty of a winter wilderness. This trip, however, was not exactly a trip to paradise.

I had recently turned fifty. Of all the visions David and I had had for the future, I could not have imagined driving alone into a blizzard in a foreign country—one I now called home. That first big milestone—and the realization of aging—made me impatient with the drive and impatient to pursue my unfulfilled dreams. The continuous fight with the logging and mining companies gave me serous concerns over the viability of the wilderness aspect of my business.

The first meeting was with the licensee's timber planner, to address the threat of clear-cutting a large block next to my property and along the lakeshore. We were going to walk through the area on snowshoe, though I had no confidence that this man would address my concerns.

The January nights are long and the days short in Northern British Columbia. As I crested the pass going down into the valley, my pulse began to race, as it did every time I reached this point on my journey home. The morning was still dark, but I could visualize the graceful beauty of the cobalt blue lake that lay below. The edge of dawn crept up over the mountaintops on the eastern shore as I drove onto the barge. The night sky broke slowly during the remaining 60-kilometre (40-mile) drive to the pullout by the trailhead to the lodge. I tucked my truck in tightly, to allow the timber company's vehicle to pull in beside me, and turned the heater on full blast, noting I had just driven 1,160 kilometres (720 miles).

I was glad I was early. My forest company contact would happily drive right on by if I had been delayed. The forest district manager, the government's representative, had told me earlier, "All the forest is sold; now we just decide how much to remove and when." This year, 2003, the logging company had decided to clear-cut several blocks in the Morrison Arm of Babine Lake. I collected my thoughts, determined to demonstrate how clearing the area adjacent to my property would affect my business, the wildlife corridor, the salmon run and the forest.

When the planner finally arrived, he was late, and he'd brought two young helpers to carry the maps. I was outnumbered again. For every question I had, they would have ten ready answers. I stepped out onto the snow-packed road, leaving my backpack in the truck. I'd take it in to the lodge later.

As the shadows turned into an unhurried dawn, we strapped on our snowshoes, climbed over the compressed 6-foot snowbank and headed into the dense forest close to my property. The snow was 4 feet of dry powder. In any other circumstance, I would have enjoyed the hike.

The temperature was −24°C, and my breath crystallized onto my scarf and inside my nose. We walked between the big trees, heavy snow falling onto our snowshoes with every step. My legs grew tired from lifting the loaded snowshoes over fallen trees and branches.

The young men moved especially fast through the snow-covered terrain, trying to wear me out, but I stayed with them without breaking a sweat. Or so I wanted them to think. I was in good physical shape for a fifty-year-old, but I didn't realize my sweat was freezing to my skin. Unfortunately, my long johns were still in my pack in the truck.

"All the trees need to come down because they are susceptible to mountain pine beetle," the planner explained. The trees did not necessarily have beetles, mind you, but he supposed they might someday.

"Can you show me what a beetle looks like?"

"Dang, we forgot our hatchet," the three men answered in unison.

I helpfully offered the small sheath hatchet from my belt. They skinned a patch from a few trees, to no avail. They could not find one measly beetle. I kept up a steady campaign.

"Why not cut all the pine that *does* have beetles, and leave the ones without, and leave the spruce and balsam as well?" I asked. "Logging roads and clear-cut blocks around the lodge and to the lake would create a security risk in the winter. Vandals would be able to find my place."

No response.

The head man handed my hatchet back and said with a sneer, "Nice little hatchet." The men smiled at each other, turned their backs and carried on.

We hiked several miles around the proposed cut-block. The men, who were supposedly here to address my concerns, did not attempt to address any of them. The head man just said, "We are here to make money, lady."

By 3 p.m., the sun was going down fast. We hiked back to the road. The company men took off their snowshoes, got into their brand-new company truck and drove away. I put on my 40-pound backpack, cinched up my snowshoes and broke trail two more miles through the forest.

Night had fallen when I reached the lodge, and the temperature had dropped to –35°C. At the porch, I turned around and let the weight of my pack pull me down onto the upper steps, so I could release it and unstrap my snowshoes. To say this fifty-year-old woman was exhausted would be putting it mildly. The thought of a nice warm fire kept me moving. I was frozen, discouraged and alone in the dark in the middle of a giant forest with no one to talk to, not even my dog. With great relief I found the key to the back door in its secret spot and took my gloves off, cold fingers fumbling to find the lock.

When I opened the door, a cloud of thick oil fumes poured out. I shined the flashlight into the back room and saw a calamity. The place was destroyed. All of the dozen or more coal oil lamps were on the floor, glass and oil everywhere. I stared in shock.

"Who did this?" I shouted to no one. "Who would do such a senseless, mean thing?" I stood in the room, afraid to open the next door.

I was starting to feel ill from the fumes, but I could not head outside. I had to go through the kitchen to reach the wood heater in my bedroom. I had to build a fire, or I would die of exposure.

When I had reached the lodge and took off my snowshoes, my only thought had been of collapsing in front of a warm fire, secure in my own space. This was not meant to be. Someone, or something, had been there before me.

I tried not to breathe in the oil fumes as I walked carefully over the oil lamps and debris in the back room and slowly opened the kitchen door. I stopped at the sight of an even bigger disaster. Every cupboard door was open, with all the contents pitched onto the floor. My glass knick-knacks were smashed, mixed into the chaos of food, flour, broken glass jars, and cardboard and plastic packaging.

I thought of my grandmother's china with a flood of dread. I kept the precious porcelain in the dining room, safe inside my old hutch. With my hand on the doorknob, I prayed that the old tea sets, which held so many warm memories, were still in one piece.

The vaulted room swallowed light and sound. I pointed my flashlight through the blackness, and a wave of relief replaced my fear. The English teacups and Franciscan dinnerware glinted behind the leaded glass doors of the hutch. I slowly realized the devastation was not the result of human wrath. A human would certainly have smashed all of these treasures. And no one had opened any doors.

It must have been a wild animal. It was a strange relief.

My frosty breath danced through the faltering beam of my flashlight. As I approached the bedroom door, I thought I heard something, but dismissed it as my imagination. I would not allow myself to recognize the reality of something being with me, in my house.

I opened the bedroom door and quickly scanned the room in the dim light. Curtains had been torn off their hooks and shredded. Picture frames lay on the floor, the glass shattered. My antique candelabra had fallen and broken, along with everything else that happened to be hung or sitting on any surface.

A loud noise came from the adjoining bathroom, and I could fool myself no longer. I was not alone.

I had to get my gun.

Being a good citizen, I always keep a trigger lock on each of my guns. The RCMP had told me that I would be held responsible if my gun was ever used illegally. I kept the keys to all of the locks in the same place, for easy access—a glass dish with a lid on the windowsill. Of course, this delicate glass bowl now lay in a thousand pieces on the floor, its contents scattered, the keys to the trigger locks nowhere to be found.

With my flashlight fading and the noise in the bathroom becoming louder and more violent, I had to think of another plan, and fast. I was literally freezing. I cracked open the bathroom door. A pair of red eyes reflected the weak beam of light, accompanied by the most frightening sound a person could ever experience: the gnashing of teeth. We've read these words in Grimm's fairy tales, but to actually *hear* the gnashing of teeth was beyond description.

I slammed the door shut. As I tied the faulty latch closed with a piece of shredded curtain, the animal screeched like a cat—a very big cat. I searched again for the gun keys, to no avail. I needed a plan, and now.

I crunched over the kitchen floor, down the back steps and through the deep snow. In the starlight, I pushed snowdrifts aside with my hands and feet so I could pull the shop door open. I like to hang old fur-animal traps on the outside wall of the shop for decoration, which I then throw in the shop for safekeeping over the winter. With my almost worthless flashlight, I finally located the rusty metal jaws. As I left the building, I stumbled over a 5-gallon bucket of tar. Carrying the traps and the bucket, I headed to the house, formulating a plan along the way.

It was −35°C inside and out. Only willpower and adrenaline kept me moving. Hypothermia was a definite possibility. My teeth were chattering and violent shivers shook my body. Things fell from my hands, and I couldn't think fast or well. I had to form simple verbal directions and tell them to myself out loud.

The thought of a fire overpowered any other ideas, including my plan. By the time I waded through the deep snow to the house and the bedroom, I had forgotten why I carried a heavy bucket of tar. Large clumps of snow fell from my frozen pants as I stepped over the trashed kitchen, but I didn't care about anything except getting warm. In slow motion I walked into my bedroom and closed the door. I lit a candle, crushed some newspaper and lit a fire in the wood heater.

Meanwhile, the creature in the bathroom was breaking, ripping, tearing, pounding and scratching. As the cedar kindling started to crackle and joined the symphony, I rummaged through the kitchen rubble for bait.

My flashlight was useless by then, so I lit another candle. I remembered the can of tuna in my backpack. Back at the bathroom door, I used my buck knife to stab a couple of holes in the can of pungent fish. It took more strength than I thought I had to open the jagged, toothy jaws of one of the traps, and I then held them open with my feet so my numb fingers could wire the can in place. When it was set, it looked frightening. I suddenly remembered why I thought the tar would come in handy. With the end of the trap's chain wired to the handle of the bucket of tar, the wretched deathtrap was finally ready. Now I had to place the trap in the bathroom without springing it or letting the beast out.

That night I did one of the bravest things I have ever done in my life: I opened the bathroom door. The horrible racket abruptly stopped. I slid the trap inside and quickly closed the door. With the tar bucket on my side of the door, the beast wouldn't die where I could not reach it. I fumbled the door shut again.

I built up the fire and peeled off my frozen jeans, revealing patches of frozen skin. The animal resumed his clamour and the noise filled the bedroom. I wrapped myself in a blanket and put my hands over my ears. I could see the fire but not hear it; could see the flames but not feel their heat. The vast glacial space inside the lodge sucked all the heat away. The walls of big logs were frozen completely and would take hours to warm. To get my body temperature up, I crawled into my frigid bed. At some point, the beast stopped its racket and I passed out.

I woke six hours later, snug in a small spot of warmth—as long as I didn't move. I was glad I had piled my entire collection of eiderdown comforters on top of the bed.

The house was still freezing cold. I had left the damper open to burn hot and the flames had gone out sometime in the last two hours. Any degree of warmth it had generated was gone too. Into this dark, frozen house I crept. Even with several candles lit, it was hard to see in the blackness, and I certainly could not see across the room. It was as if I were in a continuing nightmare—in my home, my bedroom, my personal space. Here, where I kept all the treasures and memorabilia collected through the years. Baby pictures, carnival glass, Grandmother's gaudy candelabra, Mother's fancy doilies—all these things were soothing company. But in the candlelight, I witnessed a frozen whirlwind of chaos. I stood in the middle of an alien place, the years of memories and treasures smashed and shredded around my feet.

I brought a candle to the silent bathroom and opened the door. The trap was empty, and so was the bathroom. The only proof of the animal's presence was a heap of white gypsum board and bath powder mixed with the perfume bottles, shampoo and bathroom items scattered everywhere. Behind the door, in the linen closet, I found a gaping hole ripped through the wall, exposing the pipes and the dirt floor of the basement. I nailed a board over the space, left the trap set and retied the door.

I had to meet the assistant manager of the forest district at my pullout by the proposed cut-block at 10 a.m., so I had no time to waste. Though I went out cold and shaken from the ordeals of the last fifteen hours, I still had the presence of mind to mark my path, never the same route, with bits of plastic ribbon on the way out. This would help me traverse in the dark.

A plow came down the long empty road, pushing a ton of newly fallen snow. The driver stopped to say hello. André was a French Canadian. He regularly plowed the pullout where I parked my truck. I told him about the beast in the house, asking if he had any idea what it could be.

He stepped down from the big rig. In his heavy accent, he said,

"Sounds like a cat—a lynx? Or it could be a wolverine." He paused, then added, "I'll put a .30-06 rifle in your truck this afternoon. Since," he just *had* to continue, "all your guns are locked up, right, and no keys to be found... eh?" He snickered.

I thanked him graciously.

—

The assistant district manager arrived on time. We soldiered through another gruelling snowshoe hike around the proposed logging blocks, all within walking distance of Ookpik Wilderness Lodge. I again expressed my concerns about the damage my business would suffer if the blocks were clear-cut to the lake. The lodge would be devastatingly exposed. I would have to hire a security guard during the winter when I was working down south. The noise generated from the logging traffic would not be a wilderness experience tourists would be willing to pay for. The meeting was just a repeat of the day before, although the government official seemed more sincere.

After another full day in the woods, the assistant district manager thought a partial cut would address my concerns. He figured that all timber more than 8 inches in diameter could be selectively removed. He didn't say anything about all the trees to be removed to make the meandering skid roads. But at least he didn't say all susceptible timber, which the logging company men had suggested the day before. I would meet with his boss the next day to discuss today's events.

We went back to the pullout. The sun was going down for the second day. With their work done, the forestry men took off their snowshoes, got into their truck, and drove home to their families.

I was going home too. I returned to my truck in the shadows of the late afternoon to pick up the rifle from André. The gun gave me courage as I followed the ribbons through the forest in the twilight. Every step took me closer to my home, where an unknown wild animal possibly waited.

Snow fell in small fine flakes. A vast silence swallowed the faint sound of my snowshoes moving in the deep snow. The punishing day and previous night were now taking their toll, and I felt like I was eighty years old instead of fifty. I took a long time to reach the lodge, partly because of my physical exhaustion, partly because I stopped to remove the trail markers, and partly because I dreaded facing the monstrous mess left by the beast, but mostly due to a primal fear of the unknown.

It was dark when I collapsed onto the back steps. I removed the snowshoes and took the safety off the rifle. In the back room, the smell of lamp oil lay heavy in the air. I could taste it on my tongue and I wondered if I could ever use this room as a pantry again. The crunch of broken glass under my heavy boots broke the silence. I refrained from immediately lighting a candle for fear of igniting fumes.

As soon as I reached the kitchen, I closed the pantry door and lit a candle. The beast had obviously returned. The earlier path I had cleared through the mess had disappeared. The kitchen looked as if someone had tossed the chaos of this morning into a blender for good measure. A candle in one hand and the gun in the other, I moved cautiously into the bedroom, off balance, feeling helpless.

I lit more candles. The cold sucked the flames small. Without real light, I couldn't see if I was alone or not.

Suddenly, a piercing noise came from the bathroom. The beast had returned. The door was closed, so I had time to find my dim flashlight. Holding the rifle ready and the light straight on, I cracked opened the bathroom door.

The beast was thrashing about in the trap, one back leg caught in the iron jaws. The moment the door opened he charged through, dragging the trap with him. Just as I leaped out of the way of his razor-sharp teeth, he stopped short against the weight of the 5-gallon bucket of tar.

I was going to shoot him right there, but I was afraid the blast from the big gun would make an even bigger mess in my house. Looping a rope through the handle of the bucket, I dragged the wild beast outside.

With tears blearing my vision, I shot the creature. The explosion sent red bits of bloody muck into the frozen air. It was so dark, little else was visible. I couldn't tell what kind of animal I had killed with the big gun. Tears burned my cheeks and froze to my glove as I wiped them away.

I returned to the house to tackle the next priority—making a fire. I had to get some heat into my bones, and I had to rest. Another meeting awaited me the next day.

I swept up the mess on the bathroom floor. The plywood was still in place, and I couldn't figure out how the beast had gotten back into the bathroom. It finally occurred to me that, because the vaulted living room was not touched and the doors were closed, the animal must have travelled from room to room via the attic.

The last thing I did before going to bed was to set all my traps, every shape and size.

Before I left in the morning, I nailed or tied all the cupboards closed. The lodge looked empty and unprotected without the glass knick-knacks that had stood guard along the sills and shelves. I hated to leave, knowing I would be gone for weeks. I tried to determine what I had shot with the big gun, but it was still so dark, I could only see frozen and matted, bloody fur and guts. I kicked snow over the carcass.

The bits of moonlight illuminated my way as I trudged along in the stillness. It had been over two days since I had had my truck running. I could only pray the diesel engine would start in this extreme cold. It did not.

I pulled the emergency blanket and small propane heater out from the homemade camper of my truck. With the engine covered and the heater under the oil pan, I struck a match and prayed it would not blow up. After thirty minutes, the engine finally started. I sped off to catch the barge, 50 kilometres (30 miles) away. With the heater on full blast, I became warm for the first time in two days. I met André on the road, thanked him, and gave him back his rifle. My meeting was in Houston, BC, another 110 kilometres (70 miles) away.

Crossing the lake by barge at this time of year was always an amazing experience. The sun was still low on the horizon, casting its beams through the small frozen icebergs that rolled alongside, reflecting prisms of colour. I had time to think about my forthcoming meeting with the district manager of the forest.

At the meeting, I pled my case as best I could. He said he would work on a solution. In the end, he told me I had to attend another meeting in three weeks where I would learn about his decisions. I couldn't stay any longer, because my job down south was waiting for me. I would resume my appeal in a few weeks. I filled the next several hours on the highway south strategizing my concerns. By the end of my journey, I had come to the conclusion that the only way for me to deal with this dreaded meeting was to make sure I had enough time for another trip out to the lodge.

*Ookpik Lodge in the dead of winter.*

# CHAPTER 28

# More Beasts

The weeks away had renewed my determination to survive both the loggers and the wild animal that had invaded my home. This time I had my trusty 24-pound Nuk at my side. At least now I was able to talk to him instead of myself.

The long journey north, much of it spent scraping freezing fog off the headlights and windshield, seemed to take forever. After two nights of barely sleeping in the hot-then-freezing truck, I pulled into the rest stop near Houston, BC, where the meeting was scheduled.

I changed from my wrinkled, dog-hair-covered attire into a grey wool suit and red shirt. I looked like a new woman—business-like. I also took time for a small ceremony to build up my bravery. Under my shirt, on a smooth leather strand around my neck, hung a leather pouch given to me by my daughter many years earlier. Inside were tiny things that were important to me; each held a bit of spiritual energy.

I had also brought war paint given to me by my Navaho son-in-law. He had explained how and why to use these natural pigments, and I had used them as teaching tools in years past, convinced of their power. I needed all the help I could get. As I mixed small quantities of vibrant colour, the task and the smell of the paint calmed me. On my shoulder, I painted two dots of brown pigment representing my parents, a blue stripe representing my son, a red stripe representing my daughter and three yellow dots representing my grandchildren. Strength and confidence flowed in my blood. Only I would know that my closest family accompanied me in spirit, giving me courage. I left Nuk on his blanket, curled up within his luxurious fur coat. I looked back to see him tuck his nose under his long fluffy tail.

In my briefcase were five copies of my twenty-page illustrated document outlining my formal concerns. I was as prepared as I was ever going to be.

Behind the carved and varnished closed door of the forestry building's main conference room, I recognized the deep voice of the head company man. Then I heard all the men laughing. As scary as it was to face the unknown beast back at the lodge, opening this door was even more terrifying. I waited a moment until the laughter subsided and stepped in.

At the table were four men from the logging company and two from the Ministry of Forests. I knew that calling me in for this meeting was just a formality. The meeting was a charade. Logging the area had been already decided, but government rules required this final meeting. I was surprised no one had ever confronted them before. No one had ever challenged the clear-cutting practices in this forest. No one but me had ever filed a Forest Practices Board complaint in the Morice Forest District. With 60 per cent of the forest in the area's watershed already gone, it was about time someone asked questions.

The meeting lasted two hours. The men had to give up something just to get me off their backs. I was giving them too much paperwork to process. In the end, they agreed to reduce the proposed new harvest from 100 per cent to 30. All merchantable timber was to be taken; in other words, as the forestry man had suggested at the last meeting, all trees less than 8 inches in diameter would be left—*if* they were not in the roadway, he clarified this time.

Even so, the removal of old-growth would affect my business. The guests of Ookpik Wilderness Lodge would no longer be surrounded by a pristine wilderness. One side would be partially harvested. And with so much of the forest removed, the damage from the wind could be disastrous.

—

Leaving town with a heavy heart, I travelled as quickly as possible on a highway covered in ice and snow. I arrived at the barge as the sun was going down and caught the last crossing before morning.

Traffic on my forest service road seemed heavier than usual—26 kilometres (16 miles) into the homestretch, I crested the hill with a view of the valley towards home and my stomach turned over. The sky above my area was lit up. I assumed it was a wildfire and barrelled onward. As I turned the last corner before my pullout, I slowed down. An active logging site was lit up like a carnival with floodlights wired to ugly, smoking generators. Monster machines were busy cutting down trees, and fresh dirt sullied the pristine snow. A new road had been carved into the land towards the lake.

Less than three hours after the meeting had concluded, the logging show was already underway. It was as if everyone at the meeting but me knew the blocks near my place would be cut, no matter what.

After parking my truck, I strapped on my snowshoes and headlamp and set off down the trail. The forest, normally so quiet, was now filled with the screeching of machines. Ancient trees came crashing to the ground so close to me, it was as if a beast was loose in the woods. I stumbled along the path in a daze. Nuk hung his head low, staying near my side, uncertain about the human activity.

As I approached the lodge, Nuk raced ahead and began barking madly at the back door. Worried about the traps I had set, I forced him off the porch and hurried inside. I closed the door behind me and stepped into the unknown.

I was stunned to see the place trashed again. The floor I had swept looked as if I hadn't touched it. And two of the traps in the pantry had animals in them, frozen and dead. That made three. I now recognized them as pine martens, though in their frozen, stiff state, their lush brown fur was no longer luxuriant. Their frosty bodies, about 2 feet long, sharp vicious teeth exposed, were corpses transformed from exquisite, agile animals to demons with savage faces.

I began to push open the door to the kitchen when I heard a noise. Peering through the crack, I saw another beast. Outside, Nuk's frantic barking began anew.

I had set a trap in the kitchen, and like all the other traps, I had attached it to the leg of the table, so the animal caught in the trap would not run off and die in some awkward place. For this trap, I had run out of wire and resorted to using a heavy extension cord, which the pine marten had chewed through. He'd freed himself from the weight, but as he toured the kitchen dragging his leg caught in the trap, he had squeezed through the handle of a twenty-cup aluminum coffee pot. Now he was running around and around with the trap banging the pot, and trailing the yellow extension cord behind. The chaos brought the animal, the pot and yellow cord alive as one.

What to do? I no longer had André's gun, and my guns were still locked, the keys lost. I grabbed a big stick and tried to hit the beast but managed only to beat the coffee pot to death. I think the poor marten died of a heart attack.

That was four.

Nuk was extremely curious when I took the carrion out of my home and looked for a place to cache them for a future burial. Before I opened the back door, I picked up Nuk and carried him over the kitchen disaster and into the bedroom. He was trembling now, upset with the smell of death.

The rest of the day was filled with simple duties, the painful sounds and reminders of the logging operation kept at bay by my hard work. I needed water and wood. Nuk kept me company. He seemed to soon forget the two-legged and four-legged intruders.

The lake remained frozen solid, so I gathered three metal pails of snow to melt on the woodstove. Melted snow does not amount to much, so I also brought in two 5-gallon buckets of snow. Darkness soon crept through the chaos of my house. I took candles from the ruined candelabra on the floor and placed them into cans, shedding little light, but some comfort.

The snow was in no hurry to turn into water. I threw more wood on the fire, and the melting snow started to shift in its pots. I sat in front of the blaze with the stove door open, trying to get warm.

The sound of the giant machines cutting down trees invaded my home. A short high shrieking noise was immediately followed by the crash of a tree, then a rumble of sawing. Then the tree, now a stripped timber, echoed with a sad hollow boom as it joined a pile of wood. With less than a twenty-second pause, the process began again.

With my face in my hands, I began to cry. I had killed four beautiful wild animals, and I was exhausted. Nuk kept bumping my knee and rubbing his face on my leg. I was moved by his sensitivity, but nothing could stop the sadness.

After a while, my chest shuddering and my face wet, I opened my eyes, and saw—nothing. The candles were lit but all I could see was a thick, blurry haze. I blinked my swollen eyes and dabbed my stuffed nose. Smoke was everywhere. I jumped up, ran through the smoke to the attic access in my closet, and climbed the ladder into the empty room above.

To my horror, sparks were shooting through the darkness and flames licked through the stove stack. I jumped down the ladder, then threw the half-melted pails of snow and ice into the stove and closed the door. The steam hissed and the hot metal popped. With my flashlight and fire extinguisher, I ran back up the ladder to put out the fire in the attic. I had never used a fire extinguisher before. It stank and it was messy, but it worked.

The attic was another battlefield of destruction. The marten had torn apart the stovepipe that came through the bedroom ceiling and joined the brick chimney. I searched the house for a way to fix the pipe so the stove could work for the short time I needed it on this trip. An hour and a half later, I attached the last of several hose clamps over the temporary aluminum-foil Band-Aid.

Back in the bedroom, I started to shovel out the firebox filled with ash and slush. Then I heard another animal in the attic above.

The thought of having a fifth animal trashing my home gave me the energy I needed to set another trap, in the middle of the night, in a house that was now, once again, as cold as the ice *inside* the stove. I returned to the attic and placed a trap on the board used as a walkway through the attic. Three wire coat hangers, untwisted, attached the trap through the attic access to the rod in my bedroom closet.

It was midnight when I shovelled the ash and slush out of the stove and into a bucket. Trying to get a fire relit was a test of willpower. Finally, with a meagre fire burning, I took off my filthy, frozen and wet clothes and climbed into bed. The logging continued. I passed out to the screams of the old-growth forest.

I woke to the barking of the dog and the banging of the trap in the attic. The animal thrashed and pounded the wooden walkway, an ideal sounding board directly above my bed. It wouldn't stop. I lay there begging the thing, "Just die. Please, just die." Nuk sprung onto my bed.

On and on went the horrible melee. The animal was fighting for its life. Finally, the noise stopped. Amazingly, I still had tears to shed. There was another poor animal dead by my hand.

Or so I thought, until Nuk charged into action at new sounds coming from a different area. The animal in the attic fell through the access into my closet, where he ripped and tore at my clothes. Leaping out of bed, I grabbed my flashlight and cracked open the closet door. The furious beast jumped towards the light. I slammed the door, placed a piece of kindling through the handles, and backed away. I ordered Nuk to return to the bed.

The marten ripped his way to the floor and began eating through the bottom edge of the wooden doors. Teeth, claws and chips of wood flew across the carpet. Any minute, this fifth beast was going to appear in my bedroom to rip my throat out. I knew he was in the trap and attached to the clothes hanger rod by wire, but his rage was terrifying.

If I left him there, not only would he suffer, he would also ruin all my clothes. And the wooden doors would have to be replaced. I wanted to crawl back into my soft, warm bed. The room was so cold.

As I put on my housecoat, the beast continued his destruction. My resolve returned. This was my house. Those were my clothes. I had to do something. I took one of the 5-gallon buckets of ice and slush into the bathroom. I brought all the candles into the room and lit them, then placed the bucket in the tub.

I laced up heavy leather high-top mukluks and put on moosehide snow gloves. Opening the closet doors, I reached in as high as I could and grabbed the wire holding the trap. Carefully, I pulled my clothes, which were now shredded rags, away from the trap, wire and animal. As slowly as I could, I took the furious beast, his teeth snapping, into the bathroom. He was climbing his own body trying to get to my face.

The moment I dropped the marten into the bucket of water and slush, I realized my method of murder—drowning—was not going to work. The trap and the beast were too big. I dumped the bucket of ice water, complete with marten and trap, into the bathtub. I ran to get the other two buckets of ash and slush. The water level still wasn't high enough. I went back to the stove for the pots of water and poured everything into the tub.

The poor animal thrashed about. Sobbing, I grabbed a large piece of firewood and held the animal's head under the water. Watching this beast struggle, clawing around the wood with his razor-sharp claws, was heart-wrenching. In a small voice, I begged him, "Please, just die." I told him how sorry I was. Finally, he stopped moving. I looked at Nuk, with my guilt rising in my throat. He stood on the bed, cocked his head, and jumped down to my side. Relieved he still loved me, I patted his head and placed the marten into a bucket. We took it outside to lie with its kin, frozen like cord wood.

I built up the fire and took off my armour. Going back to bed was the only thing I could do until the house warmed up. Nuk reclaimed the stuffed chair in front of the fire and nestled in.

The next day I tackled the trashed rooms, keeping an eye out for the trigger lock keys. My bedroom was first. The destroyed curtains and shredded clothes went into the fire. I picked up slivers of glass and wild animal scat from the carpet. Then I cleaned the kitchen—again. Shattered owl salt shakers, shards of coffee mugs: It took hours to shovel and sort broken glass jars and the food they had contained. Little families of glass owl knick-knacks I'd collected, given to me by clients and grandchildren, mingled with the wreckage on the floor. I picked out the few unbroken pieces, the baby owls, remembering how every year when my grandchildren came to visit, they would scrub the entire owl community that sat on the windowsill. They would carefully dry each little owl face and set the owl back onto the shelf right where the little family wanted to be. This chore was now up to me. I bathed the remaining owlets and set them on the sill, alone and orphaned. Finally, after burning any rubble that could burn, I placed the rest into rubber totes, to be hauled out by boat in the spring.

Most of the house was still as cold as a winter den, but the thermometer on the belly of one unbroken owl now read 8°C in the kitchen and 10°C in my bedroom. Even so, I had never needed or loved my mukluks more.

# CHAPTER 29

# King Daddy

**A**ll was silent. The timber saws had stopped. I had no more tears to shed. Deep under the eiderdown, I fell into a dark abyss, neither asleep nor awake, but in a place of vacant numbness. I felt empty and hollow.

Ultimately, I slept. I dreamed all five of the beasts came back from the dead. They had reclaimed my kitchen and threw anything left into a garbage heap in the middle of the floor.

My dream changed to a semi-conscious state as Nuk began to whimper and nudge at the bedclothes. I sat up and shook my head, not sure if the sounds were part of my dream. Nuk barked once and raced to the bedroom door. Something *was* in my kitchen.

How could I do this again? How could I even move? I wanted to just cover my head with pillows and give up. Then something big hit my bedroom door, sending a zap of adrenaline through me. I was now fully awake. Nuk came back to the edge of the bed and tugged at one of the blankets.

It was four in the morning when I crawled out from under the covers, encouraged by Nuk. I slipped on my headlamp and cracked open my bedroom door. Nuk and I peered through the opening into the kitchen, scanning it with bright light. I ordered Nuk back, which he did with a sniff of disgust.

What I saw in the kitchen was a bona fide nightmare. The biggest, maddest, monster King Daddy of them all, maybe 3 feet from head to tail, stood on his hind legs, looking straight at me. The pine marten hissed and snarled a soft, almost quiet sound. He was expressing his ownership of the place and challenged me.

Then he ran directly towards me. I quickly closed the door and he crashed into it. Thankfully, my hands were still on the door, or it would have flown open.

I pushed the firewood box against the door and fell back on the bed, too exhausted to do anything more. I crawled into my eiderdown cave and forced myself into a meditative sleep. Nuk went back to his chair, whined a few times, then resigned himself to passivity.

After an hour or so, the sound of gnawing and digging at my bedroom door woke me. It was still dark. The digging and chewing became more violent. I slammed the wood box against the door and the noise stopped. I heard a small scurry and *clunk*, then nothing. I went back to bed. Nuk didn't make a sound; he was done.

Twenty-five minutes later, the noise resumed. On and on, all night, the wild animal rampaged in the kitchen.

I searched all corners of my brain, under, around and through, for all the reasons I was here in the deep woods, alone. I felt totally empty, drained of all emotion. A gloom filled the emptiness and melancholy seized the opportunity to fill my psyche. My husband was dead, my children grown and far away, the old-growth forest that surrounded the lodge violated, and I was a killer. Those beautiful creatures would no longer frolic in the forest. Part of the life experience I strove to maintain was now gone.

The long night of the north was breaking. I could allow my heart to break with it, or carry on. In the early morning twilight, I got up to stoke the insatiable fire, and realized the noise from the kitchen had stopped.

I moved the wood box and opened the door. Nothing stirred. Had King Daddy left? Had it all been some horrible nightmare after all? Carefully stepping around the traps, I carried Nuk quickly outside. I tried to make myself feel normal, like nothing had happened. It was necessary to regain some control of my situation. Back in the kitchen, I shined my light around. The reality of my night was easily apparent. Most chilling was the shredded carpet under the bedroom door, where the marten had tried to dig its way into my room.

I heard small noises behind the propane refrigerator. I opened the outside doors and hoped the marten would leave what was, after all, *my* house. The temperature dropped in minutes, making the pantry and kitchen a frozen extension of the icy world outside. I draped a blanket over the bedroom door, and Nuk and I retreated to the relative warmth of the bedroom. Nuk stopped being excited by the noises in the kitchen. Maybe he figured I had taken in another pet. I found a book I had not read yet, sat in my big chair next to a bright window, and prayed the new pet would leave sooner than later.

Hours passed, and the creature resumed a steady barrage. When I looked into the frozen room, snow was banked against the kitchen cabinets. While winter confiscated my home, the animal pranced around the trap set to kill him. Ice crystals hovered above him like a magic protective dust. He stopped when he saw me and gnashed his teeth, saliva stretching between each sharp tooth. A gust of wind brought in more snow. My captor was clearly not moving out, and I was running out of firewood.

The puffed-up marten felt my fear and charged straight at me. He leaped log by log up the wall and in a split second was at the log above my door. I closed the bedroom door. I could hear the marten as he chewed and clawed, trying to get in to challenge his captive. I was indeed afraid. He pried a piece of moulding off the casing and it dropped onto the kitchen floor.

Finally, I had had enough. I was not going to let this animal tear my house apart. With my trusty big stick still covered with specks of blood, I opened the door. He had jumped over to a log wall less than 3 feet from my face. I raised my arm slowly, preparing to strike. He looked not at the stick but right into my eyes. Swinging as quickly as I could with all my might, I hit his hindquarters. As I drew back for a second assault, he leaped for my face. By the grace of God, I was able to step back into the bedroom, and then *slam!* He hit the door and fell.

I shoved the now empty firewood box back in front of the door and added Nuk's big heavy chair. My heart was pounding so hard I could feel it in my throat. With no firewood, the outside door open, and the exposure from the thin bedroom door, the temperature was dropping fast. Thoughts of surrender crossed my mind, but I picked up my book and sat wrapped in a blanket, still hoping my captor would simply leave.

The light shifted through the room as the winter sun waned. Try as I might to distract myself, after four hours I was still on the first chapter of my book. I fumbled and dropped it. Awkwardly, in my down parka and with my legs wrapped in a blanket, I reached for the book and tripped. As I struggled to untangle myself, something glinted at me from under the bottom log of the wall.

The shining object came into focus. I crawled on my hands and knees and reached under the log. Jammed tight were the keys to my gun locks! The monsters had hid them in their rampage. With a stupid grin on my face, I told Nuk, "Look out, King Daddy!" Completely ensnared a moment ago in the marten's trap, I was now filled with optimism. I had a way out.

I took all three of my guns out of the enclosed glass case in my bedroom and laid them out on top of the bed. I now felt powerful and in charge. The question was which should I use, the shotgun, the .22 rifle or the Winchester .357 Magnum? I decided to be conservative and use the .22.

One minute I was a pitiful wimp ready to give up. The next minute I had my gun loaded, and I was all pumped up and thinking like Arnold Schwarzenegger. I pulled the empty wood box to the side and stepped out into the marten's domain. For the first time, the big animal raced to his hideout behind the fridge. It was as if he knew he was now in danger.

I quietly called in a cool, coy, confident voice, "Come and get it."

Jumping up onto my built-in breadboard, I gained even more confidence. In a deeper voice, I called slowly, "Come on out and make my day!"

Not a peep came from my adversary. With the safety off my one-shot .22, ready to take aim, I placed a second bullet between my lips and jumped down from my perch. Tense and alert, I searched for the creature that had been holding me hostage in my own home for eighteen hours.

Approaching the propane refrigerator, I lay down on my stomach on the cold floor. I saw heaps of waste under the appliance and feet with claws digging into the debris. I was afraid that if I shot him while he was under there, I might hit the copper propane line and blow us all to kingdom come.

To get a clean shot, I tried to shove him out with the barrel of the rifle. He would not come out. With my cheek pressed against the icy dirt, I aimed the gun away from the copper tubing and fired. Instantly, the beast leaped out, doing a Tasmanian devil dance, spinning in circles directly in front of my barrel.

Then he stopped and stood on his back legs to his full height. This gave me just enough time to get the extra bullet out of my mouth and into the chamber. With only one bullet in the gun, I had to make this shot clean. I had to dispatch King Daddy before he took control of the situation and my castle... again. With his head in the crosshairs, I pulled the trigger.

—

King Daddy was the largest of all the martens who came into my home—the acreage around the lodge and the logged areas close by were clearly his territory, and the others his females or offspring. I somehow knew I would have no more intruders, but I felt terrible that the forest had lost these beautiful wild creatures.

That night, the house quiet and the fire once more built up, Nuk and I had a long, peaceful winter nap. The next morning, the sun rose just a bit earlier. The days were getting longer. After about eight hours, I once again had the house cleaned and warm. With no fresh sign of uninvited creatures, Nuk and I finally felt at home.

On my heavy wooden block usually used for kneading bread and making sticky buns, I skinned the last beast. From the tip of his nose to the tip of his tail, that pine marten was 27 inches long. Nuk hid under the bed during this procedure. Maybe he thought he would be the next to go. As I dropped the meat into the pot of boiling water, intending to make a meal for the dog, I wondered about my sanity—the soup smelled good! However, Nuk refused to eat the meat, and there was no way I could bear to eat it myself.

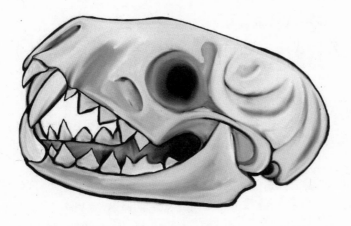

*This is the skull of the big male marten.*

It took many days and nights of contemplation to clear my conscience. I had no choice but to kill the animals, and I am sorry I had to do it, but King Daddy was the only one of the six martens for whom I shed no tears. He was an adversary I will respect forever. I left the bullet hole in my floor to remind me how strong I can be. I kept his skull to show how fierce King Daddy was, and his fur to remind me how beautiful and grand he was. The only crime these forest dwellers were guilty of was searching for a new home in the wrong place, after the destruction of habitat by the loggers.

I closed up the lodge again and went south a few days later to finish my winter job. I counted the days until my return: only sixty more rotations of the earth. Even with all the work, the risks, the dark moments and the disappointments, there was no place I would rather be.

# CHAPTER 30

# Housework and Making Bread

I used to think of housework as cooking and cleaning. In my previous life, I would just clean the house and go to the store and buy a loaf of bread. But the realm of housework in this new world took on several categories of definition. The commute, maintenance and repairs were new major categories. Food preparation and housekeeping were secondary. The only way to get a fresh loaf of bread out here in the wilderness took many more steps to consider and pursue.

Early spring was the time to stock up the pantry for the coming season of fishermen. It was best to get loaded with supplies and have as much prep work done as possible before clients entered the scene. It was hard work living at a place with water access only. First of all, even though I was used to boats, I had never had to rely on a floating vehicle to bring home all of my provisions.

After I crossed the water to the village, which had very few groceries and no other supplies, I had to drive 80 kilometres (50 miles) to Houston one way, or 142 kilometres (88 miles) to Smithers. Smithers had the best and freshest produce, so my choice would usually be to go the extra distance. After all, it would be a full day either way.

I only got to town once every two to three weeks—or whenever I would run out of coffee creamer, whichever came first. I placed all food, hardware and supplies into boxes, plastic tubs or ice chests. Everything had to be packaged to travel safely under all weather and hauling conditions.

The clerks at the grocery store probably thought I was a little eccentric. After finding a quart of precious cream misplaced with canned goods two days too late, I learned to be very fussy. It was necessary to ensure the eggs and dairy products were stored properly as soon as possible. I had to make sure the heavy items were double bagged. It was difficult to deal with a split bag during transfer from wheelbarrow to boat, and more than once I had to use a big salmon net to fish out the groceries from the muddy bottom of the lake.

The groceries were the easiest part of my housework. Transporting boxes of groceries, supplies, dog food and the dog into the truck was not bad. The most difficult housework was propane. I'd roll the 5-foot-tall tanks from the fuel station in Houston to the edge of the truck tailgate, which was 3 feet off the ground, and tip them onto the edge. Bending over from hips and knees, I would grab the bottom edge of a tank. Then, keeping my back as straight as possible and using every single ounce of muscle, I'd raise the tanks one at a time into the truck canopy. Miraculously my back didn't go out. Loading the 185-pound tanks of propane, and securing the 40-pound tanks of gas and diesel fuel so they didn't leak, was housework to the extreme. I used sixteen propane tanks per season at the lodge, transporting three tanks at a time.

Driving back to the *Rip* at the village marina, I would be fully loaded with everything I could possibly need for the next few weeks. It was important not to forget anything, because coming back was expensive. I learned from experience how upsetting it was to forget the very thing you most wanted, so I'd strive to be organized and remember everything I needed. There was no one to blame but myself if I forgot the cream for my coffee, God forbid.

Taking the provisions and fuel out of the truck and hauling them down the dock to the boat was a chore all by itself. Lifting the boxes, bags and tubs into the boat and stowing them, and making sure not to drop the heavy propane tanks so they didn't go right through the floorboards, was hard, gravity-defying work.

I'd haul the gas cans down the dock, balance myself off the stern of the boat and fill the boat's fuel tank, being careful not to spill any of the gas into the water. Finally, I would strap the remaining full tanks of gas and diesel cans onto the back step of the boat.

Inevitably, someone would be watching. In the beginning, they would ask if I would like help. It was important for me to decline in the most appreciative way possible. Humour worked best: "No thanks, I have to work off all the ice cream I ate in town."

The real reason I didn't want any help was that I didn't want to owe anyone anything, and I had to be self-sufficient. The marina was in a small village, and people talk.

The best part was that I got to take my boat up the lake and go home. No matter what the weather was like, I had the best commute. Coming home was a wonderful thing. Landing the boat was a discipline. Remembering everything I had learned about boating and adjusting for the wind, I usually had a perfect landing at the lodge dock. It was a little more daunting landing at the village with spectators, surprised to see a woman driving the boat. I messed up a little more often there, but not much. I always went in slowly.

Once I had docked at the lodge, I would use my trusty two-wheeled wheelbarrow to get all the perishables out of the boat and into refrigeration. If I had loaded the boat properly the ice chests would be on top. My goal was to trek up and back the 300-foot dock as few times as possible. The wheelbarrow was often overloaded and difficult to push up the dock and over the bumpy trail full of roots.

The eight steps into the house added up to more than eighty by the time all the groceries and supplies were inside. The fuel was next: three cans would stay in the boat, the remaining I hauled to the gas house. The last things to bring out of the boat and up the dock were the dreaded propane tanks.

I used a small hand truck. I'd untie the tanks, and I'd roll them one at a time over to the 3-foot side of the boat. Lifting up the bottom, I'd balance one on the gunnels. Carefully jumping onto the dock, while maintaining the tank's balance, I would slide each tank to the dock. It would land with a heavy thud, often just missing my toes. Rolling it onto the hand truck, I'd tie the tank on so it wouldn't bounce off when going over all the roots in the path. The 300 feet of dock wasn't bad. The 100 feet up to the lodge was a test of willpower.

Finally, I'd place the propane tank onto the platform where it lived. Tipping the brute onto the edge of the platform and untying it, I'd shove all 185 pounds home. Somehow, I got it done. The next two tanks usually waited on the dock till the next morning.

Back in the kitchen I'd refill the rubber tote with the 22-pound bag of flour I just hauled up the back steps. Later, with no bread in the house, I would pour some flour into my bread bowl, reach into the propane refrigerator for the milk, mix in all the other ingredients, warm up the propane oven and then bake the bread. The reward was not feeling guilty for the calories in the hot bread, dripping with butter and heaped with fresh raspberry jam.

CHAPTER 31

# Bears, Bats and Beloved Children

I tried to save August for my friends and family. It was a good month for that because the weather was warm, the mosquitoes were gone and the fish were harder to catch, so I'd have fewer clients anyhow. My daughter, Amanda, and her children came at that time, making August a very special month for me.

One summer, Amanda had come to pick up my granddaughter Silver, who had stayed several weeks and filled every day with the joy and happiness only grandchildren can give. Amanda came a couple of weeks early to visit before heading south. She brought my other two beautiful grandbabies, Chavala and Cyrus, and her dogs.

One afternoon during that visit we experienced a horrific thunderstorm. I was completely content. A rare visit with my daughter in front of the blazing fire was a treat. The excitement of the lightning bolts illuminating the dark clouds filled the room. Even the powerful thunder shaking the very floor didn't bother me. Amanda was more concerned about the storm and being alone in the middle of the wilderness. Cyrus was the youngest and his eyes bulged every time the thunder rolled. The dogs hid under the couch.

Amanda was sitting in the window box with her arms wrapped around all three kids. I was happily chatting away as the storm raged outside.

"Mom, what if there is a fire? What are we going to do?" Amanda said.

"There's no problem. Don't worry about it," I replied.

At that very moment I saw a brilliant lightning bolt strike the top of the giant pine tree that held the golden eagle's nest. A fireball blew up and filled the sky. I left the children with eyes unblinking and mouths gaping as I ran to the radio phone and called the emergency fire number. As I was giving them the latitude and longitude, we all watched as lightning struck a second tree 50 feet from the first.

We all watched as the fire blazed. I was glad the eaglets had fledged. Silently, I considered potential horrors, and the need for an evacuation plan to get my family to safety was the priority. All the while I had to act like everything was under control. (The possibility of losing the lodge, and my entire financial world going up in flames, was a shocking realization that only came to me later.)

On cue, the clouds unlocked a deluge. Rain pounded the forest and hit the lake so hard we couldn't see where the sky ended and the lake began. Steam billowed above the flaming eagle nest like a glowing orange halo, merging into the heavy vapour and low-lying clouds.

A helicopter surprised all of us with its sudden clattering as it broke into view. We cheered from the deck in the pouring rain as the helicopter lowered a giant basket to the lake, scooped up hundreds of gallons of water and dropped the load onto the flaming trees. After three water bombs, the craft took off, leaving the fire still smouldering.

We watched as the chopper flew south into a huge thunderhead, and I was thankful for how incredibly brave and determined the crew was. Darkness fell, along with a few more lightning bolts and pounding rain. But we felt secure in the knowledge help was just one helicopter away.

In the early morning sun, the forest sparkled and steamed with the promise of a warm day. No fires were evident, and late summer was in full swing. I made banana pancakes for my family.

I really wanted to take advantage of the break in the weather to continue staking out my angling guide territory. There was a little lake about 20 kilometres (12 miles) north I wanted to investigate. Not wanting to miss any time with my grandbabies, I got up at sunrise, tiptoed around the lodge and, with the Winchester in one hand and the fly rod in the other, stepped onto the back porch. Through the sunbeams, looking into the misty, dripping forest, I saw a mother black bear and her cubs rambling along the trail towards the lodge.

I decided it wasn't the best time to leave Amanda and the kids. I backed into the house and bumped into Amanda. With sleepy eyes she said, "Where are you going?" With all the nonchalance I could muster I replied, "Nowhere now. We have company."

About that time Nuk rousted Amanda's dogs and they all started to bark. It wasn't long before all were up, peering out the windows. I recognized the mother by the white blaze on her chest. She had come to share the saskatoon berries with her cubs. We watched the big mother bear waddling around the yard with her three frisky cubs bouncing beside her. Just off the front porch, my best patch of berries grew. With her huge paw, the mother bear brought down a branch loaded with fat berries. Using her lips and big, flicking tongue, she carefully removed each one. The baby bears tried to copy her, jumping up and tumbling back down. We watched until one cub was able to keep hold of a branch and place it into his mouth. With teeth clamped, he pulled the branch through and watched with a bewildered look, as all the leaves and berries landed on the ground beside his fat little rump. The other cubs had no trouble licking up the berries.

Sitting inside, we all laughed till there were tears in our eyes. The mother bear heard us and promptly took her cubs back into the woods.

After a quick cup of coffee, I left my family eating breakfast with a promise to return before lunch. I tied the red canoe to the stern of a dory and headed for Morrison Landing, where the truck was parked. Halfway across, I was surprised to see a big black bear swimming from the direction of the lodge.

My lucky day! I had seen five bears and it wasn't even 8:00 in the morning. I pulled the canoe out of the water, dragged it up the grassy bank and heaved it onto the truck. I was hoping I'd find a perfect little lake: never fished before, filled with hungry wild rainbow just waiting for anything I cast their way—the best little fly-fishing lake ever. It took no time at all to tie down the canoe. The sun filtered through the forest onto the road, a kaleidoscope of light and colour.

Twenty minutes later, I was untying the canoe and tugging it down a rather steep grassy bank from the forest service road to the lake. The bank was slippery in spots, and I was glad I had left my rifle in the truck. I used both my hands to keep my balance and pull the canoe. I slipped in the slick mud and landed on my rump with a soft thud. Then I heard a loud roar and looked up to see my sixth, and biggest, bear of the day. It was standing on the roadside looking down at me. I found myself down the bank, in the canoe and out on the water in a matter of seconds. The trout were jumping like crazy. My rifle and rod were still in the truck, so I sunbathed for an hour waiting for the grizzly bear to move along. I made it back to the lodge at lunchtime and told my bear tales over peanut butter sandwiches on homemade bread. The children were excited to hear the stories. My daughter was not impressed. From then on, she took bear spray along when she and the kids went to the outhouse.

—

I worked hard to book every week during June, July and September. Booking the lodge was a full-time job. Everyone I knew and everyone I met heard my spiel. It was easy for me because I loved it so much—the excitement bubbled over, and I found it effortless to talk about what I considered to be the most beautiful place on earth.

The local hardware store in my old hometown on Whidbey Island was a great spot to talk up the lodge. For one thing, the employees loved to fish. They had fished all over and were ready for something new. Most of the men just fished for fun, but the owner was more competitive. He decided the group would come up in August. I told him the fishing slowed down in August—the water was too warm and the fish went deep. Nothing I said would deter the boss from choosing August.

"If there are fish in the lake, we will catch them," he said.

So for the sake of my mortgage, I booked them, even though Amanda and the kids would be visiting. Babine Lake had lots of fish, and some big ones. My brother Bob had caught one of the largest rainbow trout ever with a fly in August of the previous year. It weighed in at 13 pounds, 7 ounces. The fish just don't bite as readily in August as in the spring and early summer.

Upon arrival, the six men moved into their cabins with excitement. They ate supper with pleasure, quizzing me on the best fishing techniques for the lake. The boss looked uncertain, however.

The other five men went out on the lake the next morning. The boss not only didn't trust my advice, he actually took one of my small boats to the village—an hour and a half away—and then drove his truck to Smithers, another two hours away, to ask the local hardware store owner what gear to use on Babine Lake. As it happened, to my secret delight, the man at the hardware store had never fished Babine Lake and had no idea.

While the boss was gone for the whole day, his companions caught lots of great fish using the tackle I had suggested. And little Cyrus, only six years old at the time, caught a lake trout almost bigger than he was.

These men taught me an extremely important lesson I would use successfully for the next several years. When asked a question like, "What kind of fly would you use right now?" I learned that I should answer like this: "My *dad* says to use a minnow-patterned bucktail fly with a long shank and, this time of year, it should be coloured with yellow and olive green."

If by chance I were to say the same thing, but leaving out "My dad says," the men would usually look at me doubtfully. From then on, I always fielded questions asked of me by my male clients by saying, "Well, my dad says..."

In truth, my dad did say. He taught me everything I know about fishing. He taught my children and my grandchildren as well. What I give him the most credit for is teaching me how to navigate in big water and to keep the boat in just the right spot so *he and my brothers* could fish. My dad taught me everything I needed to know about being an angling guide.

Although a lot of my time was consumed taking care of my guests, having Amanda and the children at the lodge the same week was a pleasant distraction. The week went smoothly, and the fishermen caught fish. After I received a call on the radio phone, we added four more for dinner Saturday night. The headcount would be sixteen.

Amanda thought it a good idea to take Silver, Chevy and Cyrus for a boat ride to let me fly into action that Saturday after lunch. It seemed like a great plan. When I was basting the turkey for the last time and putting the homemade bread into the oven, Amanda came blasting through the door.

"Mom," she said, "Chevy has just been attacked by a bat!"

The boatload of dinner guests was just landing at the dock. The fishermen were already waiting for dinner on the deck; the bread and the turkey were ready to come out of the oven.

"Mom," repeated Amanda, slow and clear, "Chevy was just attacked by a bat! You know, the kind that suck your blood or *carry rabies!*"

I heard that loud and clear. I dropped everything and got onto the radio phone to contact the provincial poison control centre.

"It is completely out of character for a bat to attack in broad daylight without provocation," the nurse said. "If you do not have the bat in captivity the child will have to get rabies shots. There is no exception because there is no cure. If the bat did have rabies the child will die without treatment." I called the hospital in Smithers and told them Chavala was on her way.

The next few minutes went by in a blur. At this point I couldn't leave the lodge, with so many people waiting for dinner. One of the fishermen offered to take Amanda and the children across the lake. While we were getting them ready to go, Amanda explained what had happened.

Amanda and the kids took the boat up the Morrison River. On their way back they stopped at an old, deserted dock about 8 kilometres (5 miles) from the lodge. They were just hanging out. Amanda was sitting with her feet in the water, Chevy was playing with her mother's hair, Cyrus was sitting beside her talking about his big fish, and Silver was sitting in the boat whittling a stick. Amanda noticed what she thought to be a bird circling in front of her when suddenly it shrieked and dive-bombed right towards her.

Amanda said it was a nightmare. Full bat form, wings spread, mouth open with teeth exposed, screeching—and getting bigger and bigger as it got closer. Amanda ducked, and she grabbed Chevy. Even so, the bat flew straight into Chevy's long, black hair and proceeded to tangle, fight and squirm.

Amanda pulled at the wiggling mass of nasty bat wings and teeth until she managed to untangle it from Chevy's hair. Without thinking, Amanda threw the bat as far as she could.

As it turned out, the hospital had to order the serum from Texas. Amanda waited in Smithers three days for it to arrive and Chevy got her first shots. Amanda then decided to go back to her house in Washington State and take Chavala to her own hospital, along with the serum she purchased in Canada for $300.

Back in the US, the doctor examined Amanda's hands. Discovering several scratches, he advised her of the possibility of contracting rabies herself. After the initial contact with the disease, there is a ten-day window to be vaccinated. After that there is no cure. The doctor had more serum rushed from Texas. This batch cost $3,000. The day Amanda started her treatment was her ninth day.

Chavala and Amanda had the full series of rabies shots: five shots at a time, three times a week for six weeks. About halfway through, Chavala, who was only seven, had reached her limit. She had to be held by several nurses at every appointment for the shots.

During this period Chavala, by coincidence, also had to go to the dentist. At the dentist she panicked and was literally foaming at the mouth as she tried to get away from the dental chair. Amanda could only say, while looking at Chevy's frothing mouth, "Don't let her bite you."

There were three cases of potential rabies incidents that year in BC; Chavala's was one of them. We'll never know if either Chavala or Amanda had contracted rabies, but if they did, the serum saved their lives.

The fishermen ended up taking stories of rabid bats, as well as trophy rainbow trout, home. Many of these same fishermen became good friends and booked the lodge over the several years—but always in June, and after that first year, they left the boss-man home.

# CHAPTER 32

# Ice Cream Sundae

Two weeks later, with the rabid bat not quite forgotten, I went to bed with the screened window open. I couldn't hear a thing through the lodge's thick log walls if the window is closed, and I like cool night air. In the morning the loon family called out their welcome to a new day. I felt the waft of fresh air as it drifted into the bedroom.

Sitting up in my grand bed and enjoying a supreme view, I would marvel at the beauty of each day. The low silhouette of the Sleeping Giant across the lake, framed with a cerulean blue sky, was warmed by the luminescence of the morning sun. The lush, thick forest eased itself to the very edge of the shoreline.

With each cool night the willows at the water's edge turned to waves of yellow. Shiny black rocks lay along the shore as if placed by hand to enclose the lake, which reflected the hints of fall.

A black bear ambled out onto the beach and wandered along the shore, then stopped to eat a spawned salmon. He thought he was alone.

Mist seeped out from the forest floor and began to join the vapour that rose off the warm surface of the lake and mixed with the cool air. The suspension of water collected into several separate and gently moving columns. This parade of seemingly supernatural figures moved down the river valley and out onto the larger body of water in front of the lodge. The current of the river pushed and twisted the misty pillars as they swirled gracefully down the centre of the lake. Watching this phenomenon, I felt as if I had been given a precious gift.

Later I collected my wet laundry and hung it out to dry. I loved my 50-foot pulley clothesline attached to the stump of my beloved pine tree. The morning was so glorious, I decided my wood gathering could wait. I slipped my kayak into the vapour hovering over the cove. The mist there was only 8 inches or so thick. As I slid into it and swirled the particles with my paddle, I felt a part of something great. Most of the time, I was able to see over the fog to the other side. Passing through the columns, I felt like I was one with them.

The loon family would visit with me now and then. Most of the time the adults were a bit standoffish, but the babies, now almost grown, were quite interested. They called out in their melodic way, and it carried softly through the mist.

I had a lot to do that day and forced myself back to shore. Grudgingly, I stowed the kayak. I refused to believe I had just finished one of my last trips for the year in my favourite craft. It was time to put all of the canoes and the kayak under the house for winter storage. Stopping for a coffee break, I laid out the plan for the day. It was essential to get another cord of wood split and stacked to prepare for winter visits. There would be only a few weeks left at the lodge.

As I gathered my tools, I hummed along with the remaining hummingbird population. Everywhere I looked many of the wildflowers still bloomed. I loved the variety and beauty of the flora, but perhaps not as much as the hummingbirds did, bouncing from one spot of colour to the next.

I pushed my wheelbarrow down the path and into the forest. The Steller's jays called and I remembered that I would need to refill their feeder soon. I stopped to watch the cedar waxwings in an alder nearby. How delicately they were painted, with a white eyebrow over black eyeliner. Their bodies were grey, soft and thick, and I assumed they were this year's young gathering the nourishment necessary to migrate south. With just the very tips of their tails a vibrant mustard yellow, they could be Japanese silk embroidery. How perfect—how perfect they all were.

The sun warmed the giant bumblebees buzzing over the wildflowers. The forest floor was dusty and dry. I gathered the fallen, dead and dying trees. Every trip to the woodpile absorbed my labour without a visible enhancement.

Grouse were plentiful, exciting the dog, who seemed to think I needed protection from them. Fat, shiny crimson rosehips were ready for harvesting. Every year at this time I'd pick my share—rosehips are a tasty way to get your vitamin C.

I always left the rosehips that grew around the house on bushes for my own comic relief during winter visits. It was truly a delight to watch the grouse leap and stretch their long necks to reach the red hips, and even funnier to watch as they twist and wiggle their fat bodies, with little wings spread out, till the rose hips give up their hold on the bush.

After what seemed like hours hauling wood from the forest, and drinking two full bottles of water, I moved to the chopping block. I enjoyed splitting the wood and stacking it—my body got into a rhythmic groove, splitting the rounds and creating a nice, straight stack, allowing my mind to reach a state of peace. It was a mantra of sorts. Having a sharp axe helped too.

Just when the large axe got too heavy, I picked up the lighter hatchet to make the kindling. The fabulous smell of cedar was heady, and it split like butter. A small wedge of cedar makes a nice big bunch of kindling.

A large shadow crossed overhead, and the dog flinched. An eagle called to announce his arrival. The sun was high. The day was hot. The work was almost done. Life was magnificent and bright—a treasure. These were the memories that would carry me along during difficult times.

Hauling the wood up the steps and into the house, I felt so happy. To be able to carry this heavy load, to always carry such love for this place. Sweat dripped between my shoulder blades. The freshly split cedar filled the box for the cookstove and perfumed the entire house. The only downside was all the cedar chips in my socks and around my wrists. This was not a wonderful feeling, but it gave contrast to my glorious day.

The eagle kept chirping nearby, but I couldn't see him. Red-winged blackbirds flew back and forth through the willows, their distinct melody piercing the air.

Only the itching cedar in my socks could have pulled me away from this beautiful afternoon. I went into the house, peeled off my sweaty clothes and started a bath. The tub filled very slowly because there was no water pressure in the system—it was gravity-fed. I meandered out to the kitchen for some juice, then took my glass out to the front porch, where I stood naked, revelling in the feel of the breeze on my sweaty skin. I felt so free. All the biting bugs had retired for the year. I could see north and south for miles, with no boat in sight.

The eagle called out urgently. Curious, I hopped down the front steps and into the yard toward the back dock, trying to figure out where the eagle was.

The cool earth felt good under my bare feet. Reaching the dock, I decadently strolled, bare-naked into this world, surrounded by dragonflies and water lilies. Standing with my feet slightly spread, I gazed across the lake in awe.

I watched an osprey hover and dive for his supper. When he hit the water, I remembered *my* water running in the tub. I raced back up the dock laughing, and at that moment the eagle screeched overhead. There he was in the tall pine above, in all his glory. The master of all birds, it was the golden eagle who was looking at me. I waited, not wanting the moment to end. I felt fearless, yet some part of me was afraid. I felt unloved, yet full of love.

Both hot and cold, like a hot fudge sundae—it felt delicious.

Suddenly, without a thought, I shouted in a full, thunderous voice, pouring out my joy, "God I love this place!" Silence. Then, softly, "God I love this place," my echo replied.

The bald eagle and golden eagle were permanent residents and used the pine in the yard as a lookout.

# CHAPTER 33

# Masters of the Forest

O ne late September, with all the guests gone, I found a few relaxing days of freedom from my chores and just sat in the living room and read. The cedar crackled and snapped in the fireplace and the ambience of the fall-coloured forest made me feel decadent and wonderfully lazy. With a hot mug of jasmine tea and the bonus of a bestseller left behind, I was in heaven!

Outside, Nuk came to the back door and whimpered—his signal that a grizzly bear was in the yard. Although he would bark and confront black bears, for obvious reasons he was not about to confront the Master of the Forest. I was not surprised by the possibility of a grizzly, because the salmon were spawning and the dead fish were washing up on the beach lately.

At the back door it was confirmed. A big old grizzly stood at the foot of the stairs. Squeezing the dog through the door, I locked it fast and stared through the windowpane. On all fours this bear was as long as my stairs were wide—6 feet!

I propelled myself into the bedroom, where I kept my guns. I had bought the Winchester Defender for exactly this occasion. I had taken it out of the locked glass case several days ago and concealed it behind the La-Z-Boy chair in the corner of my room for easy access. I thought I should at least get the thing out, find the keys and remove the safety.

The grizzly huffed and puffed and tossed things about, making a chilling racket. I ran to my new hideout for the keys: in the bathroom behind a painting. I hurried back to the corner behind my big recliner, and I rested my hand—the one holding the keys—on the sill of the ventilation window. I would need this ledge to balance myself as I reached for my shotgun. The window was open, and the screen was

6 inches from my face. The cool barrel was finally in my grip. Then I heard a *woooof*. My head turned towards the window and to my horror, I saw the bear's snout pressing on the window screen. It was the biggest grizzly I had ever seen.

The window was 14 inches wide and 4 feet tall. The grizzly's head was so wide his ears spanned the width of the window. I watched his nostrils flair as he sniffed. His top lip was sticking out and pressing the screen, exposing giant, sharp canine teeth.

The outside air was being sucked *into* the window. As he tried to smell me, I could smell him. His breath smelled like dirt, but his body reeked of decomposing fish. I wondered if he could smell my fear.

My muscles were stone. I could not move. My hand, holding the barrel of the gun, would not move. One hand squeezing the barrel of the gun, the other hand inches away from the teeth of the largest predator in all of North America, I stood frozen.

The bear began to dig a hole in front of the window, moving huge quantities of dirt with each swipe of his giant paws and deadly claws. He then moved on to a 3-foot stump cut into the shape of a chair. He ripped it to pieces in seconds. I smelled wet soil and damp wood, and the stench of rotten salmon lingered. I remained frozen in fear.

The grizzly finally moved down the trail and around the side of the next cabin. I could hear him banging the propane tank and I saw a log fly through the air. He had pulled it out from under the cabin.

I dropped the gun down and collapsed into the old chair beside the window. I could not raise my hand to close it. My body hurt all over from the tension. I kept thinking about moving to get the shotgun, in case the bear came back and decided to come through the picture window beside me. But I could not move. I told my legs to stand, but they did not respond. I remember opening my fist. The trigger lock keys had dug deep into my callused palm.

I sat for almost an hour before I was able to get up at all. I was wet with sweat and shaking like a leaf. I went into the living room to tend the fire and collect my cold tea and book. As I looked out at the peaceful forest, without a breath of wind, I admired the secrets it held behind the coloured boughs. I stayed in the house for the rest of the day, pleased the grizzly chose to eat ants instead of me.

The next day I filled in the hole under my bedroom window and disposed of the chair made from the old stump, which was beyond repair. He had trampled and destroyed the raspberry bushes by the back steps. I would have to plant new ones the following year. I put a new piling under the cabin and learned that it was a good thing the bear had pulled it out. The foundation log was full of ants. How a big bear can make a meal out of ants I will never know.

For the next two days I had to take Aspirin for muscle pain. At least I could now say I know what a grizzly's breath smells like. As terrifying as it was to come face to face with this 900-pound grizzly, a few weeks later I experienced the pounding presence of an animal weighing at least 400 pounds more!

—

In the early winter, when the frost crackles on the forest floor, the moose would begin to rut. I'd hear them call for their mates through the forest. The leaves that usually muffle animal sounds would have fallen.

I was on my way to another forestry meeting. Hiking the trail to my truck this time of the year has added concern. Not only are the bull moose in a ferocious mating mood, but black bear and grizzly hunt a last meal before their winter rest. One would rather not run into the mating monster or the beast looking for a buffet.

No human but me saw the deep tracks in the snow. No one felt the eyes I felt on my back as I passed through the woods. The whisky-jacks called out to warn me. I should have paid heed.

The vibration of the ground was my first clue. As the rumble became louder and the ground began to tremble, I crouched behind a wind-blown root ball. Holding onto Nuk with all my strength, I froze in place. I watched two massive bull moose racing as if the devil himself were on

their backs. The only reason they didn't see me was because their lust took over their usual caution. What I saw will be forever branded into memory.

The 1,300-pound animal in the lead carried a gigantic rack. His muscles glistened and rippled in the filtered sunlight. Riding on the shoulders of this enormous creature were two swirls of steam—a moving form of mist holding onto its host.

The second bull was not as large, though he would also have made an enviable trophy. He also had similar mist creatures on his shoulders. In just a few seconds the two were gone, leaving only their deeply pounded tracks and my wonder at the existence of the strange mist creatures riding their backs.

# CHAPTER 34

# Pack Rats and Marilyn Monroe

In late September, adolescent pack rats leave their homes in search of mates and new places to set up housekeeping. Pack rats are beautiful creatures that look like chinchillas: big black eyes and lush, grey fur with black tips on each strand of hair. To look at them you would think they were adorable, not horrible. And if they didn't stink so bad, people would be wearing their pelts like mink. Although the pack rat is not as aggressive as the pine marten, unless cornered, the damage can be worse. It's critical that you don't allow these creatures to move in when you move out for the winter, or your home will be ruined. Everything in it ripped up, shredded and sprayed—the smell everlasting and worse than the damage inflicted by the pine marten. Pack rats live in family units; there could be ten or more in a family. They have horrid scent glands they use to mark their territory. I have seen cabins destroyed in one winter of rat infestation. I was glad my smaller cabins were tightly fitted and pack-rat-proof, but the basement under the lodge was a different story. It was impossible to secure.

Obviously, I tried to avoid this sort of intrusion. I was told by my friend Alex Michelle to trap one and hang it in the basement and all the rats looking for a new home would carry on and go elsewhere. I really didn't want to kill anything, but I just could not afford to burn down and rebuild the lodge, or have a cabin taken over by pack rats. So I took Alex's advice and hung up the next pack rat trapped in the basement. Unfortunately, another rat was soon passing through.

One fall, late at night, Nuk woke me with a low growl and then began a full-on barrage of barking at the guest bathroom. With my flashlight, I could see the door was ajar and I barred Nuk's entry. I cracked it open a bit further to see a large pack rat on my bathroom counter, in the middle of my substantial seashell collection. The stinking male had a shimmering shell in his mouth and weighed at least a pound!

I closed the door tightly and tried to think about what I was going to do. First it was necessary to confine Nuk. I didn't want a "fox hunt" in the house, with a stinking mangled bush rat smearing residue everywhere. And I had just a couple more weeks until I would leave for the winter months. I sure did not want the rats moving in while I was away, especially not the smelly creature now hanging out in the bathroom. What to do?

Earlier in the year I'd had a family with five home-schooled children as guests. The boys were enthusiastic about all the different varieties of bugs in the north and spent their days, butterfly nets in hand, chasing the endless supply of bugs. They'd ask me for some small jars and nail polish remover. I happened to have a gallon of acetone I had used to refinish my boats. They were thrilled. They would drop a cotton ball soaked in acetone into a jar and put a bug inside. They replaced the lid and in seconds the bug was dead. The boys would then remove the bug and pin it to their specimen board. I was quite impressed at the time, and now it gave me an idea.

It was 3:00 in the morning and pitch-black outside. I found a 5-gallon bucket used to haul water from the lake and a leftover butterfly net. When I came back in I opened the door, ran inside the bathroom and jumped on top of the toilet seat, holding the long-handled net. The furious rat jumped to the floor and began leaping at my bare toes. Nuk, locked in my bedroom, was responding with alarm to the ruckus in the next room.

A couple of swats at the angry beast with the butterfly net proved ineffective, so I flipped the bucket on top of him. Now I had an enraged rat under a bucket. I slid the bucket out of the bathroom into the kitchen, slipped a thin cutting board under it and then flipped the bucket right side up.

Now what? I wondered. I was alone, and I had a very nasty rodent captured precariously, and I couldn't let go of the top. The rat was leaping up

*My daughter and I released this pack rat on the other side of the lake, hoping he would not swim back.*

and banging on the lid. On my counter was the acetone I had lent to the boys. Next to it was a roll of paper towels. I put my foot on top of the cutting board, wadded up a ball of paper towel, shoved it into the bucket and closed it up again. The rat shredded the paper in seconds. I took the jug of acetone and with all my dexterity, I slide the cutting board to the side just an eighth of an inch and poured in as much of the acetone as I could.

My plan was to asphyxiate the rat humanely, as fast as I could, so it wouldn't suffer—or escape and bite my throat. Unfortunately, the immediate death I had hoped for was not to be. The rat went insane. It took all my strength to hold the board down on the bucket. I could not bring myself to sit on it in my nightgown. The rat was fighting for its life. I felt terribly sad, and if I could have let the beast go, I would have. I promised to get a live trap for the following year. Finally, the noise subsided. I opened the lid and watched the poor pack rat gasp his last breath, and then die. Nuk went back to bed as if nothing had happened.

I was going to hang the second rat in the basement, as Alex Michelle had suggested, but the chemicals made it an unrecognizable smell and the wandering vermin would not respond to it. So, the next morning I gave the animal a decent burial and begged its forgiveness. While I was cleaning up the mess in the bathroom, I found a silver serving spoon that must have weighed at least 4 ounces mixed in with the shells on the counter.

In the silverware drawer I found two shells. How did the pack rat get into my silverware drawer? It had not been left open. It must have gone into one of the cupboards then into the drawer from the back.

Thankfully the rat had been in the bathroom only a few minutes. Even so, it took me days to get the smell out of the room. I still feel guilty for killing the poor thing. True to my promise, I have never since killed a pack rat. I bought a live trap so I could trap them and take them to the other side of the lake and let them go. There seemed to be more and more of these creatures each year. It occurred to me that maybe I should spraypaint them pink to see if they were repeat offenders.

—

In the fall the weather was never predictable, and most people had put away their boats. One October, I was thrilled to make a reservation for some union planermen association officers and their wives. They would fill the lodge and all the cabins for three nights and would come in private boats, which took the pressure off me. I could focus on everything else to make their stay warm and comfortable and not have to worry about getting them to and from the lodge in unpredictable weather.

The wives decided ahead of time that we should have a costume party on the Saturday night. I had a nice supper waiting for them on the Friday night, with fresh hot bread. The next morning, after a big breakfast, the men got on with their meeting. The women went back to their cabins to get their costumes ready. Dinner would be a big deal with a roasted turkey and all the trimmings. Elvis, Sheriff Dog, the Prince and Princess of York, along with other celebrities, greatly enjoyed their dining experience. I served dinner as Marilyn Monroe. After dinner the men went out for a smoke and the ladies sat by the fireplace, laughing and telling stories. I began cleaning up the kitchen when all the lights started to flicker and the generator started to misfire.

On the way out to the generator shed, I heard my father's voice saying: "Fuel, air or electric. Those are the reasons an engine does not work."

In my rush to make a perfect dinner and get my costume together, I had forgotten the fuel. I should have emptied the diesel jerry cans into the generator's tank before dinner. Now, I was standing in 2 inches of newly fallen snow in red high heels with a matching red jerry can of diesel, filling a bone-dry 55-gallon tank. Fortunately, the generator started right up. I went back into the lodge.

I straightened my blond wig, stomped the snow off the red shoes and went back to washing dishes. No one had missed me. Before I could finish, two of the women came into the kitchen and insisted I come out to see the snow falling. Playing the ever-smiling host, I followed them to the porch. The women had turned out the lights, blown out all the candles and lamps. Without starlight, it was jet-black outside.

Everyone became oddly quiet. I was glad to make out the muffled rumble of the generator humming in the background. Then, *ka-boom!* A rocket shot up in front of the deck and through the snow-filled air, exploding into a million brilliant-green lights. Fireworks! Every single snowflake took on the colour of every rocket. I had never seen anything like it! All the colours dancing in the snow-filled sky! It was magnificent.

My October guests left the next morning, under dark skies and through rough seas. I went back into my warm kitchen and stoked the fire, thankful for the late-season income and not having to be out on the water.

The next day I stripped the linens from the cabins and winterized all four. I drained and disconnected the waterlines and sink plumbing, removed all bedding and food, and prepared one cabin to serve as an emergency shelter: Every year I set the first cabin up with food, bedding and wood just in case a lost or stranded stranger wandered into camp. I figured it could be the difference between life and death in the dead of winter. I am pleased to say that although a few unknown travellers used the accommodation, I never came back to a mess. On the contrary, one spring I came back to a heartfelt note thanking me for the warm refuge.

Over the next few weeks, my days were filled with the duties of closing up the lodge. I was going to work for the guide outfitter again this year. As a precaution, I would have to drain the water pump on the beach and would have to re-prime it again when I got back from working at the camp. That was when I'd also fully winterize everything.

With the chores done, I was able to relax and enjoy the beautiful cool days. The snow had melted away and left the mornings cold and brisk.

It had been more than twenty days since I had seen or spoken to anyone. If I didn't have a dog, a secret observer would have found me talking to myself.

I loved to walk the beach with Nuk that time of year. The lake was low thanks to a summer of little rain, so there was more beach to wander. Nuk was elated over the smell of the spawned-out salmon on the shore. I tried to flip the reeking carcasses into the water before he rolled in them, or the grizzlies showed up for a treat. Often our walk would end with a sand-scrubbed bath, in cold lake water, for my four-legged companion.

On the way back, coming up onto the grassy shore directly below the front deck of the lodge, I stopped and stared. My heart began to pound.

"Someone has been on my beach!" I cried out to Nuk. "A human has been on my beach! Someone was here!" Someone had dug seven small holes all in a precise row, and then placed several stones around each hole, creating an unusual design. It was certainly not the pack rats—unless the acetone genetically re-created a monster capable of sacred geometric design.

Nuk felt my anxiety and looked at me nervously. I ran up to the lodge for my camera, a big lump in my throat. With the camera in hand, I went back to the holes, still asking myself who or what could have made them.

Who could have come to my beach, by boat, and done this without me seeing or hearing them? Or maybe the reincarnated pack rat had marked my beach as belonging to a murderous villain!

I searched for pack rat scat to no avail and took several pictures of the scene, then went into the lodge to consider the possibilities. Finally, reason prevailed. The fireworks! The holes had been dug three weeks prior for the rocket-launching pad. Then the area had been covered with snow that night, and it didn't melt for a week or more. I had been busy winterizing and had not walked the beach since. Case solved.

Walking along the shore the next morning, I thought of how odd it was, that I didn't mind seeing signs of bears eating the salmon on the beach, but to think a human was walking around unannounced was quite unnerving.

# CHAPTER 35

# Fall Rains Fall

The guide outfitter offered me another season as camp cook. I was surprised it was not going to be on Babine Lake. I had expressed my concerns to the head guide outfitter about being the only woman in a one-cabin camp, but he assured me I had nothing to worry about. I brought Nuk and my shotgun anyway.

We packed into two trucks and drove several miles up a dirt road, then pulled off to start unpacking and loading half of the cargo and men onto an amphibious vehicle, which then departed for the hunters' cabins across a small lake located between Houston and Topley Landing. The machine had eight tires and a stick in place of a steering wheel. The other half of the troop and I waited for the return of the strange vehicle.

Thirty minutes later we listened to the noise as it came forth, filling the empty forest with such a racket. Then the awkward machine emerged and headed straight towards us. Once we were loaded, we travelled over a trail that was half creek, slopping from puddle to pool and through deep mud. I thought my back was going to give out. We finally came to the shores of a pristine lake.

We unloaded again and reloaded everything onto a small barge. I couldn't see anything on the other side that resembled a landing or a cabin, but off we went. We tied the barge to an old fallen log and unloaded again onto the grass.

One of the guides hiked inland and then returned with a four-wheel ATV with a trailer. We loaded the gear up once again and continued our journey, following the trail on foot. Soon we entered a clearing with a new log cabin in the middle of it. Two of the hunters and a guide immediately hiked out to a satellite camp. I didn't see them again till the end of the week.

Inside the cabin, I saw that no windows had been cut. Without any light, except from the window in the door, it felt ominous, as if the last guests were Hansel and Gretel. Once we lit all the propane lamps on the walls, however, the cabin was bright and seemed almost cheery. The smell of fresh-cut wood was lovely, and there was clean sawdust still on the floor. It was a little dark while I set up the food supplies and my space, but I tried to make the best of things. With seven days' work ahead, I needed to start with a good attitude.

The cabin was built in a long rectangular shape. On the far end was the kitchen area, with a small single bed on the side. This was my space. The area by the door had six bunks belonging to the remaining four hunters and two guides.

I was soon to find out all the hunters were Mormon—they were apparently strictly observant—and that suited me fine. No goofy jokes, no bad language and no bad habits to put up with in close quarters.

I hung a curtain to ensure my privacy, and Nuk slept under my bunk. The days went by slowly. A couple of the men shot a moose, and all were happy to eat my fresh bread and sticky buns.

When I arrived home from the camp-cook job for my two days off, I found that torrential rains had filled all of my boats. Bailing them was no easy task, even with my 12-volt bilge pump. But I usually enjoyed this chore because of all the wildlife I'd get to visit with while working. I had often seen beavers, muskrats, golden eagles, ospreys, loons, bald eagles, bears, moose and deer, along with passing fish, frogs and dragonflies. Today would be the exception to my enjoyment.

This time, water filled not only my four Carolina dories but the ski boat, *The Duck* and *Dandy Rip* as well. I had flipped the kayaks and canoes over before leaving, thank goodness. All but two of the boats should have been pulled out of the water by now. The problem was that I had taken the extra job as a camp cook, cutting short the time I had to do this yearly chore.

Each fall I was sadly reminded of the logging company's error that had blocked the natural flow of the creek behind the lodge, which thereby redirected itself to fill up Ookpik Cove with mud. The marina in Ookpik Cove was a single dock, six feet wide. It began at the lawn above the high-water mark through the reeds, settling into the mud-filled shore and extended out 300 feet. After a long, hot summer and dry fall, the dock system floated out over the shallows until the end, where it was a paltry six feet of water. With seven spaced boats still tied to the dock—each boat 15–20 feet long—I needed over 180 feet of floatable surface. I would pull the boats in by hand, as close to shore as possible. The dories with the least draft would be placed closest to shore. I started bailing the boats that were moored in the deeper water and worked my way in towards the beach.

The work took three times longer than usual. With just two days a week to get my winterizing jobs done, I was way behind. Finally, the boats were bailed. It began to rain harder. I would have to haul them out the following week for sure.

My house batteries were low, so I needed to start the generator. When it was running, it was important to do as many chores that took power as possible. First, I put all the work batteries on my chargers—the ones I needed to bail the boats and run the depth sounders for the dories. Fortunately, my house batteries were hooked up to charge automatically. Then I ran down to the water pump at the lakeside and flipped the power switch to the "on" position. After that, I ran back to the house through the pounding rain and flipped the power toggle, which sent current from the generator to start the water pump.

As the pump was filling my cistern for the last time this year, I vacuumed the carpets. Starting in my bedroom, I did an extra-thorough job, because this would be the last time I vacuumed till next spring. In the living room, I glanced outside to see if the rain had slowed down.

To my horror, I saw the last dory had sunk. The gunnels were totally underwater. I ran down to the dock without a raincoat. I could not believe my eyes. The boat I had just bailed had somehow filled completely with water. Magnified in the water, the bilge pump rested quietly, right where I left it an hour before. Back in the basement, I retrieved the battery I had recently placed on the charger, tossed it back into the wheelbarrow and rushed, out of breath, to reattach the battery to the bilge pump.

I could not figure out why the boat sank. The pump started gushing out water as soon as I attached the battery. This didn't help because the boat was completely below water level. I had to sit on the bow to bring the gunnels above water. Moving ever so carefully, I was able to bail by hand as well.

Hundreds of gallons of water had filled the boat. The only thing that saved the engine was the prop touching the bottom of the lake. Otherwise, the motor would have been submerged. Gradually, the water receded. Right about then I realized I had left the house water pump running to fill up the cistern. I jumped too quickly off the bow of the dory and onto the dock, which tipped the boat sideways and allowed the lake water to fill the dory once again. Back it went to the bottom.

I ran to the lodge feeling as though I was in a bad dream. At the power panel I flipped the switch, turning off the water intake pump. Too late! The cistern had overflowed. Gallons of water had flooded the back part of the house, and in some places, it was 2 inches deep.

With furious sweeping and mopping, I flung most of the water outside. I laid every single towel I owned on the carpets and stomped water from the rugs. Wringing them over and over, I finally managed to get most of the standing water up from the carpets.

The rain was still coming down. The last dory was still sunk. The other boats I had bailed earlier now had an inch of fresh rainwater in them. I trudged down the muddy path to the dock to continue bailing the dory. Finally, with a sucking noise, the dory popped off the muddy bottom of the lake.

As I walked up the dock to check on the other boats, I continued to wrack my brain trying to figure out why that one dory had sunk twice.

Back at the troublesome dory my curiosity was satisfied. The bilge pump was back-siphoning. This meant the valve inside the pump was broken, which allowed water to siphon back through it and into the boat. Indeed, the dory had started to fill with water again. I attached the battery

to the pump and emptied the dory, then removed the malfunctioning bilge pump.

Freezing cold and exhausted, I went back up to the lodge. I changed into dry clothes and built big fires in all the stoves. It was my policy not to drink when I was at the lodge; I had to always be in control of any situation. But this was a time when a person might need a good strong drink. I settled for a hot mug of strong tea.

I had no one to blame but myself: just soggy me, and my soggy dog, and the fall rains.

—

I made it back through the stormy waters to the village, in time to catch a ride to my next hunting camp job. In one more month I would go south again to work for the winter.

The next hunt was back at the outfitter's main camp. It was well organized and seemed like a piece of cake. Here, I was not totally responsible for everything. Even so, it proved to be a long and hard job. Four a.m. seemed to come earlier and earlier each morning.

Most of the hunters got their moose. Secretly, I felt sorry for the animals. I know the guide outfitter managed his territory well and he wanted to maintain his quota, but the animals just followed eons of genetically dictated survival of the species and did not expect to be shot down as they answered the call of a ready-and-waiting cow.

Returning to the lodge, my mood wasn't much better. One moment I was thrilled to be there, the next, sad I had to leave. I felt like this every year when closing up for the winter. I had to mentally prepare myself for a heavy work schedule in a big corporation for four months, wishing I were right here at the lodge. I worried about making enough money to keep the lodge. I worried about trees falling onto the buildings while I was gone for the winter. I worried about animals, four-legged as well as the two-legged kind, coming into my home while I was away.

As the time to leave drew close, melancholy took hold. Another year spent alone. I missed David, but I also hoped to find a new companion. I couldn't envision spending the rest of my life alone. I wondered if I would be alone forever. I wanted to share my life with a man, but I didn't have the vaguest idea how to find someone who would be willing to give up his life for a life with me in the wilderness.

If I were to say, "I want a man who loves to fish, loves the wilderness, loves wildlife, loves the water and loves boats," you might think there were a thousand men who would jump at the opportunity to live a life like that. But in reality, who would move away from their family and friends? Who could live here and not miss the outside world? Not many people could, for any length of time. I decided I might have to live a life of solitude. It would be worth it, but I had to come to terms with that idea, and that was proving to be difficult.

I did love Ookpik deeply. The obstacles and back-breaking work would have been impossible to survive if I didn't have such a deep emotional attachment to the land, the lake, the wildlife, the boats and the lodge.

But I would also miss having someone to validate the wonderful experiences I had there. And OK—no one to share the chores... no one to blame for my mistakes... no one to hug... no one to bring me coffee in bed.

With all the boats winterized and put away, and the list of chores completed, I locked the doors. I loaded the few remaining possessions into the kayak, which I would be paddling to the small bay where my truck was parked. It was early in the morning and the lake smooth as glass, just the way I liked it—especially with a fully loaded kayak.

At this point Nuk took off. Knowing I was after him, he stayed just out of my reach. Nuk was usually such a well-behaved dog. I pretended to go into the house. Finally, he came, and I took him inside, into temporary incarceration.

By the time I put Nuk into the kayak, the freeboard was about 3 inches above the waterline. The wind had picked up. It looked like a following sea, but one that I could handle, even slightly overloaded.

I paddled away from the protected cove and soon began to question my judgement. The dog was nervous and not lying still in the small craft. Maybe we should have stayed in the shelter of our wilderness haven another night. A third of the way along, the wind changed to a broadside breeze. That did not make either of us at all happy. These were the moments when I'd recall my mom's words: "Is this trip really necessary?"

With virtually no freeboard, I was glad I had put on my spray skirt covering the open cockpit. That didn't keep the water from entering the forward hole, though, where Nuk popped his head up now and then, and I felt water pooling in my seat. As the craft filled with water, I was filling with panic. Even though I had a float coat on, the shore looked far away. The lodge would have looked even farther, if I'd had the courage to turn and look. Maintaining our balance and paddling as fast as I could, I finally made the turn into the bay where I had parked my truck.

As soon as I came about with the seas on my stern, the boat crested a wave and I rode it like a surfer. Panic turned to thrill as I flew over the waves and headed in to the protected shore.

# CHAPTER 36

# Three Trumpeter Swans

In the early spring of 2004, when I returned to the lodge, I hauled a dual-axle trailer loaded with building materials, along with all the usual supplies. I arrived at the barge landing at 5:30 in the morning on May 3. I was the first rig to show up and I wasn't sure the barge was even going to operate, until a parade of pickups filled with forest planners and tree planters started to arrive.

I became concerned because the industrial-sized barge had not started its engines. My apprehension grew when I saw the lights come on in the tugboat, attached to the small open barge. They used this vessel early in the season when no log trucks were hauling. All the forestry workers had first rights to the space on the barge, so I figured I'd have to come back for a later crossing, but I was in luck.

After all the trucks were loaded, the captain signalled for me to drive on.

Everyone had to back onto the barge to make it easier to off-load on the eastern shore. That meant I'd have to back the truck—with a camper attached, while pulling a 25-foot trailer—down a curved hill and into the centre of the small barge, with trucks on either side. In the dark! Dread filled my body as I watched my old logger friend Gerald push in the side-view mirror on his brand new truck.

All I could do was chant my dad's words: "Keep 'er straight—use your mirrors." Focused on the captain's hand signals, I manoeuvred the truck and trailer perfectly into place. The loggers clapped their hands. I wiped the cold sweat from my brow and thanked God, and my lucky star—my Pa. I couldn't have done that without his guidance.

Year after year the spring chores had become easier to handle, and I had become more confident and secure in my ability to deal with things on my own. With the majority of fishermen coming in June and July, half of the summer was gone before I realized it.

I had some extraordinary guests that year. Some honeymooners in their early twenties coming in late for breakfast; some second-honeymooners in their eighties napping in the afternoon sun; an art professor and company from London, England, who had never been in the wilderness before; a family from Germany with two young daughters who played Mozart on the piano for me; my good friends Betty and Bill coming to visit by floatplane; the local RCMP and conservation officer and their families for supper and stories—each and every one of my guests was a delight to host, and they were delighted to visit.

August arrived and my family came on their holidays. That filled my world with joy. When my parents, my son, my cousins Josh and Zack, and Amanda and the grandchildren left, I missed them, but felt no despair. My life set into a pattern. I was content.

In the fall I revelled in the days of isolation. Reading, writing and painting filled me with happiness. My life was almost complete. I was still working hard negotiating with the logging and mining companies and going to land use planning meetings every other week or so, but it felt like I was on the right track and better things were happening. Feeling like I was doing everything I could possibly do, I had reached a measure of composure. Looking at a clear-cut forest no longer made me physically sick. I could look into the mirror and see a person who was doing the best she could, and I would hear Pa's voice. When I was a little girl playing in the mud in my best dress, he would say to my mom, "Nancy, she is as good as she can be."

Coming back to a cold, empty house no longer made me feel depressed and alone. Feeling strong, confident and comfortable in my surroundings gave me a new level of commitment to my home and my way of life. For the first time, I felt calm. I could accept death. If the Grim Reaper came for me, I would go with no regrets.

In the fall, the sun would go down early. All the boats would be winterized. Going to meetings this time of the year was an extremely difficult and time-consuming ordeal. Leaving in the dark and coming home in the dark was my only option. Without the boats, I had to hike out to my pullout on the forest service road or kayak over to Morrison Landing to the truck, depending on what time of the year it was and what I was packing out or in. This particular time, I was taking the kayak out.

Because Nuk always knew when we were leaving, I had learned to trick him onto the leash. I dragged him down the dock and held him in the small boat and cast off by starlight. The trip went quickly. The air was brisk, I could smell the fall leaves decomposing, and the water was like black ink with pinpricks of starlight.

After hours of driving, I arrived at the logging meeting. It was 9 a.m. and everyone was having a first cup of coffee. Me too, four hours late.

The meeting was predictably uneventful. They called it consulting. I called it worthless. Even so, I had to attend, or they would interpret my absence as approval of their decisions.

Running to the truck and then racing just slightly over the speed limit, I barely made it to the barge to cross the lake. I turned off the headlamps to keep from blinding the barge hand. It was pitch-black. The barge spotlight finally struck the opposite shore. Upon landing, a weight usually lifted from my shoulders. But on that day, I felt irritated about the wasted time, money and stress.

The oncoming traffic boarding the boat was unusually heavy as the workers went home. I was the only one getting off the barge onto the eastern shore. This was the last boat for the weekend—no one missed this boat. I liked travelling into the bush on Fridays, after everyone else had already left.

It was mid-October, only 5:30 in the afternoon, but looked like midnight. I was going back to the lodge, looking out over the same black water with pinpricks of starlight. It felt like the day had never happened. I had just lost a day. Retrieving my paddle, which I always left inside the truck to keep a porcupine or beaver from chewing it up, I was ready.

I put Nuk in the kayak with me and I shoved off. There was no wind. The dark skies were clear. I was looking forward to the paddle home.

As I came out of the protected cove, my first concern was Moose Point, the spot where pregnant moose go to have their calves every year. Because it's almost completely surrounded by water, it's a safer place to bear young. I always looked to Moose Point with a little tribulation. The previous spring, I had been broadsided by a strong breeze that blew me close to this shore, and a mother moose stomped her broad, sharp hoofs into the water to warn me to go no farther. The closer the wind pushed me towards the shore, the more violent the mother moose became. By the time I was near enough to see the whites of her eyes, she was slamming her muzzle into the water, flinging spray up into the wind. I don't remember ever paddling harder in my life to get away from being stomped to death by this hysterical 800-pound animal.

It had been a long day fighting the logging company for sustainable practices. I was exhausted. But with each paddle dipping into the black liquid, a bit of stress washed off.

The silhouettes of the hills behind the lodge illuminated as the moon began to rise. Beams from the lower edges of the horizon shot across the lake between the tall trees. My heart swelled, leaving no room for the day's worries.

There was no wind. Nuk was content and I was on my way home.

With the water still warm from summer, the cold air made a mist rise. Through the vapour, lit by moonbeams, we cut through the surface. I was euphoric with the splendour of the moment. In the hush, I slipped the paddle quietly into the water. The kayak slid along the surface in silence through the rising fog. It became thick. The moon lighting up each droplet magnified the density.

It was glorious. Still, enclosed within this blanket of mist, a strange loneliness enveloped me. I paddled in blindness for some time. A small cleft dividing the fog appeared. In this space without mist, three trumpeter swans flew directly towards the kayak. They spoke soft words, their giant white wings pushing the fog aside as they soared in my direction. They swooped up when they saw me in their path and rose over my head. I could feel their passing with the gentle breeze that brushed my face.

I was never so alive. The loneliness disappeared with the mist.

I could now see the lodge lit by a full moon. As demanding as my life had been alone, I would not change it.

In the black magic of the night and the soft glowing light of the full moon, the craft slid onto the soft moss. Home.

# CHAPTER 37

# Time Changes Everything

How easy it was to fly through all those years, which left me with so many different memories. The learning never stopped. Unfortunately, neither did the forestry, logging, mining or LRMP meetings. The combined projects turned into a nightmare that lasted several years.

But in the end, being a part of developing the Land Resource Management Plan was rewarding. At the table sat some extraordinary people, who were not getting paid, representing non-extracting resources. There were also many conscientious government workers who did their best, considering the situations they were placed in. I like to believe the forest has benefited from our diligence over the years. The areas with a visual quality of interest to tourism and stakeholders are finally under management to reduce impact from industry. Buffer zones are now in place to protect culturally significant landmarks. We fought to ban the use of MSMA (monosodium methanearsonate), an arsenic-based pesticide. We succeeded in placing a 500-metre buffer zone around all special features such as waterfalls, petroglyphs, trails, campsites and cabins; and 1,000 metres around all lodges, with a total of 4,023 hectares of conservancies and parks on Babine Lake, along with 128,179 hectares of parks in the Morice Forest District. Roughly 800 square kilometres (495 miles) of new parklands were created with my help. These sanctuaries will be there for our children's children.

I like to believe the years of my life donated to this project were well spent. Whenever I look at a forest harvested or old-growth, I know I did everything in my power and tried to make a difference. Thankfully, in 2022 the Morrison mining outfit, and the open-pit mine 4 kilometres (2.5 miles) away from the lodge, was denied yet again, nineteen years after I first started fighting Pacific Booker Minerals in 2003.

I also did my very best to save the Ookpik Wild Orchid. Its real name is Platanthera orchid, but I called it the "Ookpik Wild Orchid" at every logging and mining meeting. It was my heartfelt description of what would be lost with the devastating extraction.

The ten years I spent alone built the person I have now become. The beautiful dream that maintained my sanity after losing David was Ookpik Wilderness Lodge, and the fascinating world around it. Every year it was harder to leave, and the desire to return more powerful. To say the lodge grew on me would be an understatement.

—

They say that when you stop looking, that's when someone finds you. In the fall of 2004, I became reacquainted with a man I had worked with at the guide outfitters: Helmut, the hunting guide. Tragically, his lovely wife, Mary, had suffered an aneurism that took her life. I later met Helmut again at the hunting camp as a widower, which gave us common ground.

One day, Helmut came back from leading his party through a morning hunt. I noticed the guys were all laughing. Unbeknownst to Helmut, they had placed a big wild daisy in the barrel of his rifle, slung over his shoulder. A few minutes later he came into the cook shack and asked for my phone number. I gave him my true address instead: City: 015-719-154, Lot: 6736, Cassiar District, BC. After enjoying the look of surprise on his face, I gave him the GPS co-ordinates to the lodge. I figured if he could find me, and still wanted a date, we might be compatible.

A few days later, sure enough, I heard a knock on my front door. With our mutual affection for the wilderness, we fell in love, while picking wild mint on the shores of Babine Lake. We were both in our early fifties and knew from experience just how precious every day on this earth was, and we planned to share the rest of our lives together.

We were married August 20, 2005, at Ookpik. At the ceremony, we sent our love to the two people we wanted to be remembered at our wedding, Mary and David. We promised to always welcome their memories. And from 2005 to 2018 we lived, loved and laboured at Ookpik Wilderness Lodge. I believe I chose Helmut because he was stubborn as a mule, had his own opinions and a strong personality. They say you pick someone like yourself, and in these ways, we were alike. For the first few years we argued like two thunderheads colliding. Ookpik's demands kept us together, and our love grew with each challenging day and each enchanting night. We weathered the storms and wove our ideas together and became stronger, better people.

Although I had promised Helmut that living here at a fishing lodge, he would have all the time in the world to go fishing and hunting, I had neglected to mention, "After the work got done." Of course, he was able to enhance not only the infrastructure at the lodge, but the quality of living there. With that renowned German ingenuity, he made everything easier. In the fourteen years we were there together he built a new front deck with a hot tub, constructed a big woodshed, and made repairs to roofs, plumbing, stairs and trails. He also took on the massive and continuous dock work and, of course, he found the time capsule hidden within the infamous grey water pit under the 40 pounds of nails. He also gave me the time necessary to write and illustrate the children's books trapped for so many years in my scribbled notes.

Helmut did get to fish whenever he found time, and to hunt with his bow and arrow. Pictures of his trophy moose capture anyone's attention. And he was able to share his wonderful children, Christoph and Jenny, with me and with Ookpik.

As time moved on, we worked harder, our naps became longer, and the days seemed shorter. Every morning the work list loomed, and every night new chores were added. The propane tanks and jerry cans of fuel got heavier with each trip. Suddenly, in 2017, we woke up and found we were getting too old for all this. The promise of an easy life floating about in Helmut's neglected sailboat started to call.

After we decided to move on, every experience was amplified. Smells seemed more distinct, sounds more pronounced. Our eyes seemed to see more, to register details within our memories, desperate not to forget. Helmut tried in every way to help me accept leaving my home in the wilderness but, with every inquiry into the sale of the property, sadness crept back until I recognized the darkness that encompassed grief.

—

In 2018, on our way back to Babine Lake from Helmut's home on Vancouver Island, we had endless discussions on what to do next. Oddly, I started this story with David and me wanting to sail into the sunrise, and twenty-five years later, Helmut and I were planning that same dream. We agreed to set sail sometime soon for the Sunshine Coast. We would visit all the beautiful places Helmut and his late wife, Mary, had travelled in the coastal waters of the Pacific Northwest. And we would spread David's ashes at Chatterbox Falls, a place he had always wanted to go.

That night we found ourselves on a small lake south of Quesnel, BC. We were driving north for a second load of the personal property we had both accumulated over the past years. We had prospective buyers for the lodge and needed to clear out some of our possessions. I was in a dreadful mood. It was difficult not to choke up with every flashing thought. I was mourning the pending loss of the lodge.

Helmut was hungry as we drove through Quesnel. We saw a hand-painted sign, PANCAKE BREAKFAST, and Helmut made a quick right-hand turn. We found a small farmers' market selling pancakes for a charity event. Helmut ate with gusto. Not feeling hungry, I thought about the buttermilk syrup I used to make for my guests. Afterward, we walked around the market to stretch our legs a bit. The air was crisp and fresh with morning dew sparkling on the recently mowed grass. There was a fragrant ribbon wafting along in the calm air.

I found the source. It was an essential oil soap booth. I was drawn like a child to a display of lollipops and stood gathering the colours, shapes and smells to heal my aching heart.

"How ya' doing?" the ambitious marketer asked me.

I put on a sincere smile over my depression and said, "Nice soap." She encouraged my better nature. "Nice day, going to be a nice spring..."

I had just decided to buy three bars when she asked me where I was from, and I said, "Babine Lake." Then this young lady stood up and started to tell me a very long story. Her body and face lit up with animation as she began.

"I have a very big family and our men get together and go hunting and fishing any chance they get. But the trip to Babine Lake has become a traditional holiday story.

"That trip, the men decided to rent a houseboat on Babine Lake. They had a great time until the breeze picked up and the motor conked out. The boat started to drift towards a rocky shore, and someone radioed a 'mayday.' A woman answered, and soon a big powerboat came alongside and tossed a line.

"She pulled their houseboat through the choppy water into a narrow channel, and the wind subsided. The channel opened up into a long, narrow hidden body of water. They had no idea who she was or where they were going. Grandpa says, 'Trust is an easy thing when you are lost at sea.' They saw no signs of humans or community anywhere. An hour later, the rescue boat slowed down. Only then did they see a beautiful log house and four small cabins tucked into the tall evergreens. This lady tugged and pushed their big craft into a hidden marina carved out of the wilderness. After securing the boats she shook their hands all around with a big, 'Welcome to Ookpik!'"

The young soap seller stopped and asked, "Have you heard of that place?" I just smiled and said "yes," and she carried on with her story.

"Our men were glad to be on solid ground and she took them for a walkabout ending with an invitation to dinner. They learned their rescuer's name was Caroll and she lived way out there in the middle of nowhere by herself.

"The description of the dinner they were served varies from year to year, but they always make it sound like it was an abundant and delicious feast! And every year after Christmas dinner, when we're sitting around, Grandpa and the guys start talking about the Wild and Crazy Wilderness Woman!"

This happy, funny soap lady ended her story by asking, "Do you know Caroll?"

It was like a hypnotist snapped his fingers. I had recognized the incident from the beginning with fondness and had lost myself in the memory. And with her scents and her story, this master soap maker had brought me out from the depth of my gloomy depression and onto the surface of the present.

I handed her the appropriate cash for the lovely soaps, along with my business card.

"Glad to meet you," I said.

A smile floated on the surface of my sadness that day and the next. Anytime I needed a boost while packing up my memories, I opened the bag of soaps and drew in the heady scents.

—

Alex and Hazel Michelle from the Tachet Band, along with the rest of the many people from the four bands of the Dakelh (Carrier) Nation, bought Ookpik Wilderness Lodge in late 2018. Last I heard they were still deciding on how to use the lodge itself. But for Alex and his extended family, I feel the land was what they truly desired. The traplines, hunting trails and the Grease Trail would now be reconnected. The forest could now begin to heal.

The day we signed the contract to sell the lodge, Helmut drew water from the lake and we filled the hot tub. Knowing it would be our last dip, I maintained the flames for two days. When the water reached 103°F we slipped into the tub for the last time.

As we sat there, Helmut and I watched the moon as it rose to its apex. We saw the moonlight reflecting over the lake and casting shadows through the trees. We listened to the hoot of an owl on the western shore, and then heard a reply above our heads in a tall pine. Reluctant to leave the embrace of this experience, we lingered.

Clouds blew in and we could hear a stiff gust of wind hit the trees and move on. A thunderhead loomed at the southern end of the arm. We heard the rain hitting the lake in the distance, then get closer. As we watched the small storm rage up the lake, with lightning bolts punctuating its itinerary, knowing we should get out of the water, we challenged Mother Nature. Helmut held me as I cried, and he promised things would be OK.

Ookpik Wilderness Lodge, nestled in northern Canadian boreal forest, was my home for a quarter of a century. For the first ten years, it was crucial to allow love for the lodge to be all-consuming. Like a wild morning glory, it took root in and around my soul. I had to encourage and nurture its growth with each beat of my heart. I needed the strength it gave me to survive each difficult day and to conquer the frequent challenges of life in the wilderness.

A more difficult place to live would be hard to find, and yet the rewards were innumerable. Every waking moment brought a new element to behold in the ever-changing trees, wildflowers, bushes and wild animals, in the sky and the forest. The magnificence of the shifting weather surrounding Ookpik peninsula helped to push the blood through my veins and rooted my feet to the earth.

To be greeted with the splendour of the first morning light breaking over the hillside as it splashed onto the surface of the lake, and the last ray of an exquisite sunset casting great shadows through the forest—these were the gifts of joy bestowed upon me. This was my reward for the faith I maintained in the majesty of this place for twenty-four years.

Ookpik will be impossible to forget, and there will always remain a spot of emptiness, a black hole in me where the morning glory grew. Yet all the pain and the beauty of wilderness-living has filled my heart, which will beat forever in the rhythm of the northern lights.

# Acknowledgements

My grateful thanks to the following people: Bob and Nancy Simpson, Amanda and Jason Lovendosky, Silver Daher, Chavala and Cyrus Reyes, JR Simpson, Keith Simpson, Jenny and Christoph Hofmeister, and Chevy, Nova, Nahla, Amari and Lincoln. I wish to give a special thanks to Helmut, who gave me fourteen extra years at the lodge I may not have been able to endure alone.

I would also like to thank all of my guests at Ookpik Wilderness Lodge, particularly Scott Wakefield and Paul Messner, who came every single year, bringing delightful new clients. Each one became a friend and helped me pay the tax man, the insurance guy, my mortgage, fuel costs and to generally stay afloat for the first ten years at the lodge. I am eternally grateful for the wonderful friends I made at the Ookpik dining table. Remember, save your forks—there are better things to come.

My illegible journals would still be in a box somewhere, destined for the landfill, without the individuals who helped me polish these memories into a book people can enjoy. I would like to thank all the people who read my stories and gave me advice. My thanks to Jim Senka, who was always there to help this book along. I give my utmost gratitude to a world-class wordsmith and sister-in-law, Martha Cochrane.

This book would not be possible without the choices made by my publishers and editors: Anna Comfort O'Keeffe, Pam Robertson, Ariel Brewster, and everyone at Harbour Publishing who made the work involved a pleasure indeed.

# About the Author

**A**fter fifteen years of teaching art and culture to elementary students, author and illustrator Caroll Simpson moved off the grid to a remote fishing lodge on Babine Lake in northern British Columbia. On the shores of this wilderness, with water access only, she operated a successful fishing business for over twenty years. During this time, Caroll wrote and illustrated children's picture books published by Heritage House. Her works include the Coastal Spirit Tales series: *The First Beaver* (2008), *The First Mosquito* (2010), *The Salmon Twins* (2012), *The Brothers of the Wolf* (2014) and *Whale Child* (2017). Simpson also wrote and illustrated two board books: *Creatures of the Sea* and *Creatures of the Land and Sky* (both 2017). Caroll now lives on Vancouver Island with her husband, Helmut.

Carol Simpson
2022